Dedication

To Katrina, Meabh and Deirbhile.

LEGENDS OF IRISH BOXING

Stories Seldom Told

Barry Flynn

Appletree Press

First published in 2007
By Appletree Press
The Old Potato Station
14 Howard Street South
Belfast
BT7 1AP

Tel: +44 (0) 28 90 24 30 74
Fax: +44 (0) 28 90 24 67 56
Email: reception@appletree.ie
Web: www.appletree.ie

Design © Appletree Press, 2007
Text © Barry Flynn, 2007
Photographs © Barry Flynn except where acknowledged

Legends of Irish Boxing – Stories Seldom Told

ISBN: 978-1-84758-049-8

Desk and Marketing Editor: Jean Brown
Copy-editor: Jim Black
Designer: Stuart Wilkinson
Production Manager: Paul McAvoy

9 8 7 6 5 4 3 2 1

AP 3437

The Publishers would like to thank the following for permission to reproduce work in copyright

John McNally Collection: pages 12, 14 & spine
John Caldwell Collection: 24 & back cover
Jim Jordan Collection: page 39
Harry Perry Collection: pages 42, 47
Gerry Hassett Collection: pages 50, 52, 53
Sean McCafferty Collection: pages 62, 63
Eamon McCusker Collection: pages 70, 72
Eddie Tracey Collection: pages 81, 82, 84, 86
Neil McLaughlin Collection: pages 88-89, 93, 94
Philip Sutcliffe Collection: page 111
Paddy Maguire Collection: pages 114, 116 & back cover, 118
Kenny Beattie Collection: page 128
Barry McGuigan Collection: page 152 (left)
BarryMcGuigan.com: page 152 (right)
Michael Hawkins Collection: page 162
Gerry Storey Collection: page 187

actionimages.com: pages 151, 174, 176, 180, 182
Belfast City Council (Michael Donald): pages 26
Belfast Media Group (Andersonstown News): pages 16, 36, 125
Belfast Telegraph: pages 10, 26 (left and centre), 32, 35, 56, 58, 66, 86, 97, 101, 107, 120, 122, 142, 184
Holy Trinity Boxing Club: pages 144
istockphoto.com / Tom Tomczyk: page 6, / Piotr Sikora: page 8 & front cover / Jon Helgason: endpapers
Irish News: pages 78, 102 & back cover (Brendan Murphy), 130 (Brendan Murphy), 149
North Belfast Partnership: page 67
PAphotos.com: pages 21, 34, 44, 46, 51, 74, 90, 104, 134, 136, 146, 152 (centre), 156, 158, 160, 166, 168, 189

Contents

Foreword

Mr Pat McCrory M.B.E.

To those of us in the boxing fraternity there is no greater pleasure, besides watching a skilled exponent of the game in action, than to take a wander down memory lane to reminisce about former boxers and their exploits. I commend Barry Flynn for providing us with a valuable reference book that will prompt many a discussion – or even argument – wherever old fighters and their fans gather to talk about the sport. It would have been an impossible task to include each fighter from this island who would have been worthy of inclusion in this book. However, this collection has covered most of the greats, from all the Olympic medal winners to the cream of the professionals. I do hope that Barry will continue to add to this collection in future years as Irish boxing goes from strength to strength.

The reader will welcome the refreshing approach adopted by Barry in which he places each of the boxers within the context of their times and brings out their very different personalities. While we can all admire their performances in the ring, I believe that this book helps us to acknowledge their human side and the great characheristics that gave inspiration to generations.

This book demonstrates very clearly that boxers come in all types. However, they do share common attributes in the pursuit of success, namely dedication, bravery and discipline. They provide an example to us in the sport and to the wider community in general. May they continue to do so in the future.

I wish Barry good luck with this book and look forward to reading more of his future endeavours as he plays his part in putting on record the story of Irish boxing.

Mr Pat McCrory M.B.E.
Honorary President Irish Boxing Association (Ulster Branch)
Secretary Amateur International Boxing Association

Rinty trained on the Cavehill by cutting trees

Rinty Monaghan

The Beginning and the End

The question as to where to begin a book on Irish boxing legends can be answered quite simply by one name: Rinty Monaghan. In essence, John Joseph 'Rinty' Monaghan is the natural starting point. His popularity and career blazed the trail for the many Irish boxers who would follow in his wake.

In October 1947, Rinty won the National Boxing Association – later to become the World Boxing Association (WBA) – flyweight crown. His victory in London over Dado Marino was the most significant breakthrough for Irish boxing in the twentieth century and made Monaghan an instant legend. On 23rd March 1948, at a packed King's Hall in Belfast, the remarkable flyweight retained his world flyweight crown when he dispatched the durable Scot, Jackie Paterson, in the seventh round. As Patterson was prostrate in the smoke-filled hall, Rinty jigged in the ring, and on receiving the belt led the crowd in a rendition of 'When Irish Eyes Are Smiling'. Rinty Monaghan's achievement in winning a world title was truly ground-breaking in Irish boxing history. He also claimed the British and European titles during a career that spanned sixty-six professional outings, losing on just eight occasions.

He began his boxing career in Ma Copley's famous boxing booths in Belfast and, unbelievably, had his first paid fight at the age of fourteen in 1934. That first taste of professionalism – a drawn contest with 'Boy Ramsey' – was the beginning of a sparkling career that saw him command a huge following in his hometown. A short break for military service during World War Two interrupted his rise to the top. During 1945, Rinty fought on four occasions, his only loss coming to Joe Curran in Liverpool. The King's Hall became his fortress and eventually he scaled the heights to bring a world crown to his native Belfast.

Rinty Monaghan's career is epic in its telling. A distant era of boxing, showmanship, fearlessness and bravery. His last outing in the ring took place in September 1949 when he drew with Terry Allen at the King's Hall. As a consequence, he took four major titles – British, European, Commonwealth, and World crowns – into his keeping, until chronic bronchitis forced his retirement. He later worked as an entertainer, taxi driver and garage attendant in his native Belfast. He died at his home in Little Corporation Street on 3rd March 1984, aged sixty-three.

Fifty-nine years after the epic encounter with Patterson the Monaghan family, together with the great and the good of local boxing, gathered again at the King's Hall for the unveiling of a plaque sponsored by the Ulster History Circle and Belfast City Council. The plaque was erected in tribute to one of Belfast's most fondly remembered sons who, in 1948, inspired future generations of Irish boxers, many of whom are detailed in this book. Rinty Monaghan's legacy is contained within these chapters.

John McNally

The Man Who made Olympic History

Belfast's John McNally's place among the immortals of Irish sport was assured on the afternoon of 2nd August 1952, when he claimed the bantamweight silver medal for Ireland at the Helsinki Olympics. In doing so, he became the first man from these shores to win a boxing medal at a modern day Olympic Games. He achieved the breakthrough for Ireland and staked the nation's claim among the elite of world boxing.

His feat lit the flame on a glorious decade for Irish pugilism, which saw names such as Gilroy, Caldwell, Byrne and Tiedt follow in his wake to achieve Olympic glory in Melbourne in 1956. The anomaly today however is that the man who first put Irish boxing on the Olympic map is a largely overlooked figure. He has never milked the limelight of his achievement and remains an unassuming character in his native Belfast. His story is a remarkable one: a man who scaled the heights in sport and then hung up his gloves to use his musical talents to lead 'The Freemen', one of Ireland's most popular folk groups in the 1970s.

From battling boxer to principal banjo player, John McNally's life has been one long, rich tapestry.

Born in 1932 in Cinnamon Street in Belfast's Pound Loney area, McNally first acquired a taste for the boxing game as a juvenile with the local Immaculata club. The Pound Loney district was a close-knit myriad of mill streets in the lower Falls area which has now virtually disappeared from the city's landscape. Its toughness and poverty, as well as its community spirit, were renowned and it was a natural breeding ground for excellent boxers.

As John explained, there was only one place in the area that a lad with an interest in boxing could go to learn the game.

"I'm a Pound Loney man through and through and it was only natural that I joined the Immaculata club in Devonshire Street when I was quite young. I stayed there for a while but then there was a bit of a disagreement within the club and I was unhappy with a few things, so I left to join the St Mary's club in King Street, where I went on to win an Ulster juvenile title."

All was not plain sailing for McNally's career. One episode whilst at school illustrated to him the primacy that the authorities felt that education should have over boxing. Having won the Ulster juvenile title, the progression to national honours was no foregone conclusion.

Left

Ireland's Olympic Team, 1952. John McNally is pictured second from left, front row

"I was at the time a pupil at the Christian Brothers' School in Hardinge Street but, due to my examinations, I was not permitted by the Brothers to go to Dublin to compete for the Irish title. That really upset me inside but I did learn the lesson in hindsight that there was more to life than boxing."

McNally's natural talent in the ring began to tell and by 1951 he had progressed further to claim the Ulster and Irish junior flyweight crowns. This achievement put him in the running for a place in the Irish Olympic team and the following year he duly won the Irish senior bantamweight crown and was picked for Helsinki.

For a young man who had held an ambition to travel Europe, the Olympic Games in Helsinki were a world away from the hardships of post-war Belfast. A city which was recovering from the devastations of the war was a far cry from the opulence of the Olympic Games.

"It was just a dream come true to represent my country in the green vest on a stage such as that and I was never so proud," he said. "Literally, I found it hard to believe that I, a lad from the Pound Loney, had been picked and was going to travel to the Olympics in Finland. The honour was something I cherish and always will."

The fifteenth summer games took place in Helsinki from 19th July until 3rd August 1952. The Irish Olympic squad went to the Games in hope rather than expectation. However, the eight-strong boxing team was made up of a virtual who's who of Irish greats with Andrew and Thomas Reddy, Terry Milligan, Peter Crotty, William Duggan, John Lyttle and Kevin Martin competing along with McNally for honours. Fortune was on McNally's side as he was awarded a bye in the opening round of the bantamweight competition. In his next bout, he was a unanimous winner over Alejandro Ortuosto from the Philippines.

Next up was the quarterfinal where the experienced and fancied Italian Vincenzo Dall'Osso was waiting for the Belfast boy. While McNally was not expected to come through the bout, the Irishman was at the top of his game and felt very assured and confident. As he explained, a tough international battle prior to the games had put him in the right frame of mind.

"In the warm up to the Olympics, I had represented Ireland against the American Golden Gloves Champions in Dublin," he said. "I came up against a guy from New York called Jack Carabino and he gave me the hardest fights that I had ever experienced. He had one of the most vicious punches I had ever

felt but I fought back with all I had that night to claim victory. After I had got the decision over Carabino, I felt so confident that I believed that I would be unbeatable in the Games."

Accordingly, Dall'Osso was out-pointed convincingly as McNally used his left jab effectively to swing a unanimous decision from the judges. The semi-final saw McNally go toe-to-toe with the tough Korean, Joon-Ho Kang. In the early part of the contest, McNally had to deal with some clever attacking from the Korean, but gradually he began to assert himself and, with some clever defensive boxing, soon took command. At the mid-point of the second round, McNally unleashed a vicious onslaught that floored Kang and thereafter the decision was a foregone conclusion.

Ireland had not claimed a medal of any colour since Pat Callaghan and Bob Tisdall had claimed gold in track and field events at the 1932 Olympics in Los Angeles. With a medal – and his place in boxing history – now assured, McNally was determined to leave Helsinki with the Olympic title.

It was not to be as in the final McNally lost on a controversial decision to the local favourite, Finland's Pennti Hamalainen. As he recalled, there was great suspicion of a 'home-town' decision regarding the outcome of the contest.

"The fight took place in a packed and partisan arena and when the split decision was called in favour of the Finn the place erupted in celebration," remembered McNally. "It was the last day of the Games and the host nation had not yet won a gold medal so there was a lot of weight on the Finn's shoulders to deliver.

"The Finn had been cautioned at least eight times during the bout for hitting with the inside of the glove and for using his head to open my eye, which in today's rules would have lost him points. When the final bell rang, we shook hands and I went back to my corner and we were all convinced that I had got the decision, but I knew that the pressure was there with the home crowd expectant.

"It came down to the three judges and the British judge gave it to me, while the American and the Austrian gave it to Hamalainen. He got it on a split decision and I could not believe when his hand was raised, it was like a nightmare come true. I was devastated and in floods of tears because I was convinced that I had won the gold medal. I was so low that I still find it hard to think back on those few minutes as it really was a hard blow to take after coming so far. The fact was that, regardless of how I felt, I had no time to compose myself as everything was working like clockwork and I had to carry on with the formalities. Immediately after the fight, they held the medal ceremony in the ring but I was so cut up about the whole thing that it was all a blur to me. My silver medal was no consolation and the fact that the crowd were in raptures only made me even more depressed."

Left

John McNally pictured in 1954 during his professional heyday

Above

John McNally with his Olympic medal

The loneliest place for any boxer after a devastating defeat is indeed the changing room. McNally retired from the ring that afternoon only to be accosted by one of the Game's doctors who ordered immediate medical attention for his scarred back. Once there, whilst trying to control his tears, an act of kindness by an anonymous American boxer touched him greatly.

"After the ceremony, I came out of the ring and the official doctor took one look at my back – which had been shredded through rope burn – and ordered me to go to the dressing room to be tended to. Once there, a medic took out a bottle of pure alcohol and told me to lie face down on a bench and warned me that the alcohol would sting my back badly. I recall there was a boxer lying meditating on the bench beside me preparing himself mentally for his own final bout and he held out his hands for me to grip. The alcohol really did hurt so much that I felt that I was about to scream so I squeezed

that boxer's hands very hard in a reaction to the pain.

"Only later did I come to realise that the man who offered to hold my hands that day was the legendary Floyd Patterson, future heavyweight champion of the world. It was an act of kindness that I have never forgotten and I have always held him in the highest personal esteem."

Nearly half a century after his Olympic dream was shattered, John is philosophical about the defeat.

"My attitude to life has always been to never look back in anger," he explained. "I just thank God that I had the chance to go there and represent my country. Ireland in the early 1950s was a relative newcomer on the world sporting scene and this was a real breakthrough for the country. It was one of the hardest few minutes that I have ever endured and being so young I was just devastated. In retrospect, the experience has stood me in good stead and helped me cope with adversity in later life."

Ireland had declared itself as a republic in 1949 and very little was known about the island on the world stage. One story McNally relates illustrates that point to perfection.

"It was only after the final in Helsinki did I learn that the Olympic officials knew so little about Ireland that they thought the name of the National Anthem was 'It's a long way to Tipperary'. Indeed they had that record lined up to play should I have won – in which case, maybe the silver medal, in reality was just meant to be."

Given that the only athlete from either Britain or Ireland to claim a gold medal at the Helsinki Olympic was a horse called 'Foxhunter', ridden by Harry Llewellyn, McNally's silver was big news across Ireland. Little did John know what awaited him in his native Belfast.

"When we arrived back in Dublin, my father arranged for me to stay a couple of days with some friends of his. Now I realise that it was only to keep me out of the way while the homecoming was arranged. Eventually I took the Belfast train and I could not believe the numbers who were there to greet me. The crowds were so excited that they actually broke through the railings at the station to get to me. I was on top of the world that day and never felt so happy – it was only then that I realised how significant an achievement it all had been."

However, the fact that McNally had represented with distinction an all-Ireland team did not meet with the blessing of all in his native city. Politics in Belfast were never far away from the reality of daily life and McNally recalled one episode that caused him grief on his return from Helsinki.

"I had been invited to the Ritz Cinema, where a number of prominent dignitaries were to make a presentation to me on the stage. The film to be shown was the premiere of *Jim Thorpe – All American* which was about the Native American who was stripped of his own Olympic medal because he had played professional baseball. I remember it so well; I was standing there in my Olympic blazer when my trainer approached me to say that a politician was refusing to go on stage with me unless I removed my blazer, as it had a Tricolour badge. My trainer was the type of man who would always try to smoothe over everything and he suggested that I just took the blazer off to avoid any embarrassment, which, to my regret, I did. Only after I had left the cinema that night did I get really wound up and angry about the whole thing and realised that I should never have taken the blazer off."

After the heights of the Olympic Games, McNally joined the paid ranks in what he still feels was the greatest mistake of his career.

"There are no friends in a professional boxing ring and all the enjoyment you get as an amateur vanishes. In reality, you become just another means to an end for others and that is a fact. I was boxing out of London and not really enjoying my sport: it was a different game to the one I loved and I never settled as a professional."

Once he had hung up his gloves, many people in Ireland got to know John McNally better for his banjo playing, than for his boxing. He was one of the founding members of the legendary folk band 'The Freemen', who played widely throughout the country in the 1970s and toured Europe extensively. Many followers of the band would have had no idea that the talented banjo player was also a legend of Irish sport.

Today, in his mid-seventies, John is a picture of health and as he talks it is with the enthusiasm of somebody who has lived life to the full. Apart from turning professional, John's other regret in boxing terms is that he felt that he never got the recognition in Ireland that his feat in Helsinki deserved.

"I feel some time like the invisible man of Irish boxing," he explained. "I was the first to win a boxing medal at the Olympics for Ireland and sometimes it seems that it never happened. Recently, a wall mural was painted in Belfast in tribute to the champions who had come from the Immaculata club and I was not included. I am a man born and bred in that area and I represented that club so I feel again overlooked. I am not bitter for I have had a life that others can only dream of and my achievements will always be in the record books."

Perhaps it is in keeping with the unassuming and polite nature of John that this is his philosophy. On the reasons why Belfast, and the Falls Road in particular, has over the years produced so many fighters of note, John is sure in his response.

"In one word it's poverty that has been the biggest factor in creating the conditions for boxing to flourish. There is no doubt that times were very hard back then and people had to adapt to survive and that is why so many became great fighters."

When asked about the most important advice he could ever give to a boxer, he recalled something that was said to him by an Egyptian fighter at the weigh-in for the 1952 Olympic Games. The Egyptian had been on the end of some insults from Iranian fighters in the queue, yet he refused to become involved in the petty insults. Instead he just remained quiet and ignored the abuse. McNally asked the Egyptian why he did not defend himself, and with a glance in McNally's eyes, responded.

"Irishman, I will do my talking in the ring and remember this always: when somebody has beaten you, take your hat off to them; when you beat somebody, take your hat off to them also – but make sure it fits your head when you put it back on."

That gem of civility is something that has stuck with Gentleman John since 1952 – and you can tell!

Tony Byrne

"Sock it to him Anthony!"

On 6th December 2006, the Co. Louth town of Drogheda honoured one of its most famous sons. Tony 'Socks' Byrne, a bronze medallist for Ireland at the Melbourne Olympics, returned home from Edmonton in Canada to witness the unveiling of a statue dedicated to his name.

For Drogheda, it was a case of déjà vu as it had again delved deep in its pockets to honour the man who put the town's name on the Olympic map. The campaign to have the statue erected was a carbon copy of the one which had raised the finance to send Tony Byrne to Melbourne in 1956. Back then, a sum of £653 was secured by the 'Send Byrne to Melbourne' campaign – an unbelievable figure which was sufficient to finance many athletes in those days.

In 2006, a sum of almost €30,000 was raised to finance the statue which stands proudly by the town's Scotch Hall. A fitting and permanent tribute from the people who remain dear to the heart of Tony 'Socks' Byrne.

Born in Hardman's Gardens, Drogheda, on 7th June 1930, Anthony Byrne joined the local Tredagh Boxing Club in the town at the age of twelve. Under the watchful eyes of Ray Everitt and Jimmy Carroll, Byrne learned his ring craft. On leaving school at fifteen to take up employment, he soon found that his job as a message boy interfered with his ability to train so he left boxing for a period of three years.

At eighteen, Byrne joined the Irish Army and was afforded an opportunity to resume his boxing career. In a period of six months, 'Socks' won Army titles at junior and senior level and complemented these with Irish titles at the same grade. In 1951, he gained his first green vest and went on to make twenty-nine appearances for Ireland, losing on only three occasions.

In 1956, the Drogheda man won the Irish senior lightweight crown by seeing off the challenge of the reigning champion, Steven Coffey. Byrne had been voted the best boxer of the championships and was selected on to the Irish team for the Melbourne Olympics. The scarcity of money in the Ireland of 1956 was the greatest barrier to Byrne undertaking his trip of a lifetime. However, the town of Drogheda was determined to fund Byrne's trip and the 'Send Byrne to Melbourne' campaign was established.

"Everyone in the town threw their weight behind the fundraising effort for me," recalled Byrne. "The factories, pubs, shops, businesses all held events and in the end a sum of £653 was raised which was more than enough to see me there and back. I have the town of Drogheda to thank for my Olympic

Left

Statue of Tony 'Socks' Byrne in his native Drogheda by artist Laury Dizengremel

experience and the people couldn't have been kinder to me. For a man who had never in his life been more than a mile away from cow dung, I just could not explain what a trip to Australia meant. We went to America first and our only knowledge of the States had come through the Hollywood movies."

At an event that autumn held at the Gate Cinema, the funds raised were presented to the President of the Irish Boxing Association, Chief Superintendent PJ Carroll, and Tony Byrne was on his way to Australia as Ireland's chosen lightweight. He was named as the Irish team captain and remembers well carrying the Tricolour around the Olympic Stadium. A flag, together with a blazer, tracksuit, vests, shorts and tie he retains in his Edmonton home to this day.

"I had been the number one choice by the IABA for the Games and holding the flag in the Stadium is an honour I will never forget. After we left the Stadium there was an army truck outside and a soldier was collecting the flags and placing them neatly into the back. I remember that the Irish flagpole was jutting out and Harry Perry said to me that I should take it on to the team bus as a souvenir of the Games. I grabbed it and it was quite a struggle to get the pole into the bus. So this guy was watching us trying to get it on to the bus and he suggested that we lose the pole and keep the flag. So we did and to this day the flag I held in Melbourne is a permanent fixture in my home."

Byrne's first bout in Melbourne saw the Drogheda man drawn to meet the Czech Josef Chovanec. Byrne was victorious in the bout as his opponent was disqualified in the third round and led by the referee to his corner. Standing just three rounds away from a bronze medal, Byrne was drawn against the American champion, Louis Molina.

A tough battle ensued with the American which Byrne won on a points' decision. He, along with John Caldwell, Freddie Gilroy and Fred Tiedt, was now into the Olympic semi-finals and one fight away from a crack at the gold medal.

Byrne's opponent in the semi-final was to be the West German, Harry Kurschat. In an international earlier that year, Byrne had defeated the German who had beaten Kurschat in their national championships and expectations were high. It was not to be however as the German displayed greater technique and scoring ability to get the decision over Byrne on points. In the other semi-final, the talented Scot Dick McTaggart saw off the challenge of the Russian, Anatoli Lagetko, and subsequently took the gold medal with a win over Byrne's semi-final opponent. Sitting in the arena that night watching the finals, Byrne saw McTaggart crowned also as the most stylish fighters of the Games. In January 1957, Byrne was afforded an opportunity to meet the new golden boy of British boxing.

At the Royal Albert Hall on 30th January 1957, Byrne met McTaggart, who was representing England as a member of the Royal Air Force. The Drogheda man caught the champion in the second round and sent him to the canvas. He was awarded the bout after three bruising rounds and the Scot was left to think how lucky he had been to win the gold medal in Melbourne. Strangely, with the scarcity of televisions in Ireland, the fight was witnessed live by hundreds of people on the television of the McKinney family in Drogheda's Pearse Street, such was the interest in 'Socks'.

Before Tony Byrne left the Olympic Games for Ireland with Harry Perry, the Irish team witnessed a water polo match that has gone down as one of the most famous events of the Melbourne Olympics. Byrne recalled the clash betweeen the USSR and Hungary in the Olympic Pool that became known as the 'Blood in the Water' match. The Melbourne Games were over-shadowed by the Russian invasion of Hungary and the match between the two sides ended in chaos.

"The crowd was all for the Hungarians after what had happened with the invasion the previous month. Hungary were winning and the match degenerated into a bloody fight that threatened to turn into a riot in the crowd. I could not believe what I was witnessing and the police came in to restore calm. I will never forget that day as it showed what could happen when sport and politics mixed."

Being an Olympic representative from Drogheda meant that you were quite a popular character in your hometown. Byrne's arrival back to the Co. Louth town, on 16th December, was to a massive civic reception hosted by the then Mayor, Alderman Lawrence Walsh. The Olympic hero was paraded through the crowds to George's Square led by the Drogheda Brass and Reed Band. The people of Drogheda paid tribute to 'Socks' and a presentation concert took place in his honour at the Gate Cinema the following Wednesday evening.

By 1957, Tony Byrne was employed by the local Galbraith's bakery. He worked as a deliveryman paid on a commission-only basis. One event in 1962, which led to him departing the company, changed his life forever.

"I was basically employed on a commission basis so there were no real fixed hours to the job and I did not work on a nine to six basis. It suited me as I could train also and keep the job going at the same time. Sometimes I would start later and work well into the evening in order to see clients but this did not suit my manager and we fell out over it. Eventually the firm told me that I would have to follow their rules and work as they saw fit and I thought it was unfair. So I said to my wife Honor that that was me finished with the bakery and the very next day I was at the emigration office and on my way to Canada."

Above

Hungarian water-polo player Ervin Zador nurses a gashed eye after being sucker-punched by Russia's Prokopov. Hungary won the match 4-0 but the event goes down as probably the most violent encounter ever seen in an Olympic team sport, an event that 'Socks' witnessed. Just prior to the Olympic games, the USSR had invaded Hungary to crush a anti-Communist revolution. Hungarian players feared they wouldn't be able to return to their country after the games. This only added to the hostilities between the two teams.

In 1962, Ireland was haemorrhaging its greatest export: its people. For Tony Byrne and his family, a new start in Canada was a very hard experience as he recalled.

"We went out to Edmonton as Honor's sister had settled there some time before. I got a job as a lumberjack and it was hard going in the beginning and homesickness was always there. As you settle you meet up with Irish people and they can point you in the right direction to get better employment. The one thing that we all found hard to come to terms with were the Alberta winters as the place froze over for four months each year.

Tony and Honor had four children, twins John and Anthony, together with Ruth and Lisa. In the 1970s 'Socks' was associated with his local parish's boxing club where his sons all tried their hand at the sport. Tony was working as a truck driver and he found it hard to devote his time totally to the club.

"The thing about Canada is that people find it hard to appreciate the sheer size of the place. In Ireland we could have fought every night of the week and the furthest spot we went to was Belfast. Over here, if you wanted to arrange a competition in Alberta sometimes it would be necessary to travel all day and night to fulfil it. It just became impossible for me to give the devotion necessary due to work commitments."

Drogheda has never left the heart of Tony Byrne. Nor have the people of Drogheda ever forgotten Tony Byrne. In 2005, an Olympic Golden Jubilee Committee was established in the town with the aim of raising the necessary finance to erect a suitable memorial to the achievements of 'Socks' Byrne. Under former Mayor and chairman, Frank Godfrey, and members including Joe and Isobel Lynch, Frank Maher, Sean Roma, Malachy Godfrey, Ray and Catherine Everitt, Des Byrne, Noel Carter, Ollie Connor and Jimmy Weldon the committee set about raising the €30,000 necessary to erect a bronze statue. The people of Drogheda reacted as they did in 1956 when the name Tony Byrne was mentioned. Eventually, the renowned sculptor, Laury Dizengremel was commissioned to produce the statue and the date of 6th December 2006 was set as the unveiling day.

Tony Byrne had been invited to Ireland to a number of events organised in Dublin to mark the 50th anniversary of the Melbourne Games. All the great names including Ronnie Delaney, Maeve Kyle and the boxing team were feted in Dublin on 1st December. Five days later, it was an emotional Tony 'Socks' Byrne who returned to Drogheda to unveil the permanent reminder to his achievements. Fittingly, Tony invited Alacoque Everitt, widow of

A full half-century had gone by since Tony Byrne had first been honoured by the people of Drogheda. As Tony recalled, in 2006, he had returned to a changed Ireland:

"There was very little money in Ireland back then but things are a lot better now. We had to go and request some pocket money from the Irish Olympic Board while we were in Melbourne as we just had no money. Today with sponsorship and all that, the athletes are a lot better off than we were, but I can't complain. I've had a good life and am comfortable now in Canada. One thing is for certain that the town of Drogheda is special to me and I have never, ever got it out of my system."

The people of Drogheda felt the same about their most famous son as this poem by William Frank Godfrey shows:

Tony 'Socks' Byrne

Socks, how we admire you,
Hardman's Gardens has no finer son.
You did us proud in Melbourne,
And a Bronze you bravely won.
Drogheda will now remember,
Your Golden Jubilee
And erect a fitting monument,
To honour your memory.
You carried the Flag for Ireland,
In that Olympic Opening Parade
And made us all so very proud,
In Drogheda on that day.

One final query needs to be cleared up definitively about Tony 'Socks' Byrne – where did the nickname 'Socks' come from? A number of theories abounded as to how Byrne acquired the name including one that he always fought with his socks around his ankles. Another theory refers to his use of socks on his fists when punching the bags at the Tredagh Club. However, the man himself is happy to clear up the confusion for once and for all.

"The name 'Socks' came about as every time I fought as a schoolboy the crowd shouted at me to 'sock' it to my opponent," he said. "It sort of stuck and I became known as 'Socks' throughout my career."

Today, Tony, and his wife Honor, still live in Edmonton in Canada. He has great memories of a life and career in boxing that has given him much pleasure. He retired some years ago and carries a business card with him that states on the front:

Anthony Byrne Esq. Retired–
No Worries, No Work,
No Money and No Responsibilities

On the back of the card, there is a line which sums up Tony's carefree attitude to life:

If I pass out from overwork bring me to,
If I am still a little shaky, then bring me two more

John Caldwell

Pure Genius, Pure Class, Unsurpassed!

Of all the boxers from this island who have scaled the heights of the Noble Art of boxing, one man's name is held consistently in higher esteem than all others. That man is John Caldwell. Many followers of boxing in Ireland may argue differently but, when it comes down to sheer class and achievement, Caldwell's name is talked about universally with hushed reverence and awe.

Caldwell was quite simply a master of his art. A supreme boxer and fighter, his skill saw him claim, at eighteen years of age, an Olympic bronze medal in Melbourne and the world professional bantamweight crown in 1961. He enjoyed a magnificent career, as both an amateur and professional, in which he contested 275 bouts, winning on all but ten occasions. That is why he is still so revered.

Today, he is one of only two living Belfast men to have held either a WBA or WBC professional boxing crown. His achievements, in the 1950s and early 1960s, will, in all probability, never be equalled or bettered. Boxing today is a changed sport and, undoubtedly, they do not make fighters like John Caldwell any more. He represented his club, city and country with grace, style and pride. His dedication to his sport was unquestionable and throughout his career his greatness was never, ever, in doubt.

Born in Belfast's Cyprus Street off the Falls Road in May 1938, Caldwell was first drawn at an early age to the now world-famous Immaculata boxing club, which was situated off the city's Grosvenor Road. His natural talent in the ring soon came to the fore, and under the keen eye of his trainer, Jack McCusker, he came to prominence throughout Ireland.

By 1956, with a plethora of titles to his name, the Falls Road boxer held both the junior and senior Irish flyweight crowns and a place on the Irish team at the Melbourne Olympic Games was secured. The Irish Olympic squad embarked upon a journey to Australia in late 1956 and for Caldwell the experience was a universe away from the harshness of post-war Belfast. For the so-called 'baby' of the squad, it was a dream come true.

"We were away from home for six weeks and travelled to Australia by boat," remembers Caldwell. "It was a magnificent experience for all of us and stopped off at San Francisco and then in Honolulu on the way to Australia, places which we had only heard about and seen in films up until then. I was very young at the time and, at just eighteen, I was considered to be the baby of the team, which meant that I was well looked after in some respects. The athlete Maeve Kyle was brilliant and she looked after us all and you could say that she mothered me in

particular, which took care of any homesickness that I had during the visit. Everything was fabulous and the opening ceremony in the stadium stood out for me particularly."

Belfast's John McNally had claimed Ireland's first boxing medal at modern day Olympics when he took silver in 1952. For the boxers of 1956, that achievement was surpassed by the most talented fighters to have represented Ireland in a modern Olympics. The team acquitted themselves with skill and pride and surpassed all expectations, as John remembers fondly.

"As it turned out it was the most successful set of Irish boxers ever to go to an Olympic Games as, apart from my medal, we won two bronze and one silver through Freddie Gilroy, Tony Byrne and Freddie Tiedt. But, for me personally, it was such an honour to be picked in the first place and I was so overjoyed to be representing Ireland and wearing the green vest on such a stage. Just being there at such a young age was something really special and I still find it hard to explain the feeling."

In the opening round of the flyweight division, Caldwell was afforded a bye. His first opponent, Yai Shwe of Burma, fell victim to John's unique style of working inside with quick punches and then switching his attacks from body to head. Yai Shwe was duly knocked out in the third round.

In the quarterfinal, Caldwell upset the legions of local Melbourne fans when he beat their local hero, Warren Batchelor, on points. The Australian had been the favourite to win the division and Caldwell's success put him in pole position for the gold medal.

However, it was not to be as, in the semi-final Caldwell lost out to the crack Romanian Mircea Dobrescu and had to content himself with a bronze medal. The Romanian, in turn, lost out to the legendary British fighter Terry Spinks in the final and he claimed the gold medal.

Whilst Ronnie Delaney had crowned the Irish squad's achievement with a gold medal in the 1500 metres, the boxing squad's achievements represented the greatest display from any set of pugilists ever to have worn the green vest at the Olympics.

On their return, the team were held in the greatest esteem as rapturous receptions were followed by numerous civic ceremonies across the country. John Caldwell was feted in Dublin, Belfast and most warmly in his own Cyprus Street as an all-conquering hero. He recalled the experience with pride.

Left

John Caldwell (*left*) and Freddie Gilroy pictured in New York, 1956. Their paths would cross again in 1962.

"The whole of Cyprus Street and most of the Falls Road was out to cheer me on my return to Belfast. When I recall the feeling I had inside and I just think of standing there on that podium in Melbourne with my medal it just makes me so proud," said John. "It was a dream come true for me and sometimes I have to pinch myself and question whether it really happened."

With the Melbourne Olympics behind him, John continued with his amateur career and found himself a trade as a pipe fitter. He was now operating at the top of the game and with the experience of winning an Olympic medal so young he saw his career in boxing moving towards a different sphere. Naturally, the calling to the paid ranks was not far off and in January 1958, he fought his last unpaid fight in Belfast's St Mary's Hall.

It is said that there was an audible gasp among the crowd in the Bank Street venue that night when it was announced from the ring that Caldwell had worn a vest for the last time. As a boxer, he was cherished in his hometown. Given the fact that he had now turned professional – and given John's talent and the state of professional boxing in the City at the time – the prospect of spectators seeing Caldwell fight out of Belfast became a distant hope.

Family life and John's career soon coincided. John married his childhood sweetheart Bridget and made the decision to start his career in the paid ranks and base his family in Scotland. Glasgow was to be the base from where Caldwell, under the management of Sammy Docherty, set out on a new era.

The 1950s were an era when professional boxing was flourishing in Britain, and Caldwell's professional career was soon underway. In his first bout, a two-round stoppage of Englishman Billy Downer signalled the start of John's rise through the ranks. As he recalled, the training regime he followed required discipline, self-control and dedication.

"In Glasgow, I attended mass at half-six every morning. After that, I would take to the hills outside the city for the running and stamina training. I had to watch my diet and keep myself right that it was really tough going. My exercise routines were so varied and beneficial that the then Glasgow Celtic manager Jimmy McGrory asked me to go along and help the team out. I showed the players the range of exercises that I did to get fit and we all became very friendly. As a lover of football, I jumped at the chance of mixing with the Celtic players and remember playing in many practice matches with them. The one thing I remember about those training games is that none of the Celtic players were allowed to tackle me as I was in training for fights, so it was a strange experience to be able to run rings around them. Without exaggeration, I can say that I was supremely fit at the time but it took real discipline and an awful lot out of

me both physically and mentally. My trainer at the time knew me inside out and he could tell exactly what stage I was at and how I was shaping up in the run up to a bout. He always cautioned me against being overly fit and he sensed just by my mood when I had reached perfect fitness; after that it was a case of no more physical work as he was sure I was ready."

After six successful bouts in Scotland, John made his return to Belfast where he out-pointed the Spaniard Esteban Martin in late 1958. His career continued to flourish and two years later he claimed the British flyweight title when he knocked out the holder Frankie Jones at the King's Hall.

With a Lonsdale Belt around his waist, John became a natural contender for higher honours. In due course, he moved up a weight to bantamweight and a world and European title fight was arranged with the French-Algerian fighter Alphonse Halimi. The fight, which took place in London in May 1961, went the full distance and John was awarded the points decision to become the first Irishman since Rinty Monaghan in 1948 to win a world title. The fight is, naturally, well remembered by Caldwell.

"Halimi was a very, very dangerous man and a hard hitter and I know that well as he caught me many times throughout the fight," he said. "He was constantly at me – in and out all the time – and I couldn't take my eyes off him for a split second: the fight was one of the hardest of my career. I remember that after a terribly hard struggle, I eventually knocked him down in the last round and that got me the decision in the end. I felt as if I was on top of the world – which literally I was – and knew, as an Irishman, that it had been a great sporting achievement. I was the first fighter to win a world title since Rinty Monaghan, and it was everything that I could have wanted to achieve."

As champion, John won two further bouts before defeating Halimi on points in a rematch at Wembley. In February 1962, a unification bout for the bantamweight title of the world was arranged for Sao Paulo in Brazil, where Caldwell was to face the legendary Eder Jofre.

A bloody battle ensued in front of 26,000 fanatical fans, and the Brazilian gradually got on top to stop Caldwell in the tenth. John, who had been accompanied by his father on the trip, spoke of his memories.

"Eder Jofre was the greatest bantamweight and the hardest-hitter for his weight of all time," he said. "I remember the place was packed to the rafters and there were many thousands locked outside the arena. I just couldn't get to terms with him on the night, maybe it was the heat of the crowd, but it was an unbelievable occasion which I will never forget. As it turned out, it was my first defeat as a professional and it was very hard for me to take."

While Caldwell sought to regain his world title, a chance to guarantee a rematch with Jofre turned up rather closer to home – in his home city of Belfast. It was an occasion that has gone into the folklore of Irish sport.

North Belfast's Freddie Gilroy had been a friend and rival of Caldwell in both the amateur and professional ranks. Gilroy had made a name for himself in the world bantamweight division, and a clash with Caldwell for the British and Empire titles was set for the King's Hall on Saturday, 20th October. The King's Hall on Belfast's Upper Lisburn Road is an imposing cavernous exhibition centre built in Art Deco style. Owned by the Royal Ulster Agricultural Society, it is steeped in Belfast boxing history and it was only natural that the Gilroy versus Caldwell clash was fixed for this amphitheatre.

That Saturday, a crowd of 58,000 spectators had packed Belfast's Windsor Park for the Home International match between Ireland and England – a game which the visitors won three-one with a goal from Jimmy Greaves and two from Mike O'Grady. The match only proved to be the warm-up event for the eagerly anticipated fight later that evening. The Lisburn Road that day was a sea of spectators as the end of the International signalled an exodus towards the King's Hall.

At that time, the rest of the world watched as events surrounding the developing Cuban Missile Crisis brought the United States and the Soviet Union to the brink of the Third World War. Nevertheless, Belfast, in its own indifferent way, was engrossed in the clash of its own two local boxing superpowers. The prize at stake – in theory – was a crack at Jofre for the world title and a record crowd of 15,000 were in attendance to witness a fierce and bloodthirsty encounter.

That night has gone down in Irish sporting folklore as the greatest boxing occasion of the last century. Gilroy, the underdog, won the fight when Caldwell was forced to retire with a cut eye at the end of the ninth round. For the victor there was, however, to be no crack at the champion Jofre, only speculation of a rematch with Caldwell, which would have been a promoter's dream. The rematch never took place as Gilroy retired from boxing after the King's Hall clash.

Freddie Gilroy is on the record as saying that in his view the fight was a needless one that should never have taken place. There is no doubt that the media exaggerated the occasion as a grudge match between north Belfast's Gilroy and west Belfast's Caldwell. For John, due to the damage his eyes received during the fight, it was a bout that signalled the waning of his career.

"I thought truly that I was ahead when the fight was stopped, and I was definitely up for a rematch with Freddie," he said. "I had a feeling though when I saw him afterwards that he would never fight me again and I was proved right in the end. In that fight, I suffered very severe cut eyes and after that I was always having difficulty with my eyes."

While Caldwell was proved correct in his belief that Gilroy would never fight him again, his own career continued. Unfortunately, his problem with cut eyes came back to haunt him just three months later, when he was forced to retire from a bout with Michel Atlan at the Royal Albert Hall in London.

Undaunted, Caldwell won back the Commonwealth and British bantamweight titles in 1964 with a win over George Bowes at Belfast's Ritz Cinema. A year later, with two further victories under his belt, he was forced to retire in the tenth round against Alan Rudkin in a defence of his titles.

At twenty-seven years of age, John Caldwell had had enough of professional boxing. In 1965 he lost his final bout on points to Monty Laud in Nottingham, and returned to his trade as a pipe fitter in Belfast. The dream was over.

Looking back on his career as an amateur and professional boxer, John is proud of his achievements but dismayed at the treatment that he received from many in the game.

"In hindsight, I suppose that I am unhappy at the treatment I got from some managers and promoters. I never got what I felt I deserved out the game and it seemed to me that everybody got their cut of the purse before me. I felt like I was only a means to an end for some and that hurts me no end: but that's professional boxing. Saying that, I did get enough to buy myself a house back in Belfast, but it could have and should have been a lot more. But I enjoyed the whole experience immensely and have many great memories."

Caldwell retired from the fight game and returned to his trade as a pipe fitter. Today he will still receive a warm reception at any bill he attends in his native city, with those who saw him fight most emphatic in their applause. When asked about his views on boxing today, John is certain in the view that the game, in which he acquitted himself so well, is not the same one in which he competed.

"It was an entirely different set-up to the one that I became involved in fifty years ago," he said. "You had to be totally dedicated back then, clean-living and prepared to make a lot of sacrifices to survive at the top. It was a game for hard and skilful men and if you couldn't stick the pace you were found out very easily."

Today, John Caldwell is still a familiar figure around the Andersonstown Road in Belfast. A quiet and unassuming figure, many people would be astounded if they knew of the career that he had enjoyed. He remains sharp, astute, full of playful charm and possesses a fabulous sense of humour. When asked

to estimate the attendance at his King's Hall bout with Freddie Gilroy, he smiles and says wryly, "I don't know, I hadn't time to count them all. Freddie kept me too busy that night."

In June 2006, the 2012 London Olympic Road show came to Belfast's City Hall where the great Irish Olympians of the past were honoured and rubbed shoulders on a podium as they were introduced one by one to the assembled crowd. A special reception was afforded to John Caldwell as he took his bow in his native city. Afterwards, he posed for the cameras sporting his Irish Olympic towel from 1956, which had been preserved perfectly by his mother.

The year 2006 marked the half-century since John claimed his bronze medal at the Melbourne Olympics. Many things have changed in boxing, and indeed in his native city of Belfast, since that historic day but one thing has not changed. John Caldwell is still revered in Irish boxing circles – and will be for many generations. The boy from the terraced houses of Belfast's Cyprus Street has packed so much into his boxing career that his place in Irish sporting history is assured – and deserved!

Fred Tiedt

Golden Memories with a Silver Lining

The world of boxing suffered a body blow on the morning of 16th June 1999, when the death of Fred Tiedt was announced. The silver medallist from the Melbourne Olympic Games died after a long illness at the relatively young age of sixty-three in Dublin's Mount Carmel Hospital. His passing left a great void in Irish sporting history as he had been a true and dedicated ambassador for the country and the art of boxing. He had been a supreme stylist who in reality had been denied an Olympic gold in 1956 by a logic-defying decision that saw him condemned in the same manner that John McNally had been in Finland in 1952.

Tiedt was descended from Austrian immigrants who came to Ireland in the 1930s. He was born in Dublin in October 1935, one of four brothers who all made a name for themselves at the South City Boxing Club. By 1956, Tiedt had made his mark in Irish boxing and duly qualified to meet Harry Perry in the Irish welterweight decider.

Throughout this book, you will come across boxers who were to cross swords many times with a great rival within the ring. Neil McLaughlin met Davy Larmour on occasions too numerous to mention, whilst Billy Walsh and Michael Carruth's clashes held the attention of Irish boxing in the early 1990s. The names of Harry Perry and Fred Tiedt were inseparable within the boxing ring in the 1950s.

Their most significant clash saw Perry victorious in the 1956 Irish final, but the Irish Amateur Boxing Association – shrewdly, it seems in hindsight – chose Tiedt as Ireland's representative in the Melbourne Olympics. After a request was made by Perry's representatives, a box-off was organised between the two protagonists. Tiedt beat Perry on that occasion and went to the Games, while Perry accepted a compromise and dropped a division to go as light-welterweight.

At the 1956 Olympics Tiedt, in his opening bout, saw off on points the fancied Pole, Tadeusz Walasek – a skilled fighter who would go on to win both silver and bronze medals at the two succeeding Games. The Dubliner was then drawn to meet the American representative Pearce Lane. The American was the reigning US Army and Services champion, and was considered to be a tough opponent. However, it was Tiedt who made all the running in the fight and he was not troubled by Lane throughout the three rounds. Tiedt's cat-like footwork and ability to find his punches from range saw him home on a unanimous decision.

By now, Ireland had John Caldwell, Freddie Gilroy, Tony Byrne and Fred Tiedt all through to the semi-finals of the boxing event. Tiedt was to meet the Australian Kevin Hogarth in front of a partisan home crowd for the right to qualify for the final. In the end, Tiedt put on an exemplary display as he kept out of the Australian's reach for the duration of the fight. He adopted a defensive mode as he baffled Hogarth by bobbing and weaving on the ropes, then launched his own blistering attacks on the counter. A carpenter by trade, Tiedt displayed excellent boxing craftsmanship as he waltzed into the final where he would meet the Romanian, Nicolas Linca.

As Ireland's boxers fell one by one, Tiedt found himself the country's sole representative in the Olympic finals. In his semi-final, Linca had beaten the fancied Commonwealth champion Nick Gargano. The press had considered the Romanian as fortunate to come through that bout, a fact that made Tiedt favourite going into the final, which was held on 1st December 1956.

The result of the match was, as one observer described it, the only blot on what had been a great boxing tournament. History records that Tiedt was beaten on a split decision, but that result was very hotly disputed. The Romanian was awarded a three-to-two verdict and immediately there were howls of derision around the arena. The anomaly was that Tiedt had been awarded more points in total than the Romanian, but was denied on the majority verdict.

It was said that Lord Killanan (President of the Irish Olympic Council) had been asked by an Olympic official at the end of the bout to make his way to the ring, in the belief that the result had gone in Tiedt's favour. Wisely, not counting his chickens, the noble Lord retained his seat, not wishing to tempt fate. A Romanian referee was heard to say to Lord Killanan that Linca had been well beaten. However, it was Tiedt who took the verdict square on the chin. Eventually, there was to be gold for Ireland that day in Melbourne, as Ronnie Delaney raced to victory in the 1500 metres event.

Interestingly, in the Official Report on the 1956 Games, as produced by the International Olympic Committee, the fight between Tiedt and Linca was mentioned specifically in dispatches:

Welterweight – Probably the most unlucky boxer was Tiedt (Ireland) who lost a close final to Linca (Romania) after he had come through three very hard fights in his division against Aaleskra (Poland), Lane (USA) and Hogarth (Australia).

Despite the setback in the final, Fred Tiedt was soon back with his colleagues in the Irish team. It was reported that he was not made too despondent by the decision and the team began their arduous journey back to Ireland. On arrival at Shannon Airport on 12th December, where Fred's father, Ernie, and Uncle Paddy were present, the team began a crawl through Ireland where they were feted in every town as they made their way to Dublin.

From Limerick to Nenagh and then via Portlaoise, the squad eventually made their way to the Mansion House in Dublin, where a reception was given by the Lord Mayor, Mr Brisco T.D. When Tiedt was called to the stage, it took many minutes for him to work his way through the local well-wishers to receive his accolade.

The following evening, Fred was guest of honour at the annual University College Dublin versus Cambridge University inter-varsity match. His entrance to the Earlsfort Terrace venue was greeted by prolonged cheering. Ironically, that night, Tiedt was presented by a gold medal for his achievements in Melbourne, when Pat Donovan gave him the Athletic Union of Merit Medallion. On handing over the award Donovan, the President of the University College Boxing Club, told Tiedt that while he had been denied a gold in Melbourne, the University would not deny him an award.

The following evening, the same ceremony was performed by Mr Edwin Solomons, on behalf of the Trinity College Boxing Club, at the Trinity versus Cambridge annual match. The official engagements continued and culminated when the team was received by President Seán T. O'Kelly in Áras an Uachtaráin in Christmas Week, 1956. Tiedt was fast becoming a hero in his native city of Dublin.

With the glory of Melbourne behind him, Tiedt went into the ring to face Harry Perry in the 1957 Irish senior welterweight final. The match was the latest in the series of clashes between the two, and Tiedt proved to be Perry's master in the National Stadium that night and assured himself a place on the Irish squad bound for the European Championships in Prague. It also presented Tiedt with the prospect of an early rematch against Linca and an opportunity to put matters right from Melbourne.

With the confidence gained from the silver medal at the Olympic Games and with Irish boxing on a high, Tiedt was expected to go all the way at the championships. The Irish team had feasted on veal on their arrival in Prague, but it was a jaded and out of sorts Tiedt that started against the Dutch boxer, Jan de Vos. The anticipated match with Linca was not to be as the Romanian was withdrawn before the championships with a damaged hand.

The bout with de Vos did not to see Tiedt at his best. The Dutchman, who had been described as 'clumsy' by the press, held Tiedt for the opening two rounds. It was only in the third that Dubliner opened up with his jabs and found de Vos wanting. A unanimous decision was assured by Tiedt, but boxing was fast becoming a science that the Eastern Europeans were perfecting, and the Irishman's style was in need of change. Frank Cooper was the trainer of the Irish team in Prague and he was certain that Tiedt would need to adapt to progress. The twenty-four-year-old Swiss, Max Mier – a surprise victor over Scotland's Tommy McGuinness – was next up for Tiedt.

On the night that Ireland had Mick Reid, John Caldwell and Peter Burke, eliminated from the championships, Tiedt again found himself as the last Irish representative as he saw off Mier on points. It was evident that Tiedt was not at his best and his display was below par. His reluctance to come off the ropes and attack was something that would be exposed by the Eastern Europeans. His sluggish display was redeemed in the last round when he cut loose on his opponent to take the unanimous decision.

With Tiedt through to the semi-finals and assured of at least a bronze medal, things took a misfortunate turn. At the medical before his bout, an examination of his bruised hand called into question Tiedt's ability to compete. Without resorting to a pain-killing injection, Irish team manager Colonel Jim Devine took the decision to withdraw Tiedt from the fight. It was in some respects an admission that Tiedt was not producing the same blistering boxing that had seen him storm the Olympic Games. However, a European bronze, to add to an Olympic silver medal, made Tiedt a sought-after talent.

Accordingly, in 1958, Tiedt turned professional under the management of Belfast's Jimmy McAree. His first outing saw him out-point George Davis at the King's Hall, where fellow Olympians, John Caldwell and Freddie Gilroy were jointly topping the bill. A month later, Tiedt travelled to Glasgow and won his bout with Terry Lake. In July 1959, he made his debut in Dublin's Tolka Park against the Ghanaian, Sani Armstrong.

With four wins from four outings in a year, some pundits were predicting that Tiedt could become a contender for European honours. Meanwhile, others were spotting his shortcomings in the paid ranks, and the lack of an effective right hand was a hindrance. The tall Dubliner with a distinctive crewcut had still a lot to learn in the professional game and Armstrong gave Tiedt a tough fight in front of a sparse crowd at Tolka Park. The decision was a draw. Tiedt's limitations with the right hand were exposed again when, after dazing his opponent with his left on two occasions, he lacked the ability to finish the fight with a crisp right.

In November 1959 Tiedt suffered his first defeat, when Boswell St Louis beat the Dubliner on points at the Albert Hall in London. In March 1961, Tiedt was forced to retire at the King's Hall during a fight with Sandy Manuel due to a cut eye. A trip to South Africa in July that year saw him lose – unluckily – on points to Willie Toweel. This reversal was followed by an enforced retirement in the second round at the King's Hall against the

American Larry Barker. As he sat in the dressing room in the aftermath of that defeat, the superbly fit Dubliner was left to rue his luck as double vision forced the doctor to stop the fight.

"I wonder is this all worthwhile. I spent six months training for this and then something like this happens."

A defeat on points to Jimmy McGrail was followed by a victory in Belfast over Albert Carroll, which set up a crack for the Irish welterweight title against Al Sharpe, whom Tiedt had beaten earlier in his career. That fight at Tolka Park was to prove to be Tiedt's highlight in the paid ranks. Sharpe was a veteran of ninety paid fights and was a firm favourite to take his title. Tiedt was victorious on points, but the decision was widely derided by the Dublin crowd. Ned McCormack, Sharp's trainer, described the decision as 'diabolical', while Sharpe announced his retirement from the ring. Tiedt had been adjudged the winner by his own manager, Jimmy McAree, but the general consensus was that he had been fortunate to get the decision.

Regardless of the result, Tiedt's career was floundering: an Irish welterweight title was far removed from the glory of Melbourne. He fought a further four fights, winning two and losing two, and retired in his last fight against Al Sewell in the United States with an elbow injury after five rounds. It was November 1964 and his career in the ring as a professional had ended unfulfilled.

By this stage Fred Tiedt's achievements had reserved a place in Irish boxing history. He continued to play an active role in his beloved sport and oversaw the Trinity College Boxing Club for many years. That dedication was eventually rewarded by an honorary degree from the Dublin institution. He also became renowned as a respected referee in the professional ring, and was known as the consummate gentleman in his attitude and appearance. On the morning that Michael Carruth made history by claiming Olympic gold in Barcelona, Fred Tiedt was a special guest of the Carruth family in their Dublin home. The man who should have been the first gold medallist sat enthralled, as he watched Carruth take that honour thirty-six years later.

Fred Tiedt succumbed to his illness at an all too early age and his passing robbed Irish boxing of his wisdom and personality. On that famous December day in 1956, he was, in essence, the winner of Ireland's first boxing gold medal. However, at the end of the day, this gentleman will go down in history as another Irish fighter who never got the ultimate accolade he so richly deserved.

Freddie Gilroy

Socking it to the Soviets

Freddie Gilroy is a living legend in the world of Irish boxing and holds a record which is second to none. He is one of only four men from these shores to hold a Lonsdale Belt and was in his day a triple British, European and Commonwealth champion. In 1956 he was part of the most successful boxing squad to have represented Ireland, when he claimed bronze in a tally of four medals at the Melbourne Olympics. In addition, he was the victor in the greatest boxing occasion ever held in Belfast, when he stopped John Caldwell at the King's Hall in October 1962.

Remarkably, Freddie Gilroy's career ended abruptly after his win over Caldwell. A man at the top of his profession, he chose to walk away from the sport on a point of principle and left many wondering what he could have achieved if he had continued. The simple truth was that Gilroy had had enough of the fight game.

Born in east Belfast's Short Strand area in March 1936, Gilroy's family soon crossed the River Lagan and settled in Northwick Drive in the Ardoyne district. In the austerity that was post-war Belfast, Gilroy found his way to the St John Bosco boxing club in Corporation Street at the age of eleven and there began his glittering career.

"My first title came as a schoolboy when I won the club championships at the three stone twelve pounds weight," recalled Gilroy. "I then progressed on to the Down and Connor championships, which I won on four occasions, and then claimed the Ulster and Irish juvenile and senior titles. Later I graduated to the Irish team as a flyweight. I just loved the fight game and the competition with the other lads, for I just seemed to have the ability and winning titles became easy to me. I dedicated myself totally to the sport and I began to get the rewards of travel and recognition."

The highlight of Gilroy's amateur career came at the 1956 Melbourne Olympics when he won a bronze medal in the bantamweight division. The Irish team that year finished with a tally of four medals with John Caldwell, Freddie Tiedt and Tony Byrne claiming honours in addition to Gilroy. However, as he explained, his trip to the Olympics was in doubt due to a dispute which arose on a misunderstanding concerning his weight.

"We had travelled to tour the United States and Canada, the highlight of which was a match against the Golden Gloves

Left

Freddie Gilroy (*right*) lands a blow on Glasgow's Billy Rafferty in the King's Hall (British Title Fight) in 1959.

champions and a Canadian select. I was in New York airport
on the way home and decided to weigh myself on a set of
scales which were in the public part of the building," he said.
"The scales showed that I was heading towards two stones
overweight and somebody obviously saw this and word got
back to the Olympic Board that there was no point in picking
me due to being not ready. I, as an individual, always went
well overweight between bouts but I always had no difficulty
reaching weight in time, and shedding two stones would not
have been a problem. It was just the way that I was made up
and I always battled to stay at bantamweight.

"The fact was that the board indicated that I was out of the
reckoning due to the weight issue and I was devastated. I was
the number one choice at that stage so my manager Jimmy
McAree created such a fuss that the board admitted that there
had been a mistake and at the last minute they chose me to
represent Ireland in the bantamweight division."

The Olympic Games, which took place in Melbourne in
November and December 1956, were held amid the controversy
of the invasion of Hungary by the Soviet Union. The Superpower
had decided to crack down on perceived dissent by invading
its neighbour, much to the consternation of the West. The
'Communism vs. Capitalism' ideological battle was in many
ways played out at those Games and particularly in the boxing
ring. Gilroy, like most sportsmen, had no interest in the political
sphere, but he hit the headlines when he knocked out – in his
opening bout – the Russian favourite for the bantamweight gold
medal, Boris Stepanov.

"I remember there was a lot of tension in the air over the
Hungary invasion and my fight with the Russian was being seen
as a clash of East and West," he said. "He was the hot favourite
to lift the gold but I caught him with a sweet left hook in the
third round, over he went, and I knew he was not getting up.
The crowd were going absolutely wild as this was one in the
eye for the Russians; it was absolutely unforgettable and made
big news all over. In the next round of the competition I won
on points over the Italian Mario Sitri and I was now determined
to go all out for the gold. However, in the semi-final I came up
against the classy East German Wolfgang Behrendt, and he got
the decision. I thought though that it was a bad decision and I
had been robbed, but he went on to win the gold medal and I
had to be content with a bronze."

After the Olympics, Gilroy decided to join the paid ranks, for
Belfast at the time was a hotbed of professional boxing, thriving
on a diet of two shows a week, eleven months a year.

"I began fighting at bills in the Ulster Hall and I attracted a
good following with the place being packed to the rafters each

time I fought. I recall I got five pounds for my first bout, when I knocked out a guy called McReynolds, and seven quid for the second bout with Danny McNamee, but in those days that was nothing considering the money that the promoters were making. Then I was due to fight at the King's Hall in the under card of one of Billy Kelly's title fights. I was reluctant to fight as the money offered was peanuts, but I was approached by the Scot Sammy Docherty who offered me £250 to fight so I jumped at that."

Gilroy went from strength to strength and in January 1959, he claimed the British bantamweight title at the King's Hall when he stopped the ageing champion, Scotland's Peter Keenan. Gilroy was on a roll and Empire and European titles duly followed.

The next stage in his progress was a world title eliminator in London against Alphonse Halimi in October 1960. For the winner a chance to fight the then-world champion Eder Jofre was promised, and Gilroy is still to this day sure that the referee made a monumental mistake that evening. The French-Algerian Halimi, who died in November 2006, was a former undisputed world bantamweight champion. He had learned his trade street fighting in the mean back streets of Algiers and had acquired the nickname "Le Petit Terreur" in recognition of his ferocious talent. He was proud of his Jewish background and fought in shorts adorned with the Star of David. For Freddie Gilroy, this was to be his greatest challenge and it was a fight which left him sore, in more ways than one.

"I had out-boxed Halimi in the fight and I was sure that I had won," he said. "The two of us were in my corner shaking hands when the referee came over to raise the winner's arm and I'm sure in the confusion that he lifted Halimi's by mistake but by that stage it was too late to change the decision. It was my first defeat and it really bugged me."

For Halimi, his victory over Gilroy was – despite his obvious geographical shortcomings – "France's revenge over England for the death of Joan of Arc". Halimi went on to fight again for the world title and lost to Gilroy's compatriot, John Caldwell. The inevitable clash between the two Belfast pugilists was beginning to take shape.

While Gilroy was setting the pace in the bantamweight stakes, fellow Olympic medal winner from west Belfast John Caldwell was becoming prominent also in the professional fight game. A product of the Immaculata club in Devonshire Street, Caldwell, like Gilroy, had been a British and European champion and, when he moved from flyweight to bantamweight, a collision course was set for the Irish boxing clash of the decade.

In October 1962 while the rest of the world watched nervously the developing Cuban Missile Crisis, Belfast was engrossed in the clash of the two local boxing superpowers. The meeting of

John Caldwell and Freddie Gilroy captured the imagination of the country as they met for Gilroy's British and Empire bantamweight titles in the King's Hall on Saturday, 20th October. The prize at stake – in theory – was a crack at the Brazilian World champion Eder Jofre.

A record crowd of 15,000 from all classes and creeds were packed in that evening to witness a fierce and bloodthirsty encounter. The fight swung both ways many times and many observers feel that Gilroy was slightly in front as the ninth round commenced. However, Caldwell's eye was causing concern at the ringside and Gilroy was finding it constantly with both hands. Gilroy won the fight when Caldwell's manager, Sammy Docherty, retired his man at the end of the ninth round. Gilroy believed that he had been well ahead and is also adamant that the fight was a complete waste of time.

"I didn't want to fight John Caldwell at that time for I felt it was a stupid fight, a needless fight and one that should never have taken place. It was billed as a grudge fight between north and west Belfast but John and I were good friends that had travelled the world together so all the hype was way over the top. The media really built up the clash as at that time there was nothing else for them to do, and I remember the King's Hall was heaving that night and to be truthful I would have loved to have been in the crowd to have savoured the moment.

"Beforehand, I took time out of work and trained solidly for six weeks in order to lose four stone in weight and I was never as fit as I entered the ring. I knew John and his style inside out and did my homework well as I had every round clear in my head and I boxed to a plan and it worked out well."

The media that Monday was full of praise for Gilroy's performance, claiming that his powerful body shots had been the downfall of Caldwell. Many observers were sure that promoter Jack Solomons was to seek a rematch between the fighters and this led eventually to Gilroy's retirement from the fight game. The crack at Eder Jofre was perhaps high on Gilroy's agenda, but others believed that an instant rematch with Caldwell would prove more lucrative.

Solomons as a promoter was, unsurprisingly, keen to get a rematch and outlined his reasons why. "The return would be the crowd-puller of all time and I am aiming to put it on," he said. "Gilroy is a great champion and will prove to be a great world champion, but there must be a return. I don't remember seeing a better fight and Caldwell must get another chance."

Gilroy was unimpressed by the rematch prospect and felt he had been short-changed.

"I was under the impression that the crack against Jofre for the world title was in the bag, but Solomons wanted a rematch. I had already said that I thought the fight originally was a stupid idea and it was a pointless exercise. Then Solomons offered me £3,000 for a rematch and I knew that the bout was a real money-spinner, so I said I wanted £10,000 to make it worth my while but they refused to meet me. In those days, boxers were continually getting short-changed and I knew precisely how much a rematch would have generated in receipts, so I stuck to my position.

"Then the British Boxing Board of Control ordered me to defend the title against Caldwell and I told my manager Jimmy McAree that I would have to think about it. I can tell you that I thought long and hard but gave nothing away as the deadline neared."

So confident was Jack Solomons that Gilroy would fight Caldwell again that he organised a press conference in Belfast's Grand Central Hotel to announce the rematch, but the most vital person on the proposed bill never turned up at the hotel. Freddie Gilroy had decided he'd had enough.

"My manager Jimmy McAree was trying to coax me into the fight and I had already won one Lonsdale belt and was on my way to claiming a second, but I just walked away on a point of principle."

Eventually it was Caldwell who claimed the vacant title and Gilroy retired from the game at the top of his trade. The many questions of why Gilroy retired are still left unanswered but he was content that he had made the right decision.

Gilroy went back to work in his native Belfast and in the early 1970s bought the Tivoli bar in Donaghadee, Co. Down. However, the North had exploded into violence and the venture soon became a victim of the Troubles. A taste for travel, and for Australia in particular, saw him emigrate 'Down Under' in the mid-1970s but four years later, he returned to his native city and that is where he has stayed. On his return to Ireland he moved into his current north Belfast home situated near Ardoyne in the Crumlin Road district.

These days Freddie Gilroy is a picture of fitness and health. His living room bears testament to his career, with his Texaco award and Olympic medal prominent in his display of treasures. Sadly, the much-cherished Lonsdale belt he won was lost many years ago and he points out with regret that one was recently sold at auction for £58,000.

Today he keeps fit by working out three times a week in a gym in the centre of Belfast, and almost fifty years after Belfast's fight of the century he explained that he is still fondly remembered by the public.

"I would go into Belfast city centre a couple of times a week and everywhere I go people are saying 'Hello Freddie' to me," he said. "So one day I said to my wife Bernadette that I would keep a count on the number of people who greeted me during the day. It worked out that seventy-eight people had acknowledged me by name and I wouldn't have known who a quarter of them were," he added.

So it seems that time has not diminished in the eyes of the Belfast boxing fraternity the achievements of Ardoyne's Freddie Gilroy. He remains today a symbol of a distant era, of packed, smoke-filled halls where only the shrewdest and fiercest survived.

Jim Jordan

A Match for Dick McTaggart

It is said that the love of boxing is set coursing through one's veins from an early age. Sometimes in life you come across individuals for whom that adage is true. Jim Jordan learned to love the sport of boxing at a young age courtesy of his father John, who had enjoyed an accomplished career during the 1920s and Thirties. His father's love and enthusiasm for the fight game was inherited by young Jim, who went on to emulate his father's fighting achievements by carving out an impeccable career in boxing, and a love of the sport he holds to this day.

In the late 1950s, Jim 'Bap' Jordan was certainly a contender. With a plethora of Ulster and Irish titles he was making a distinct name for himself in international boxing circles. Spurred on by the heroics of the country's Olympic boxing success in 1956, he claimed a silver medal at the 1958 Empire Games in Cardiff. This was a fabulous achievement when one considers that his opponent that day in the Welsh capital was none other than the undoubted legend Dick McTaggart – a fight that Jordan still maintains he was unlucky to lose.

Born in Belfast's Milford Street, situated near St Peter's Cathedral in 1936, Jim Jordan was one of a family of ten children. His first calling to boxing was to the local Mother Cabrini club where he learned his basics before transferring to Lisburn Boxing Club as a juvenile but as a determined and proud fighter, Jim found the club's treatment less than complimentary.

"I was being looked after by Jackie Gormley at the time and was winning plenty of bouts and awards, but I left Lisburn after I felt slighted by one incident at an end of season presentation night. What happened was that I had been the most successful lad at the club by a mile and I was awarded a cup in recognition of this fact. However, it really was an insult as it was the smallest and most insignificant thing you could imagine. Then, I saw the size of the trophies that they were giving to the rest of the lads, and, to one lad in particular, which were unbelievable, and I knew that I was never going to get the recognition I thought I deserved. I said to myself that I should try and find a more suitable club in Belfast. So I joined up with Jimmy McStravick who ran the St George's club off High Street and by seventeen I had claimed my first Irish junior title."

Three Ulster senior titles in 1955, 1956 and 1957, together with a number of Irish senior honours, soon followed for Jordan and he was a natural selection for the Northern Ireland Empire Games boxing squad, the first time that a boxing team had been included in the North's Games team.

The team that went to Cardiff that year were a classy bunch, who all went on to claim medals. Along with Jordan at lightweight, Jimmy McAree, as trainer, had the formidable talent of veteran Olympic and European Games middleweight Terry Milligan at his disposal. Dickie Hanna of Lisburn was chosen as the bantamweight representative, while twenty-year-old Peter Lavery of the Bosco club was considered to be the team's best chance of glory. The final piece in the squad's jigsaw was in the form of twenty-four-year-old John McClorey, a featherweight representing the Holy Family club, who, like Jordan, was the reigning Irish champion.

A month before the commencement of the Games, while fighting in Dublin for a Co. Antrim select team against an English representative squad, Jim Jordan was to come up against his future nemesis, the Scot, Dick McTaggart, who fought for England as he was based in the RAF there. It was to be a foretaste of what lay in store at the Empire Games.

'Dandy' Dick McTaggart had won the Olympic gold medal at the 1956 Olympic Games in Melbourne, went on to claim a gold at the European championships in 1961, and was, in 1958, the top lightweight in the world. The respected BBC boxing commentator Harry Carpenter has described McTaggart as the greatest amateur that he ever saw. Born into a family of eighteen children in Dundee in 1935, McTaggart was a cook in the army who had been awarded the Val Barker trophy as the most stylish boxer in Melbourne. He was peerless in the noble art. Whilst Jordan lost out for the Antrim select to McTaggart in Dublin, it was a fight date with the Scot in Cardiff that he really yearned for.

In Cardiff, an indifferent victory by Jordan over the Welsh lightweight Joe Robson saw the Belfast fighter drawn against the English representative John Cooke for a place in the final. Cooke was highly regarded among the English hopefuls but Jordan boxed immaculately to see off the challenger with consummate ease. McTaggart, as expected, saw off his New Zealand opponent, Thomas Donovan, and the Scotland versus Ireland clash for gold was on.

In addition to Jordan's lightweight exploits, Terry Milligan had fought his way to the final of the middleweight grade, while McClorey, Hanna and Lavery – whose defeat had prompted the Northern Ireland team manager, Bill Rutherford to lodge an official protest – had to be content with bronze medals. The finals in Cardiff were held on Saturday 26th July 1958 and Jim Jordan was confident ahead of the clash with McTaggart.

"I had nothing to fear going into that final as I was a game fighter and had come across McTaggart before and felt that I could take him," he recalled. "I had not gone into that final to lie down against McTaggart, and I was going all out for gold no

'Bap' Jordan posing in his Co. Antrim vest in 1958

39

matter what. But in the end I didn't get the decision, and still to this day feel hard done by as I felt that with a bit of luck I could have shaded a win over McTaggart that day."

McTaggart was the hottest of favourites to take gold in Cardiff, but Jordan gave him nine minutes of unrelenting courage and determination. He gave his best performance of the Games but unfortunately for Jordan, the Scot had come into a rich vein of form. McTaggart meted out some neat punches in the opening round that caught Jordan but he refused to retreat and took the fight to McTaggart in the second. However, the Scot's defensive skill mopped up the Irishman's attacks and Jordan could not turn the tide. In the third, the Scot's composure saw him safely through to the end, but Jordan never stopped going forward and won the backing of a majority of the crowd in the arena for the fortitude he had displayed.

As the strains of 'Scotland the Brave' floated across the arena, Jim Jordan had to settle for second best and the silver medal. However, in the middleweight final, Terry Milligan was an impressive victor over the South African Philippus du Plessis and he took Northern Ireland's only gold of the Games. Indeed, Northern Ireland's medal haul from Cardiff ended up as one gold, one silver and three bronze, all of which were claimed in the boxing ring.

Prior to the finals in Cardiff, three of the Northern Ireland competitors had come to the attention of the professional promoters, and potential contracts were in the offing for Jordan, Lavery and Milligan. One headline of the time suggested that any of the fighters who won gold would be assured a £200 handshake to enter the paid ranks, while £100 was to be the price of turning professional with silver. After he returned home

Jordan thought long and hard about his future and, at twenty-two, took the decision to leave the amateur game behind. Much to the consternation of some observers that a promising amateur career had been cut short, Jordan explained that the economic necessities of life were foremost in his mind.

"It was costing me money to stay an amateur and I was working long hours in my day job, only to return and train at night and really something had to give," he said. "I joined up with John Kelly, the former British and European bantamweight champion as my manager and I thought that the path was assured for me to have a crack in time at the British title. All the talk after the Games of big money changing hands to turn professional never happened, and I was getting fifteen pounds a fight back then, so there was no fortune to be had. My first fight as a professional was in the Ulster Hall when I beat the undefeated Phil McGrath over eight three-minute rounds only four months after I returned from Cardiff."

While the victory over McGrath had been close, Jordan was satisfied that he had shown the ability to go untroubled beyond three rounds. In his next bout he out-pointed the rugged Ghanaian, Jimmy Sansu at the Ulster Hall and the press were glowing in their praise. In that bout, Jordan received damage to his left eye and in real terms, it was a race against time to save his career. In his next bout against Len Harvey, the third outing in a month, Jim attained a hard-earned victory but by now he was sure that the professional game would be a tough nut to crack.

"There is no point saying that it was easy to fight back then as it was not by any stretch of the imagination," he recalled. "I was working at the Ulster Hospital in Dundonald at the time as a plumber and saw myself on the hills around Belfast at six o lock in the morning before travelling to the hospital for eight. That was three or four buses there and back a day and by seven n the evening I was back at the gym for my sparring, so there was nothing easy about being a professional."

On 3rd January 1959 Jim Jordan suffered his first reversal as a professional fighter. That night in the Ulster Hall, Pat Loughran was awarded a technical knock out when damage to Jordan's left eye forced the referee to stop the bout. The problems with cuts to his eyes, which had first surfaced against Sansu, were soon to prove Jordan's downfall.

Jordan went back to his job as a plumber and did not box again for another fourteen months, when he won on points at the King's Hall over Roy Scanlon. A month later, he beat Harry Shaw in Manchester and followed this up with a victory, in the same city, over Jimmy Gibson, a fight for which Jordan received the apparent princely sum of eighty pounds. However, all was not rosy in the garden.

"I remember that I travelled to Manchester alone for that fight with Gibson and had to take care of all my expenses," he recalled. "I ended up staying in the Salvation Army hostel as it was all I could afford, and then I saw the entourage and facilities that Gibson had brought with him and I realised that things were just not right."

Those two victories were to prove a false dawn for Jim Jordan. A further victory over the rated Sammy Etioloja in Paisley in October 1960 proved to be the beginning of the end of his career. His last fight as a professional ended in defeat in the first round when Sean Leahy of Dublin stopped Jordan at Tolka Park in June 1962.

"The eyes were now causing me great problems and it was only a matter of time for me," he recalled. "I remember that fight

with Leahy so well, as I needed a lot stitches again in my bad eye and we travelled through the night to get back to Belfast. The problem with stitches is that your eyes swell up badly after they are put in so an injury can seem to be a lot worse than what it is and that is what happened. I remember getting into the house in Belfast and I didn't want to wake my wife Beryl as she was asleep, so I lay down on the couch in the living room. She heard me come in and came down and when she saw the state of my face she sobbed and sobbed, so I knew that it was time to call it a day."

Jim Jordan went back to his plumbing and put all his experience into following his brother Gerry, who was making a name as an amateur fighter in Belfast, and who emulated Jim's achievement by representing Northern Ireland at the 1970 Commonwealth Games. Today, Jim Jordan looks fit and healthy and still follows the game with great interest.

"I saw an awful lot of Europe as a boxer and I cannot complain when I look back," he said. "My highlight was standing in Cardiff beside McTaggart knowing that I had given my best against a fighter who really was super. But, as a professional, I always recall beating Sammy Etioloja in Scotland as I never felt as good in, or after, a fight as I was flying and that was something special. To young lads today I would say definitely get involved in boxing as it is a fabulous sport and take it in your stride. As a boxer, I refused to look back and always looked ahead in the belief that I was going to better all that I achieved."

For the man who lost to the legend Dick McTaggart in 1958 in Cardiff, a world of 'ifs' and 'buts' may still exist. One thing is for certain though, and that is that Jim Jordan from Milford Street was definitely a contender.

Harry Perry

From Harold's Cross to Blackrock

via Melbourne and Rome

In 1952, when Harry Perry was just seventeen years old, he received a setback to his boxing career. As reigning Irish senior featherweight champion, he was told officially that he was considered too young to go to the Helsinki Olympics. No argument, no debate; Perry was left to consider what could have been. It was a case of hard luck that made him even more determined to make the Irish team bound for Melbourne in 1956.

Seven years later, Perry suffered a further setback, this time of a medical kind. In Lucerne, Switzerland, at the 1959 European Boxing Championships, he was well ahead in his quarterfinal bout with the Dane, Benn Neilsen. In the third round, he ripped a ligament in his lower leg. He held on in great pain to claim a place in the semi-final and, thus, assured himself, and Ireland, of at least a bronze medal.

Unfortunately, the tournament doctors told him that he could not fight in the semi-final, as his injury would not stand up to a further outing. His opponent was awarded a walkover, Perry got bronze. Since those heady days of the 1950s, many observers of Irish boxing have speculated as to what Harry Perry could have achieved if he had gone to Helsinki in 1952 and had fought for gold in Lucerne in 1959.

Between 1952 and 1962, Harry Perry went to the European Championships in both Lucerne and Berlin, and to two Olympic Games in Melbourne and Rome. He was an Irish senior champion nine times at various weights in every year during this period except in 1957, when he lost to his great rival Fred Tiedt, and 1959 when he was nursing a damaged hand. He was asked to turn professional in the Gresham Hotel in 1955, only to tell promoter Jack Solomons to "wait and see". He fought in Chicago for Europe against the American Golden Gloves champions. In 2007, Perry was inducted into the Irish Boxing Hall of Fame; a worthy honour on a great career. No wonder.

Harry Perry was born in December 1934, in the Harold's Cross area of South Dublin. His father, James, owned a fruit and vegetable business and the family lived near the Grand Canal. His mother, Ellen, was a devoted homemaker who catered to the whims of the Perry clan. His first encounter with boxing came at a young age, and it was through trips to the Terenure Boxing Club that Harry and his gang gained an interest.

Left

Left to right – Tony 'Socks' Byrne, Fred Tiedt, Harry Perry, and Gerry Martinez (wrestler) during the 1956 Melbourne Olympics

"We used to go up to the club as kids and ask the guy in the gym for any old gloves or ropes going spare. So he would kindly give us the damaged gloves and we would have brought them back and have great fun on the streets. One day, a man called Gus Dorrington saw us larking around and he suggested that we took our chances at the Terenure Boxing Club, where we could spar to our hearts' content and learn how to box properly."

That was an offer too good to refuse and Perry and a number of his friends took up Mr Dorrington's proposal. After about three weeks at the club, Harry's friends had all found new pastimes, but his own personal devotion to the game had begun. Under the keen eyes of Dorrington and club coaches, Christy Carroll and Billy Knowles, Perry soon acquired the attributes that would help him survive in the ring.

"I really enjoyed the boxing club, but I was more of an observer as I sat dumbfounded and watched the older guys with the bags, skipping and sparring in the ring. There were a few lads at the club who were internationals, such as Dave Connell and Paddy Dowdall, and these guys were an inspiration. Dave had won a medal at the 1951 European Championships and Paddy had been a European professional champion. They were both great characters who took such an interest in us and they used to get us into the ring and show us all the moves."

By 1950, Harry Perry was making a name for himself in his native city. In that year, he represented Dublin Schools against London Schools in the Royal Albert Hall. Whilst there, the schoolboys were taken on a tour of the sights of London and this whetted Harry's appetite for further travel. In 1951, Perry lifted the Irish junior featherweight title and a year later he repeated that feat and subsequently, in 1952 and 1953, at senior level.

While the Helsinki Olympics were a possibility, he was not picked and today he still rues that missed opportunity.

"I thought I was going to be picked for Helsinki, but before they announced the team an American team came to fight Ireland and the officials said that all the Irish champions would be picked to box that night. Well, they announced the team for the American match and the boxer who I'd beaten in the Irish final, Tommy Reddy, was picked over me. I was taken aside and told that the officials were concerned that I would get hurt in the Olympics as I was so young, and

basically I was out of the reckoning. My view has always been that if you're good enough, you're old enough and it was a big setback, but it was a case of aiming now to make sure I made it to Melbourne in 1956."

In Helsinki, Tommy Reddy competed well, but without success, in a Games that saw Belfast's John McNally claim Ireland's first medal at boxing.

Meanwhile, Perry's successful run in the Irish senior championships continued. After he left Terenure College, he commenced employment in British Rail's offices at the Dublin Docks. In 1954, he left the Terenure Boxing Club and transferred to his own work's gymnasium to fight for the British Railways Boxing Club. Under new trainer Danno Maher, Perry improved and he duly came to prominence at a higher level. A call-up in 1954 to the European boxing team destined for Chicago has left an indelible memory.

"I remember I was picked to go to Chicago to represent Europe against the American Golden Gloves champions. In the 1950s, Ireland was not as well off as it is today and most people who went to America didn't go for a short visit. It was a great experience to represent a European team and the Englishman Bruce Wells was the captain of the squad. We stayed in New York and then went up by train to Chicago to box, and this was just fantastic for a lad from Dublin back then."

The calling to the professional ranks was never far away and one day a prominent promoter phoned the British Rail offices in Dublin and asked to speak to a Mr Harry Perry.

"I thought that the people in work were having me on when they said that Jack Solomons was on the phone for me. Anyway he asked me who was looking after me and then said that he would come over to the National Stadium to see me fight. Well I met him in the Gresham Hotel before the fight in the Stadium and he asked me why I wanted to keep fighting as an amateur? I told him the truth and that was that I enjoyed boxing, travelling abroad and the chance to win medals at major games. He said to me that if it was medals I wanted, then he would get me a bagful of medals in the morning, but the real prize in boxing was to fight for money as a professional. I was unsure and said to him that I was going to the European Boxing Championships in Berlin and if I won a medal I would then sign a contract for him."

Harry Perry duly went to the 1955 European Boxing Championships and lost in the opening round. The professional ranks did not entice him when he returned.

The Olympic Games in 1956 were held late that year in Melbourne. A chance to exorcise the ghost of Helsinki

presented itself as Perry won the 1956 Irish title at welterweight. However, his position on the Irish team was in doubt and, as he explained, the welterweight place had already been allocated.

"It was like four years previous as the officials called me in and said that they were taking Fred Tiedt to the Games as the welterweight. They explained that he was taller and they thought that he would be better suited at the weight. I was not happy and they then offered me a compromise by saying that if I could get down to light welterweight, then I could go. My club requested a trial fight with Fred and it was agreed to, but he beat me fair and square at the Stadium. Eventually, I went as the light welterweight but it was hard to drop down weight and, more importantly, to then keep inside it."

The 1987 Steve Martin and John Candy film *Planes, Trains and Automobiles* could have hardly done justice to the manner in which the Irish team travelled to the 1956 Olympic Games. Buses to Shannon, flights to New York, on to Chicago, a week in San Francisco for training, then a plane to Honolulu and from there on to Melbourne. Ireland brought its strongest-ever team of boxers and came away by finals' night on 1st December with four medals. Fred Tiedt won a silver medal, while John Caldwell, Freddie Gilroy and Tony Byrne claimed bronze.

For Harry Perry it was not to be. He was afforded a bye in the opening round of the light-welterweight division and in his first bout lost on points to the French representative, Claude Saluden. That early exit gave Perry time to take in the rest of the Games and his highlight was cheering to the Heavens as Ronnie Delaney stormed through to claim gold in the 1500 metres.

The return home to Ireland was another very complicated affair with Perry and Tony Byrne the last to leave Melbourne. It was a highly eventful road trip.

"There had been all sorts of mix-ups about our arrangements in Melbourne so Tony Byrne and I stayed on and then started off for home. In Honolulu, our plane was delayed for two days and the travel company put us up in the Waikiki Beach Hotel and that was out of this world. In New York we were delayed also and we were put up in style, so when we got back to Ireland it had been some experience."

With British Railways permitting Perry time-off on each occasion he represented Ireland on the international stage, Perry had not the concerns of other boxers as his job was a secure one. In 1959, he attended his third major games, the European Boxing Championships in Lucerne, Switzerland and won a bronze medal. That year Perry had not fought for the Irish title due to damage he had received to a knuckle in his right hand. By the time the

Above and Left

Above: Harry Perry today
Left: Harry Perry holding his trophy after winning a British Rail Boxing Finals 1960 held in the Royal Albert Hall

team was selected, he had recovered sufficiently to secure the welterweight nomination. Perry was fancied to go far in the Championship due to his wealth of experience.

However, once again, Lady Luck was to desert him. In his first bout, the Dubliner was lucky to record a victory over the Bulgarian, Schischman Mizew. That fight was too close to call but may have swung Perry's way due to a warning Mizew received in the first round for hitting after being told to break. Three right hooks to Perry's jaw in the last round left the decision too tight to call. Harry was considered fortunate to win.

His next contest was to see him an easy winner over the Dane, Benn Neilsen but during the last round a ligament snapped in his lower leg. The last minute was fought out in agony by Perry. He won convincingly to assure himself at least a bronze medal, but the prospect of a semi-final outing was doubtful.

"I was the type of boxer that was always bouncing away on the tips of my toes," he recalled. "The injury was serious as I would be hindered badly, however it turned out. They tried everything, strapped it up and put ice on it, but the tournament doctors took one look at it and said that I would be unable to fight in the semi-final."

Harry Perry, along with Adam McClean and Colm McCoy, claimed bronze medals for Ireland at the Lucerne championships. As Perry was eliminated through injury it was a case of what could have been.

"It was sad for me as I didn't get the chance to realise my full potential in those championships. It's hard being on a podium and seeing the other boxers and regretting that you didn't get a chance to box against them. I suppose that's all part of life and I soon got over it."

In 1960, Perry was to go to Rome – this time as the undisputed welterweight – to represent Ireland in the Olympic Games. However, the Irish team could not reproduce the magic of Melbourne and the Dubliner was eliminated on the tightest of split decisions by the Korean, Kim Ki Soo. Perry's swansong in international competition came at the 1961 European Championships in Belgrade. A great win over the ABA champion, Tony Lewis, in the opening round proved to be a false dawn as he was to lose in the quarterfinal to the French representative, Jean Josselin.

Harry Perry went on to win his last Irish senior titles in 1962, but his priorities in life were changing. "I married Anne and we bought our house in Blackrock and began a family. I was still boxing with British Rail and was the Railways' champion of Great Britain. Life just changes and I couldn't keep up to the training and standards that I had achieved."

Harry Perry has lived in that same home since 1960 and today he is retired and shares the home with Anne. In 1990, he retired from British Rail after thirty-three years. On his highlights, he remains sure that representing Ireland all over the world was top of the list. Whilst being part of a team in boxing is important, Perry feels that the individualism of the sport cannot be underestimated.

"Boxing is one of the sports where it's all down to how the individual performs. You are on your own in a ring and it takes skill, belief and determination to survive. Some of the greatest pleasures I have had in my career were when I read about myself in a paper if I had done well in a fight. It's nice to read things as all the work and dedication you put in is recognised. However, the opposite goes for you if you lose, but that is part of the sport."

On the downside, Perry is sure that the injury sustained to his leg in Lucerne robbed him of a chance of glory. Many observers would argue that his omission in 1952 from the Helsinki Olympics was also a chance lost. Perry's philosophy remains that, as reigning Irish champion, he had proved himself good enough. Unfortunately, others thought he was not old enough.

Harry Perry's boxing career still has moments that come back to tease him periodically since he retired in 1962. Today he is content with his achievements in boxing and has many cherished memories of a truly outstanding career.

Gerry Hassett

Been There, Seen That, Bought the T-Shirt!

Gerry Hassett is as hard as nails. Trust me; I do not use that description lightly. He is a man who turned to professional fighting at the age of seventeen and went on to box sixty-nine times in a career that lasted nineteen years. He is a veteran of the boxing booths in the East End of London. He was Muhammad Ali's bodyguard when 'The Greatest' came to Ireland. He brushed shoulders with the Kray twins and faced down two members of the Richardson Gang. He has policed the doors of the roughest establishments in Ireland and Britain. He will readily admit that he was "no angel in the ring" and was disqualified on three occasions. Oh! I almost forgot – the South African version of the mafia threatened to put a bullet in him if he did not throw a fight!

Now in his seventies he is still as strong as a bull. However, as he sits reminiscing in his Downpatrick home, sipping tea with the manners of a lord, it's hard to imagine the life that this man has overseen. In professional boxing it's a case of 'dog eat dog' and Gerry Hassett has a tale to tell. Born in the Springfield Road area of Belfast in 1933, Gerry Hassett was given the nickname 'Louis' after the great fighter Joe Louis. The name came about through his tendency to get into numerous street scrapes in and around his district. As Hassett recalled, his reputation was well known, but he feels somewhat unfair.

"I had the name as a bit of a bully when I was younger but I never bullied anyone and despised people who were bullies. I suppose I was a bit of a nuisance and one night a policeman by the name of John McNeill, better known as 'Pig Meneely', came to our door to see my father. Well, the policeman said to dad that they were fed up with me and if I wanted to fight then he would take me along to a local boxing club where I could have all the fights I wanted. So he brought me round every club in the city until I arrived at the St Matthew's club and thought that this was the one for me. Jimmy Brady was the trainer at the club and he got me into the ring for a bit of pad boxing and that was me hooked."

Remarkably, within a month, Hassett was fighting in the final of the Northern Ireland boys' championships, where he lost out to another boy who would go on to make a name for himself, Harry Enright.

"Harry beat me that night and for me, someone who thought he was a hard lad, it broke my heart and I came out of the ring and cried," recalled Hassett.

Hassett was quick to learn from his defeat and three weeks after the bout with Enright, he fought him again and this time was victorious. In his second year as an amateur, he took Ulster and Irish honours and that was the form he continued as he moved through

the ranks in boys' boxing. His first taste of 'international' boxing came through the most peculiar of circumstances, when he was asked by the Royal Ulster Constabulary to fill in on their team who were to take on the Scottish police in a representative match.

"It came out of the blue when a policeman approached Jimmy Brady and said they needed a lightweight to box in Glasgow for the police," he said. "My trainer pointed out that I was just a kid at sixteen but in the end I travelled to Scotland to represent the RUC team and that was something else."

Back in Belfast, Hassett's age was against him: he yearned to fight as a senior, but, at sixteen, he was still ploughing the junior ranks and felt he was getting nowhere. At the age of seventeen, he decided to hang up his vest and try his luck in the professional ranks. With little or no support in the offing, he appointed his father Joe as his manager and his career began.

"In those days there were plenty of guys prepared to pay a few pounds for lads to fight on unlicensed bills and when I was still an amateur I had a couple of such fights in Lurgan," said Hassett. "I then fought a guy called Hugh Smyth, then Jackie Donnelly and Fred Morton, all within about a month of officially turning professional. In those days you could have fought every night of the week and the crowds were out in force with the Ulster Hall packed to the rafters like sardines. I was getting paid a ten pound note every time I fought and that went to my father as there was little or no money coming into our house."

Hassett's winning streak came to an end one evening in May 1950, when he lost on points against Bunty Adamson, who had a significant weight advantage over the seventeen-year-old. Undeterred, he kept at the game and fought on to establish a reputation as a hardened and fearless fighter. A reputation that he admits went somewhat to his head.

"I cried after Bunty beat me and that taught me a lesson that I will never forget as it had been my own fault. I had not been keeping at my training and Jimmy Brady saw that I was messing about and he knew the defeat to Bunty would teach me a lesson. My career was not foremost in my thoughts and I remember one day I was kicking football in the street when a car pulled up and a promoter asked how I was keeping. I said 'okay' and he asked could I fight that evening against a guy called Paddy Dowdall, who had been a former European champion. I ran in and got my father and before I knew it I was in the ring fighting as a nineteen-year-old against Dowdall.

"Things in those days were chaotic and really and truly something like that should never have been allowed to happen."

For Gerry Hassett, the rules of boxing, designed by the Marquis of Queensberry, sometimes proved to be a battle to

Above and Left

Above: U.S. World Heavyweight Champion Rocky Marciano, right, charges into sparring partner, U.S. Toxie Hall. Hassett became friends with Marciano in South Africa
Left: Gerry Hassett during his bout with Jan Pieterse in South Africa, 1967

Right

Publicity shot of Gerry Hassett taken around 1965

adhere to. One moment of madness during a fight in 1953 almost finished him as a fighter. In a bout against Oldham's Harry Warner at the Ulster Hall, the referee, William Duncan, cautioned Hassett for a breach of said Queensberry Rules, and found himself on the end of a right hook from Hassett. It was a moment of madness which saw him disqualified and the powers-that-be calling for his licence to be revoked. The date set for the hearing was duly appointed by the Northern Ireland Boxing Board and it was a case of plea-bargaining. Even the sinned-against referee spoke on Hassett's behalf. The net result was a six-month suspension, but the licence was not revoked. A move to London for a time saw Hassett keep fit by sparring in the East End for a number of promoters.

"I remember that I was brought over to spar Tommy McGovern who was preparing for a British title fight, and I got twenty pounds a week plus my lodgings paid for so I was happy. It was then that I got involved at the boxing booths at the fairs which were an easy way of making a few quid on the side. I was getting fifteen pounds a night and all I did was go out on a stage and the guy would shout: 'Roll up, Roll up, who fancies their chances to make a few pounds by fighting this Irish boy?' So all these tough guys from the East End fancied their chances, but they hadn't a clue and I had them away in a couple of minutes. It didn't matter how big or strong they were as you could outfox them by skill alone and it was easy money. I always remember that I bought myself a great suit of clothes with the money I made and that was great."

With his penance completed, Hassett returned to Belfast and his career recommenced on St Stephen's night, 1953. A series of wins and defeats followed and his career became increasingly mediocre. The potential for glory had diminished greatly with his suspension and he was seen as damaged goods in some quarters. Even so, moments of class permeated the ordinary as Gerry Hassett continued into the 1960s as a seasoned journeyman. Hassett progressed through the divisions as his weight increased and he became a regular name on under cards throughout the British Isles.

However, in 1967, at the age of thirty-five, a bout was secured in South Africa, against the darling of the apartheid country, Jan Pieterse. A trip of a lifetime ensued which saw Hassett victorious when the South African was disqualified but, as he recalled, all was not as it seemed.

"I travelled out there confident and was approached before the bout and offered a package to throw the fight. The gambling thing was big in South Africa and their version of the mafia was in control of it so there was always some shady type prepared to have a word in your ear. They were talking big money – a lot more than I was on for the fight – but I refused as I was not like that. Well they thought I would bite anyhow and in the first round I hit Pieterse clean in the face and broke his nose with two punches. Anyhow, one thing led to another and he hit me with the head and the referee disqualified him. I went into that fight with a middle shade and I came out with one, so it was easy enough.

"The natural reaction from the South Africans was to get a rematch and the money they were offering was great so naturally I agreed. That was only the start of the hassle and I got word that they were going to make sure that their boy got the decision in the second fight. So I made it known that there would be going all out to win and my trainer said to me that these guys were out to shoot me if I didn't give them the fight they wanted."

Some time in late January 1968, the papers in Belfast carried stories regarding the mysterious disappearance of Gerry Hassett in South Africa. Concern was expressed that he had become mixed up with the wrong people and was in deep trouble. As he later explained, both he and his trainer felt that in order to prepare properly for the fight it would be wise to go undercover.

"There was a definite threat out on me so we decided to head to the bush to do our training from there well out of prying eyes. Eventually we made it up for the rematch and things turned out okay as regards our safety. Pieterse beat me that night in front of 15,000 spectators by half a point, but it was a gruesome fight throughout and we both ended up cut open very badly. Where he got the half a point over me I will never know as I had him down twice in the fight, but

Right

Gerry Hassett with former Deputy Lord Mayor of Belfast, Joe O'Donnell and Thomas 'Hitman' Hearns, 2004

that's hometown decisions for you. It all got nasty then and I remember offering him to go outside to finish it properly but he wouldn't have it."

No rematch took place in the car park that night but Hassett has fond memories of staying with the great Rocky Marciano while in South Africa. As he recalled, the former heavyweight champion was not all he had expected.

"He had the strongest handshake of any man and you knew that he had power in that body," he said. "But then when he spoke it was in a high pitched manner and it was hard to believe it was the same man you were dealing with. He was a real gentleman though and had a presence of a true champion."

A year and two months after his South African adventure, Gerry Hassett got into the ring at the Ulster Hall to fight Terry McTigue for the Northern Ireland area light-heavyweight title. He lost by a knock out in the fifth round and that was his last outing in the boxing ring.

A new life beckoned as Hassett started into the security business and began providing cover for events throughout Ireland and Britain. At one such event in Glengormley outside Belfast, he came across two individuals with a reputation known far and wide.

"It was a boxing bill and I was organising the security and two guys at the front were messing around and flicking things into the ring. So I went up and grabbed them and told them in no uncertain terms that if they persisted that I would throw them out the doors, no questions asked. Frank Carson the comedian was doing the cabaret at the show and he ran over and grabbed me and said to watch myself as they were part of the Richardson Gang who were over from London to look at a fighter. The situation developed into a standoff and they wanted to have a go but I was game. It was eventually sorted out but I didn't care, and would have had no hesitation in taking on the two of them. Funnily, I heard later that they actually admired me for the way in which I handled them and asked if I would be interested in doing some security work for them."

In 1972, Hassett's name in the security business was growing and he landed the plum job of overseeing the arrangements for the visit of Muhammad Ali to Ireland to fight Al Lewis in July of that year. Strangely, he remembers that Ali's private persona was totally at odds with his public face.

"I found him to be a very quiet person who didn't really want to bother away from the cameras. We were there to make things run smoothly and ensure that he got to where he needed to get there with little hassle. I recall he was ever so polite and nice in his dealings with us, but just wanted to be left alone with his thoughts away from the media."

Promoting and managing boxers became another of Hassett's sidelines. He took an interest in names such as Neil McLaughlin and Charlie Nash. However, acrimony and falling out were all part and parcel of the paid fight game: Hassett soon decided to concentrate on his security business, leaving boxing behind. Today, as he reminisces about his career, it would be appropriate to say that Hassett has been left dismayed by professional boxing. He is sure in the view that there is a level of bias which will always count against a proper decision being awarded.

"The hardest thing for me was losing fights that I knew I had won," he said. "I learnt the hard way in the early days and I admit I found it hard to keep cool, especially when the abuse was coming in from the balcony. The fight game is tough and sometimes it borders on the farcical what goes on inside rings."

Despite having been involved in boxing for over seventy years, Hassett is adamant on his view regarding the future of the game. Surprisingly, he is sure that the drawbacks of the sport outweigh the benefits.

"If you asked me what I think the best thing that they could do to boxing I would say to ban it. I have seen too many men end up badly affected by the game where today they can hardly function. I carried on too long and got out unscathed, but others haven't and they are staying in the ring and getting damaged permanently. It's not worth it and I would say that the most important thing is not to get into the ring, but more importantly get out before it's too late. I can say ban it but they never will as the fighting will go underground and people will really get hurt. All they can do is control fighting but when I come across some of the boxers I knew and see how they have coped I just find it so sad."

Therefore, it seems that time has mellowed even the fiercest of fighters, as was Gerry Hassett. The Queensberry Rules were not always adhered to strictly by the man nicknamed after the great Joe Louis in his youth. As he sips his tea in his Downpatrick home, his still youthful face bears the scars of many cuts and clashes of head. However, his eyes exude warmth that not many witnessed in the ring. Gerry's days of thunder are over but he is always prepared to contemplate a return.

"I'm thirteen stone now and still on a diet," he explained. "I have boxing in my blood and always will do. If a man came to my door and said 'would you fight next week at twelve stone?' I would be trying to get the weight off as I am game for anything. You just can't keep me out of the ring and maybe one day I will come back."

As he lifts his cup and drains off his tea, it is noticeable that, at seventy-four, Gerry's arms still resemble a rather famous cartoon sailor man. Gerry Hassett in the ring again? I wouldn't bet against it.

Jim McCourt

The Prince of the Immaculata

It is now over half a century since James Vincent McCourt first passed through the doors of Belfast's world-famous Immaculata Boxing Club. What the eleven-year-old from Leeson Street off the lower Falls Road didn't know was that he was embarking on a glittering boxing career that would see him achieve Commonwealth, European and Olympic glory. Or that he would rub shoulders with presidents and popes, tour the world with his country and finish his career with an astonishing record of 496 fights, with only fifteen defeats.

Now in his sixties, McCourt is a man who represented his country on the highest stages with skill, panache and no shortage of courage. Today he is a quietly spoken former pugilist who has seen the highs and the lows in sport and life in general. An unassuming man who is reluctant to boast of his achievements, preferring only to speak of his love for the game to which he has devoted most of his life. His story is worth the telling and preserving for Irish sport.

Born in Belfast in January 1944, the youngest child of James and Bridie McCourt, Jim McCourt attended the local St Joseph's primary school in Slate Street. The McCourts were a well-known family in the district and ran a small electrical and cycle shop from their home. Jim always had a love for sport and showed a natural talent for games and competitions as a child. Given the history of boxing in the city, it was natural that McCourt would gravitate towards a local institution that was producing fighters of note who had the ability to produce the best.

To appreciate what made Jim McCourt the boxer he was it is necessary to understand the place that Belfast was in the 1950s. In essence, the city was a pugilistic conveyor belt that produced boxers of style, class and quality. Men such as John McNally, Freddie Gilroy, Bernie Meli and John Caldwell were the heroes of that era who put Belfast and Ireland on the world boxing map.

By the time McCourt joined Immaculata, the club already had two former boxers with Olympic medals to their names, and this was a period when the pugilistic standards were sky-high across the city. For somebody to emulate such boxers, it was essential that they possessed exceptional talent. The fighters of the Immaculata club were overseen by the legendary trainer Jack McCusker and he took special notice of young Jim McCourt. McCusker knew exceptional talent when he saw it as he had just overseen the rise of a local boy called John Caldwell.

Housed in Devonshire Street in the Lower Falls district, the Immaculata Club was a dilapidated building which catered for many sports for the local boys. In an era of scarcity and poverty it provided a valuable social outlet to the surrounding district. In boxing, particularly, it was setting the highest standards in the

city. For a new boy such as Jim McCourt, a world of opportunity and glory awaited him.

Competitive action was almost instantaneous for Jim and within two weeks of joining the club he reached the final of the Down and Connor boys' championship, only to lose narrowly. That first championship experience of the Noble Art left the love of boxing coursing through McCourt's veins. He learnt his trade eagerly and progressed rapidly through the ranks, proving himself untouchable in Ulster. In 1962 he won his first Irish vest representing his country against Bulgaria. In 1963, a clean sweep of Ulster and Irish junior and senior lightweight titles made the pundits sit up and take notice that the boy from the North was indeed a special talent.

The following year, McCourt again took the Ulster and Irish senior titles and he was, by right, on his way in October to represent Ireland at the Tokyo Olympics. A trip of a lifetime to a novel Games in Japan that was to prove to be the turning point of his career. When the Games had ended, the only Irish medal claimed came courtesy of McCourt, when he won bronze in the lightweight division. His memories from the Games are fond but because he was involved in competition until the final day he never got to see much of Tokyo or savour the experience. As he recalled, he was confined largely to the Olympic Village.

"I had to stay at the arena right up to the last day to get my medal after the final, so I didn't get a chance to see much else but inside the village," said McCourt. "The gold medal that year was won by the great Josef Grudzien of Poland. I was very disappointed to lose my semi-final though to the Russian star, Barannikov; indeed many thought that I was the winner on that day."

On arrival back in Ireland, McCourt and his medal were the centre of attraction for the media at Dublin Airport, but he had little or no knowledge of the welcome that awaited him back in his native Belfast.

"My mother and father joined me on the train home from Dublin and when we arrived at Great Victoria Street I saw the St Peter's Brass Band from the parish on the platform, but I thought that they were going off somewhere to perform," he said. "Then I saw the crowds behind the barrier and the band began to play. The next thing I knew I was lifted shoulder high through the station and onto the back of a lorry and up to Leeson Street."

The strange thing for Jim McCourt was that he could not understand why he was receiving all the adulation. He felt that he had let everyone down by losing out in the semi-final, such was his confidence and style. The welcome home was something special as the tight-knit community was out in force to acknowledge his achievement.

Above and Left

Above: Liam McBrinn (author's father-in-law), Tony Flynn (author's father) and Jim McCourt, Salthill, Galway 1963
Left: Jim McCourt pictured with his parents Bridget and Jimmy on his return from the Commonwealth Games held in Jamaica, 1966

"When I arrived back in Leeson Street, there were crowds and photographers everywhere but I felt that I had failed and was still a bit disappointed," he said. "I just couldn't take it all in and but the experience was super and it began to sink in just what an achievement it was."

Whilst Jim had been disappointed to have not come back from Tokyo with a gold medal, retribution was not long in coming. In March of 1965 he was a convincing winner over the gold medallist Grudzien in an Ireland versus Poland international at the National Stadium in Dublin. It was an occasion that he will never forget as the Stadium was packed and erupted when McCourt beat the Olympic champion convincingly.

"The place was heaving that night in expectation of the fight with Grudzien," he said. "I wanted that fight so badly as I felt that I had something to prove from Tokyo. Henry Turkington was on the bill and he fought another Pole who had won gold in Tokyo. He lost however and I felt that it was up to me to prove a point. I fought a great fight and had him all over the ring, but the roars of the crowd spurred me on and I felt so happy when I got the decision."

The success story continued two years later, when he won a gold medal at the Commonwealth Games in Jamaica. In the opening round of those games, McCourt had seen off the English favourite Tony Reilly; thereafter, the gold medal was a formality. That was followed by a further – but less successful – Olympic outing in 1968 held in Mexico. Jim lost out to a West German opponent in the early rounds but felt that he was not in proper physical shape at the games due to a nasty bout of the Mexican ailment known as Montezuma's Revenge!

With McCourt now operating at the pinnacle of the amateur game, it was inevitable that he would attract the attentions of the professional fight promoters. To his regret, McCourt never took the leap into paid ranks and chose the path he was most comfortable with.

"In about 1965, the English promoter Bert McCarthy offered me a £5,000 contract for twelve fights in London," said McCourt. "In those days a fee like that could have bought you four semi-detached houses in Belfast and was not to be sniffed at. I thought about it long and hard, especially as McCarthy was going to let me train out of the Immaculata in Belfast. But some people didn't want me to go professional and I was told off the record that if I stayed an amateur then I would, on retirement, be

Jim missed his plane due to leaving his passport at home for an international against England, Aldergrove Airport, 1967

given the job of Irish Olympic coach, so I decided to stick to the amateur game. Of course the coach thing never happened as it was all speculation and I do really regret that I never tried the paid ranks, for I feel that it was the only natural progression open to me at the time."

In the 1960s, the demarcation lines between the amateur and professional boxing ranks were fixed in stone. McCourt, a joiner by trade, recalls the hardships he had to endure to keep down a job and continue a boxing career.

"Today to achieve success in the Olympics would guarantee some sort of sponsorship or grant, but in those days I was not allowed to undertake anything that would break my amateur status," he said. "When I was interviewed for television or radio, the cheque was made payable to the club. I recall on many occasions training on a Thursday evening, and then working on a Friday while fasting and travelling to Dublin to take part in a tournament that evening. If I won through to the final I had to travel back to Belfast that night for work on the Saturday and then back to Dublin to fight in the final that evening. I lost every penny for being absent from work on international duty and I had to pay my own way to Dublin to compete in tournaments."

What drove McCourt on to greatness was his love for the sport and especially representing his country at international level. If financial reward was not forthcoming, there were other compensations to be had. Jim recalls with pride sitting not five feet from Pope Paul VI in the Vatican when the Irish boxing team had been afforded a private audience with him in 1966.

"We were treated fabulously everywhere we went on international duty and it became normal to receive the best treatment," he recalled.

Indeed time has not erased his achievements as on a trip in 2005 to a function for Irish Olympic medal winners at Áras an Uachtaráin, Mary McAleese took the opportunity to tell McCourt of how she skipped an afternoon of lessons at St Dominic's High School to witness his return to Leeson Street from Tokyo in 1964.

Towards the end of his career, controversy occurred when McCourt was at loggerheads with the Irish Boxing Board over their insistence that he undertook collective training with the rest of the Irish squad.

"I just couldn't go along with it," said McCourt. "In the Immaculata, under Ned McCormick and Vinty McGurk, I had the best training available in Ireland. I was sparring with professionals like Spike McCormick, Peter Sharpe and Jim McAuley and to be truthful the collective training did not help me. My view then was that what had made me the boxer I was came down solely to the excellent advice and training I was getting at the Immaculata club. I was not prepared to change my routine. I started having weight problems when I did collective training and in the end I indicated to the authorities that I was unwilling to do it. Eventually I was called in front of the governing committee and told that I was not going to be picked unless I toed the line. I stuck to my principles and they told me that I was out of the reckoning for international duty."

This decision to stick to his principles cost McCourt dearly, and he was not picked to represent his country at the Munich Olympics in 1972. His career as an international was, at the age of twenty-eight, all but over.

McCourt left the Immaculata in the 1970s but continued to fight for the St Agnes club in Andersonstown until 1976. He also began to raise a family with his wife Mary in Belfast. Since then, apart from a couple of stints as a trainer, he has been by and large absent from the world of Irish amateur boxing.

Today his Finaghy home bears little or no evidence of the sparkling amateur career he enjoyed, which is in keeping with his own personal unwillingness to boast of his achievements. He still works as a joiner by trade but is intensely private and shirks publicity. Jim is keen to look back, in admiration, to the great boxers he has seen, and with a knowledgeable eye heaps praise upon those whom he has admired. Jim is glowing in his comments on other boxers. However, one man who inspired him to greatness still has a special place in his heart.

"The greatest boxer of all time in my view was Muhammad Ali and nobody could touch him," said McCourt. "In Irish terms, I always thought that Mick Dowling was a bit special, as was Brendan McCarthy. But the question as to who was the best boxer that this island ever produced is easily answered, and without a shadow of a doubt that was John Caldwell. John was just everything that I wanted to be as a boxer. His style and elegance inspired all of us in the Immaculata. We felt that we were privileged that he was a local lad, and to watch him in the ring was a fantastic education. He was the greatest and there is no doubt about that. John had everything and was something special. Just seeing him spar gave me such confidence and I owe him a lot."

Jim McCourt's style of boxing was regarded as very hard to compete against. His reluctance to involve himself in battles, together with his skilled southpaw approach, meant that he was a counter attacker who, while absorbing some punches himself, always ensured that his opponent shipped significantly more hits than he did. His boxing philosophy was simple: "Why should I put my face on the line chasing after opponents when all I have to do is wait for them to come to me."

Recently a mural was commissioned in the lower Falls district to the heroes of the Immaculata club and both McCourt and Caldwell are featured. They are but two representatives from a district that has given the world many of its most courageous and graceful boxers.

McCourt was emphatic on his proudest moment in his career when he said: "It has to be representing my country in the green vest over the years; nothing else came close to giving me so much pride. To feel that I gave so many people so much pleasure in the boxing ring has made me think that it was all worthwhile. I always remember my dad standing at the steps in the National Stadium as I prepared to get into the ring for an international. He never missed a bout and always claimed not to be nervous when I was fighting. One night, I was standing with him and I asked him was he nervous? He said 'no'. Then I noticed he had lit two cigarettes – one in each hand – and was puffing on both of them. He was nervous alright!"

Jim McCourt wore the green vest with pride, just as he had the Immaculata and Ulster singlets. Nobody will argue or doubt his ability or greatness. He has stood the test of time in the world of the Irish greats and his place as a sporting legend is unquestioned.

Sean McCafferty

Beating the Cubans with 'Tokyo Paddy'

When Sean McCafferty looks back on his career in boxing, he is certain when he says that he has no regrets about leaving the fight game behind. A career as a professional that saw him box eighteen times ended on 10th February 1970. He retired after he had been disqualified – in his view, and in the view of many present, unfairly – in a bout with Sammy Lockhart in Belfast's Ulster Hall. Acrimony followed with the boxing authorities, which convinced Sean that he was sick and tired of the sport he had devoted a lifetime to. His career as an amateur had been exemplary, but, as a professional, a bitter taste still lingers over the manner in which it all came to an end.

"Professional boxing is a dirty game where the god is money and nothing else counts," he said. "I was just fed up being used for the benefit of others and in reality I was just a means to an end. When you lose as a professional you're finished and good luck is the most important thing required, but if the luck is out, then it's a sorry tale."

One particular event at the World Sporting Club in London's Mayfair illustrated perfectly to Sean the difference between the 'haves' and the 'have-nots' in professional boxing.

"I remember fighting in the World Sporting Club and it was a real eye-opener for me. Barney Eastwood had hired a plane for the fighters and bookmakers from back home to go over.

The guy I fought was called Felix Brami and it was a black tie function with dinner laid on for all the guests, so fine brandy and cigars were the order of the day for the punters. I lost my bout and afterwards I sat in the lobby on my own and feeling physically sick as I had been carrying a bug. I was as white as a ghost and one of the Belfast bookmakers asked me if I was okay. I said 'not really' and I felt really ill and he said he would get me a cup of tea as it might help me. While I drank my tea I saw all the finest china, silverware, crystal and expensive wines being brought to and from the room for the guys in suits who were watching the fights. It became clear to me that I was the poor relation in that I was not even provided with a cup of tea. I was just there to get into the ring to entertain and make a lot of money for other people. In the professional fight game, if you're a winner, you're a winner and everyone wants to know you. If you're a loser, nobody cares about you."

Sean McCafferty was born within spitting distance of Belfast's Smithfield Market in December 1944. The son of Patrick and Mary McCafferty, Sean's family was one of three living in a townhouse in Francis Street, a house that at one stage was home for twenty-eight people.

He joined the St John Bosco Club at an early age and followed the usual route taken by young talented pugilists by winning the Antrim and Ulster boys and juvenile championships. By the time he had turned seventeen, Sean had a difficulty to contend with; he tipped the scales at a mere six stones.

"I just could not put any weight on no matter what I tried," he said. "From no age I was working after school in McGlade's chemist shop in Divis Street, which was a three or four miles jog for me after school, and then at night I did my training at the club, so I was always fit and lean. If I wanted to make the senior grade in boxing I had to put on some weight so I stopped training for six months and was told to eat loads of porridge. I eventually made it to flyweight and at five feet five inches was considered very tall for the weight."

Regardless, in 1963, Sean McCafferty made the grade in Irish amateur fighting by taking the junior and senior Ulster and Irish flyweight titles. He attributes his improvement to one legend in particular who was associated with the St John Bosco club.

"Freddie Gilroy was the hero for all the lads in the club," he recalled. "Freddie was training us and I sparred him all the time so my confidence was sky high as I learned so much from him. I was naturally orthodox but adapted and copied Freddie's southpaw style. He used to take me to all his professional fights and let me carry his kit bag, so I got in free. I remember the night in 1959 when he won the British title by beating Billy Rafferty at the King's Hall. My mother and father were very strict and we had to be in by half eleven every night, but I took the chance and went up to Freddie's house in Ardoyne as there was a big celebration. I stayed a bit late and remember running home to make it on time when I was stopped by a big policeman who thought I was up to no good. I explained that I had been at Freddie's party and told him about being late so he told me to jump into his car for a lift. He saved my bacon that night."

By 1964, Sean was working for the Belfast Corporation in its Electricity Department erecting poles. A full sweep of Ulster and Irish titles were attained that year and international caps for Ireland were soon added to his record. A boxing dream became a reality in the summer when he received notification from the Irish Olympic Association that the flyweight spot on the boxing team for Tokyo was his.

"It was an experience and a half to go to Tokyo," he recalled. "We were all just kids at the time but the whole thing was tremendous from start to finish. At the opening ceremony it all began to sink in as we walked around the stadium. I remember we were behind the Italians and the noise was incredible and when they set free the thousands of doves in the stadium I just thought it was unbelievable.

"Everything was so clean and new; the motorways were perfect and the village itself was state of the art. The one thing

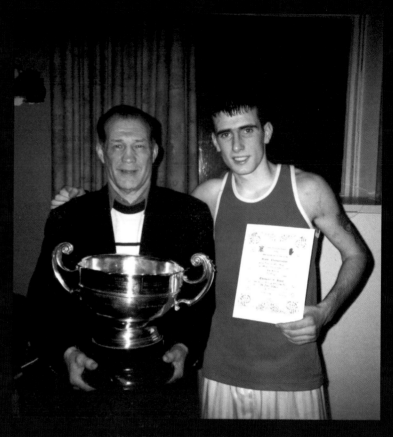

Above

Like father, like son. Sean McCafferty with his son, Barry who followed in his father's footsteps by winning the Co. Antrim title.

I always remember though is the food, which was out of this world, and the Japanese ran everything like a ship."

Sean's first contest in the Games took place in the Olympic arena on 12th October 1964, where he beat, on a unanimous points' decision, the fancied Rafael Carbonell of Cuba. A notable scalp for an Irish fighter if ever there was one.

His next fight was against Sulley Shittu from Ghana who provided tougher opposition but McCafferty won the fight on a split decision and was now one bout away from at least a bronze medal. Shittu was a class fighter and would later go on to win two gold medals at Commonwealth Games.

"Things were going really well for me and I was confident with my draw as my next opponent, the Italian Franco Atzori, was having problems with his eye and was considered vulnerable. However, they sealed the cut in his eye with some new type of adhesive and he out-boxed me in the end to get the decision. I was upset of course but the thing was that I accepted it and went on to enjoy my time in Tokyo."

While stationed in Tokyo, the Irish squad were given their own personal interpreter and the team took their official to their hearts.

"The interpreter we had with us was nicknamed 'Tokyo Paddy' as he was with us day and night. We got on really well with him and he conducted the tours of Tokyo for us. We had great times and I'd say he is the only man in Tokyo today who can do a Belfast accent.

"Another person we spent some time with was Joe Frasier. He had time for everybody and was so unassuming, but you could tell that he was destined for greatness. He was a great boxer and in the Olympic final I was never so impressed as when he stormed to the gold – he was a pleasure to watch. Even at that stage the offers for Joe to turn professional were numerous and just seeing him in Tokyo I knew he would not be an amateur for too long afterwards."

From the heights of the sporting world in Tokyo, the late autumn of 1964 was spent by Sean McCafferty in his native city of Belfast. He resumed work with the Belfast Corporation but soon took the bait and joined the paid fight game under his long-time trainer Jimmy McAree, with Barney Eastwood as his promoter. His first bout took place at the King's Hall on 12th October 1965 where topping the bill was a contest between Al Sharpe and Henry Turkington for the Northern Ireland middleweight crown.

Jonjo Donaghy was a journeyman fighter from Coalisland in Co. Tyrone and he offered little resistance to McCafferty as the fight was stopped in three rounds. Within eight weeks, Sean had won a further four bouts in the Ulster Hall and his reputation in the flyweight division was growing as many pundits were tipping him for glory.

Above

Sean McCafferty is recognised for his lifetime devotion to boxing by An Taoiseach Bertie Ahern.

On 15th March 1966, Norman Coles was knocked out in the first round, while Orizu Obilaso lasted only three rounds in May. A victory over Winston Van Guylenburg in the Ulster Hall in November saw McCafferty matched in December for a crack at Jim McCann for the Northern Ireland bantamweight title. McCann had won that title in December 1965 when he beat Alex O'Neill in the Ulster Hall. McCann had a record of nine fights with one defeat, while McCafferty was unbeaten in eight. It was a fight which generated a lot of interest and speculation which went to the wire in the favour of McCann on points.

It was a sore lesson for McCafferty who was competing in his first twelve round fight and thereafter his career was on the slide as his enthusiasm for boxing diminished. However, within a month he had stopped Reg Gullever in the Ulster Hall and followed this up with a stoppage of Welshman Glyn Davies in February 1967, the year that Sean married his childhood sweetheart, Maura Hamill.

In March that year, McCafferty won his eleventh fight when Carl Taylor was disqualified during their bout. After that came a trip to the World Sporting Club where he lost to Brami and found a completely new perspective on professional boxing. A rematch with Brami in Portrush in July ended in another points' reversal for McCafferty, while a win over Giancarlo Centa in October proved to be his final victory as a professional.

A trip to Rome to fight Franco Zurlo in December ended in defeat when Sean was knocked out for the first time and the writing was most definitely on the wall. As reality began to bite, McCafferty took a break for ten months from the game and returned to fight Bobby Fisher in Hamilton, Scotland, where he lost on points. His final bout saw him return to the Ulster Hall in February 1970 where he fought Sammy Lockhart for the Northern Ireland area super featherweight crown.

In the fourth round of the contest, with Lockhart flailing on the bottom rope, McCafferty was disqualified when he was adjudged to have hit his opponent while he was on the canvas. That decision incensed McCafferty and most of the people present and he set out to have the decision overturned. His money was withheld as the British Boxing Board of Control went about disciplining McCafferty.

"I went to the hearing confident as I was sure that I should not have been disqualified," remembered Sean. "I suggested that the television pictures of the incident would clear my name but the whole process was stacked against me with legal costs involved and it was then that I realised that I had had enough of boxing. Times were changing in Belfast and I had to think of my family first and foremost. The Troubles had begun and I could sense that there was to be little future in the fight game. It is a thing that I was proud of and I have no regrets in leaving the sport. I have always had a love for boxing but sometimes you can get fed up and, at that time, I was totally fed-up. The best times and worst times were to be had in boxing and I look at that trophy cabinet in my living room and it makes me proud. I have seen a lot of guys in my life who were class acts and I am so glad to have witnessed so much."

Of all the great fighters he saw boxing, he is sure that the best was the Joe Frasier who was in action during the Olympic final in 1964.

"He was such a nice guy but when you saw him in the ring he was special and I will never forget that."

Today, Sean McCafferty oversees the talented boxers of the Bosco club. He has passed on that knowledge at various stages to his six sons, all of whom carved out notable careers as amateurs. Unselfish dedication and great memories for a Belfastman who is in all probability still fondly remembered by an ageing Japanese man in Tokyo nicknamed Paddy.

Paddy Fitzsimons

Keeping the Game Alive

The town land of Ballymacarrett, on the Co. Down side of Belfast's River Lagan, is an area that grew in population and importance as the city's industrial revolution evolved. Many mean streets grew up around the traditional industries centred in Ballymacarrett as the area prospered and produced its own distinct identity and colourful characters.

Sport was no exception, with Glentoran football club the main focus for many working class families in the area. In the Short Strand district, an enclave nestled uneasily between the Newtownards and Albertbridge Roads, the sport of boxing was particularly favoured and produced many fighters of note. One such son of the 'East' was Patrick Fitzsimons who represented Northern Ireland in the 1962 Empire Games and Ireland in the 1964 Olympic Games. Paddy represented Ireland with grace on the highest stages and has devoted his life to the sport he loves.

As a life-long dockworker, one of Paddy Fitzsimons' proudest moments came in August 2006, when the Dockers' Boxing Club opened new premises in Pilot Street in Belfast. It was the culmination of many years of dedication by Fitzsimons and others to keep a sport alive in the area of Belfast formerly known as Sailortown. This historic district has sadly disappeared from the map of the city due to redevelopment and population displacement. Five months later, on the night of 11th January 2007, Paddy Fitzsimons stood with pride in the corner of the ring in Belfast's Ulster Hall as Ryan Green, one of the new stars in the new era for the Dockers' Club, won an Ulster senior title. Dedication by a young Lurgan boxer which had been nurtured by Fitzsimons is helping to keep the famous Docks district on the map of Irish boxing.

Born in the Short Strand area of Belfast in 1943, Paddy Fitzsimons soon blazed a trail to the local St Matthew's club situated off Beechview Street, in a place known locally as Noble's field. Under the watchful eye of Jimmy Brady, Paddy was just another youngster immersing himself in the Noble Art. He progressed through the Down and Connor championships as a boy but showed little signs of the talent that was to mature in his teens. In the early 1950s, boxing ceased in the Short Strand with the closure of the St Matthew's club. A number of the boys from the area, including Fitzsimons, moved over the Albert Bridge to the Market area of Belfast where they joined the St Malachy's club.

"At St Malachy's I was considered to be just another one of the boys and nothing made me stand out in any way. I remember I got to the final of the Down and Connor youth championships only to be beaten, but I really wasn't what you would call an exceptional boxer."

The Short Strand did not have to wait too long for a boxing club to re-establish itself. Harry Enright was the trainer who attracted the Strand exiles back when the St Matthew's club reopened in 1958. As Fitzsimons recalled, his return to the club under Enright was a move that enabled his career to prosper.

"Naturally, all the lads went back to the St Matthew's club when it reopened, but I noticed that I started to improve greatly under Harry Enright. I had just started work at the time and it became noticeable that I began to get better and better as the boys who had beaten me previously were now losing to me. There was one particular fight I recall against the lad who had beaten me on points in the final of the Down and Connor championships. The next time I met him I stopped him in the first round for something just clicked inside me and I came on in leaps and bounds."

Championship victories soon followed in abundance as a junior boxer. In one season, Fitzsimons took triple honours as Antrim, Ulster and Irish champion and the call to don the green vest soon followed. In his first season as a senior, Paddy recalled the disappointment of losing an Irish final in the National Stadium, a fight he feels he lost through his own over-confidence.

"I was fighting a guy that night called Eddie Tracey and I just was too sure of myself and I let him come back at me when I thought the contest was won. I learned a lot from that fight and went on to get my revenge over Tracey not long after that fight."

In 1962, when Paddy was nineteen, he was chosen to represent Northern Ireland at the Empire Games, which that year were held in Perth, Australia. The Games took place from 21st November to 1st December and are remembered as the 'heat, dust and glory Games'. On the day of the opening ceremony the temperature reached 105° Fahrenheit and such extremes persisted for the Games' duration.

"That was an unbelievable experience for me to travel to Western Australia at that stage for it took about two days to get there with many stopovers. In my opening bout, I boxed a guy from Uganda called Kesi Odongo and I felt I got a terrible decision and was eliminated. To be truthful, I was so sickened by the treatment I got from the judges at the Empire Games that when I returned I packed in the sport for a while. The result of that decision to quit was that I began to put on a lot of weight on so I drifted back into training; then one thing led to another and I decide to give it another shot.

"In 1963, I won Ulster and Irish senior titles and got a call up to the Irish senior team and I boxed a Welsh guy called

Above

Former World Heavyweight Champion Frank Bruno opens the new
Dockers' Boxing Club in August 2006 – Paddy Fitzsimons is pictured
on the extreme right

moved to London where he is the head coach at the Repton Boxing Club who we in the Dockers' boxing club have struck up a great relationship with."

Things went from strength to strength for Paddy and in his next bout, he was paired against a future world champion.

"After the Wales international I was paired with Ken Buchanan in Scotland and I beat him too which gave me a lot of satisfaction. I then boxed the European champion who was from Hungary in the National Stadium and that was when I felt that I was capable of going to the Olympics. That night was special for me as I really excelled myself in front of a packed stadium and the noise was unforgettable. I got the decision that night and it was a great feeling that is very hard to explain."

Further successes in the international arena left the tantalising prospect of a trip to Tokyo in 1964 well within his grasp. The Ulster title soon followed and the scene was set for a defence of Fitzsimons' Irish featherweight crown.

"In those days you were supposed to fight your semi-final and final in the same evening and the tension was high as at the end of the night the Irish Olympic team was to be announced in the ring, so there was a lot of pressure on the fighters to perform well. That night I knocked my opponent out in the first round in the final – and sure enough I got the nod to go to the Olympics."

The Irish team that represented Ireland in the Games that October consisted of Fitzsimons at featherweight, Sean McCafferty at flyweight, Jim McCourt at lightweight, Brian Anderson at light-welterweight and Chris Rafferty at bantamweight.

"I had been to Perth and enjoyed that experience very much but Tokyo was different as firstly there was the language issue and of course there were thousands more athletes. They were so well organised from start to finish. That was an all-Northern side that went to Tokyo as in those days boxing in Ireland was dominated by Belfast and the other Ulster counties," recalled Fitzsimons.

In his opening contest, Paddy was paired with the crack Pole Piotr Gutman and was disappointed to lose the bout to the fancied Eastern European, who went on to claim a bronze medal.

"For me that was a devastating experience," said Fitzsimons. "I had been really confident going into the fight with Gutman and it was pretty even until the last round when he caught me and put me down. By the time I received my count and composed myself, I realised that it was too late and I would not have enough time to save the bout.

"All the training and dedication I had put into the Games were for nothing and I had to just accept that I was out. When I look back I can say that 1964 was a bad year for me in more ways than one. Prior to the Games, my father Harry died suddenly at the age of forty-eight and that was very devastating to the family, and also I was very concerned at the thought of leaving my mother in the wake of his death.

"Also my trainer from St Matthew's, Harry Enright, had gone to Tokyo and we had a falling out over a number of things out there, so I returned home in a very despondent mood and never returned to the St Matthew's club. Let's just say that I was annoyed by a lot of things that happened after the Games but that was forty years ago and its all history now. Just at that stage in Belfast, Barney Eastwood was promoting a few professional bills and I was being approached to give the paid ranks a go."

Fitzsimons' debut as a paid fighter came on 12th January 1965 at the Ulster Hall in Belfast. His opponent that evening was a Nigerian boxer who went by the name of Simon Tiger. Fitzsimons was a convincing winner and within a week he had his second outing, this time at the Manchester Free Trade Hall against Johnny Ratcliffe, the seasoned journeyman. Ratcliffe was dispatched in the fourth round of that bout, but little did Fitzsimons know that he had just fought his penultimate fight as a paid boxer.

"The thing about my career was that I did get a few pounds in my hand for turning professional but I never signed a contract so there was nothing on paper. As soon as I began to box in the paid ranks I got the feeling that I would not like it as the entire atmosphere changed. Everybody was talking about money and all the friendships were false, so I really did miss the feeling I had as an amateur. What I had come to love as a sport had changed and there was no enjoyment to be had.

"I recall the fight in Manchester as we had travelled over on a chartered flight with a load of bookmakers from Belfast. The changing rooms were so different to what I had experienced as an amateur. They were quiet and humourless and you could feel that there was more than pure sport to the professional game."

On 30th March 1965, Fitzsimons fought his last fight as a professional when he was defeated by fellow Belfast fighter Brian Smyth and he left the ring for good to continue his career in Belfast Docks.

"That was it I thought and I told Barney Eastwood that I was finished and as I had no written contract I could just walk away and I did. After my father died I began working in the Docks but it was the type of job that if you took time off to box you lost out on your money, so I was having problems with keeping my head above water. When you consider the sponsorship that is available today for athletes it was really farcical what I had to go through. When I came home from the Olympic Games I went down to sign on for unemployment benefit and they refused to give me credit as I had been out of the country. Eventually I got a few people to speak up on my behalf and I got the money paid to me in the end."

So, Paddy Fitzsimons hung up his gloves and continued to invest his skill into the young pugilists at the Dockers' Boxing Club. Throughout the Troubles the club continued in the part of Belfast known as Sailortown. The area became a ghost town as the city ground to a halt. Throughout the darker days, the dream of rejuvenating the area and its boxing tradition had been a key aim of Fitzsimons and others such as Brian McCann.

Many years' hard work were rewarded on 4th August 2006, when the fighting legend that is Frank Bruno travelled to Belfast to open the new Dockers' Boxing Club. Present also were representatives of the Repton Boxing Club in East London, who have established a strong relationship with the Dockers' Club and undertake many exchange visits with the club.

Bruno was glowing in his praise of the work and dedication that had seen the new club come to reality.

"I am absolutely delighted to be here today to open these premises and, having had a good look around, I am confident that the future of boxing in inner North Belfast is in safe hands."

At the launch, Paddy Fitzsimons, as chairman of the club, paid tribute to all those involved in the project and he was justly proud.

"To see this wonderful resource we have here today is a dream come true for the club. The old premises had seen better times and their days were certainly numbered. This state-of-the-art facility has been a long time in planning and we are very grateful to the people who have shown faith in us and made this possible. Many people have worked hard to ensure that the future of amateur boxing for the kids from both sides of the community in North Belfast is secure for many years to come and this is a proud day for us."

From the Short Strand to the Belfast Docks. From Dublin to Perth and Tokyo. Paddy Fitzsimons' boxing career was long and varied. His skill at his craft has been exemplary and his dedication has seen a suitable monument in the new Dockers' Boxing Club established in his native city. A club that will prove to be his legacy in Belfast's Dockland.

Eamon McCusker

'The Star of the County Down'

From 'the Banbridge town in the County Down' came a boxer by the name of Eamon McCusker. A formidable and skilled exponent of boxing, he was a feared competitor for club and country for most of the 1960s. His career highlight came in 1968, when he secured his ticket on the Irish Olympic boxing team bound for the Games in Mexico City: a trip of a lifetime for somebody who describes himself as 'a mere lad from the country'. It was a trip that, although not successful in boxing terms, still brings out a sense of pride and nostalgia in an unassuming man now resident in Lurgan, Co. Armagh.

Born in Banbridge in 1945, a town nestled halfway between Belfast and Newry, Eamon McCusker was reared in a family where Gaelic football held sway. The breakthrough in all-Ireland terms of the famous Down footballers in the late 1950s and early Sixties, inspired many young lads to the local GAA fields. However, whilst a fan and exponent of the round ball game, McCusker found himself by 1959 enrolled in the local St John

Bosco boxing club. A decade of excellence and travel awaited him as under the eye of Barney and Tommy Savage, together with Jim Scullion, his skills were honed to international class.

McCusker's earliest competitive bouts were fought against the boys from the neighbouring counties of Armagh and Tyrone in the mid-Ulster championships. By 1963, he had achieved Ulster junior welterweight honours, only to lose in the national decider to the skilful Paddy Walsh. Two years later, McCusker had claimed the Irish national title and his first international vest was gained in the European senior championships, which were held that year in Berlin.

"That was a real coup for me to be selected on the Irish side as I had never fought an international and now I was going to a major championship," he said. "The games took place in what was then East Berlin, behind the Iron Curtain, and it was a real eye-opener. All the talk about scarcity and greyness in the Communist countries never occurred to us as we were given the absolute best of treatment and hospitality. At nineteen years of age, it's hard to take in the history all around but I remember posing at Checkpoint Charlie and at the Berlin Wall itself. I fought a guy from Bootle called Pat Dwyer, who was the ABA champion, and while it was close he beat me fair and square."

Left

Left to right: Bob Peden, Barney Savage (trainer) and Eamon McCusker at the Bosco Club in Banbridge.

Above

Left: Olympic Village, Mexico 1968
Middle: Eamon McCusker with boxing legend Floyd Patterson
Right: Eamon today

As 1966 arrived, McCusker's Irish title was put on the line in the National Stadium in Dublin. This time his opponent was the hometown favourite, Gussy Farrell. After a bruising encounter, the Dubliner was a convincing winner and McCusker's reign as champion was over. In a quirk of fate later that year, the two protagonists fought again in a trial for the right to represent in an Ireland under-21 team against Poland. Again, Farrell got the decision and McCusker was put on stand-by. However, prior to the trip, Farrell damaged his hands and McCusker was given the nod to travel to Warsaw.

"Poland was another great experience but I will never forget Warsaw itself as it really was something from a cold war movie," he said. "It was very dark, full of military and concrete and totally different from Berlin. I was becoming a well-travelled fighter and the squad relished every minute as everything was new to us."

While losing the Irish title in Dublin had been a set back for the Banbridge man, a trip to Jamaica to represent Northern Ireland in the Empire Games was ample consolation. That particular Northern Ireland team included the likes of Jim McCourt, Paddy Maguire, Jim Neill and Danny McAlinden and much was expected.

The trip to the Caribbean lasted a month and included a week in Canada prior to returning to Belfast. For Eamon McCusker, it was his personal highlight.

"There was constant sun the whole time we were there," he recalled. "I always travelled with low expectations and in hindsight that was my downfall as I was as capable as any in my division. I was in constant awe of the occasion and as a lad from the country, I just never got the confidence inside me to give it my best. I lost out to an English fellow called Mark Rowe in the early rounds of the competition and he went on to beat the Scot Tom Imrie to win the gold medal. Rowe was some fighter and could fairly hit, but he beat me fair and square that day and I have no qualms."

McCusker was a lucky amateur in many ways and his constant trips abroad were always with the blessing of his employers. A loyalty he repaid through forty-two years of unbroken service.

"I had at that stage begun working making ladies' shoes at the Down shoe factory," he said. "I really was treated so well by them and it helped that the boss, Sidney Betts, was an avid boxing fan. I never lost a penny by being away from work and, unlike some amateurs, there was a full pay packet waiting for me when I returned home."

In 1967, McCusker reclaimed the Irish senior title and followed this up by retaining it the following year. The *Boxing News* in London rated him as the number one light middleweight in Ireland or Britain, so a calling to the Irish Olympic team in 1968 was a foregone conclusion.

The opening ceremony on 12th October 1968 is something that McCusker will never forget as long as he lives.

"The preparations were amazing and we were all lined up in our countries outside the stadium waiting to be called," he said. "Jim McCourt was carrying the flag and when they announced Ireland into the stadium the place just erupted. Literally, the hairs on my neck were standing up and the noise was incredible. It was then that you knew that you were part of something special and it was so emotional."

Luck, or maybe confidence was not on McCusker's side and the fact that he drew the Cuban Pan-American champion in the opening round meant the odds were stacked against him.

"I fought Ronaldo Garbey in the first round and he went on to claim a silver medal," he recalled. "Again I was in awe of the whole event and really could not come to terms with the fact that I was there representing Ireland at the Olympics. I lost the bout, but in a way it was a chance for me to relax and take in the sights and the rest of the sports that were taking place, so I made the most of things."

The last quote could be taken as something of an understatement. In the following weeks, McCusker witnessed at first hand three moments of sporting history in the Olympic stadium.

"I recall we were walking around the training grounds and we saw this guy practising the high jump," he said. "We thought he was mad as he was jumping backwards and I thought he would be in with no chance. I spent a lot of time watching the athletics and when the American Dick Fosbury performed that backwards jump [the 'Fosbury Flop'] everyone was on their feet. That changed the face of athletics and I literally had to eat my words."

It was not the only piece of history that McCusker witnessed in the Olympic Stadium.

"I remember also that I was sitting watching the long jump and Bob Beamon almost jumped out of the sand pit and that was just amazing. He had been under pressure to even qualify and something must have possessed him during that jump. I knew that this was history taking place in front of my eyes and it was a joy to behold."

The third piece of sporting drama witnessed by McCusker came during the awards ceremony after the 200-metres final. As the Americans Tommy Smith and John Carlos took the stand, they made their famous clenched-fist salutes in support of the Black Power Movement during the anthem. McCusker seated in the stadium again knew that what he had witnessed an event that was to prove iconic.

The icing on the cake for McCusker occurred when he came into close contact with George Foreman, the American heavyweight hope in the Games.

"We all thought he was one of the American basketball team due to his height but when he got into the ring we all knew we were very, very wrong. He was really special and had a build and stature that just exuded class. You could just tell he was a natural and his personality was just fantastic."

Seeing Foreman lift the gold medal by beating the Russian Ionas Chepulis in the final rounded off a tremendous experience for McCusker, who had packed in enough sporting history in three weeks to last a lifetime.

However, Banbridge in late autumn was, literally, a world away from the heights of the Olympic Games. For every high, there comes a low, and, on returning to Co. Down, a loss of enthusiasm for boxing took hold.

"After Mexico, things became a bit of a chore for me," he said. "For all the glory of the Games, I was working a forty-hour week and then travelling to Belfast and back to train every other night. It was really hard going and I would be up at seven for work and had no sooner had my tea in the evening than I was on my way to training. By the time I got home it was eleven o' clock at night and I was just physically exhausted. Something really had to give."

A natural progression for an amateur of McCusker's stature would have been to the paid ranks, but, as he explained, professional boxing never attracted him.

"I was asked to consider turning professional on a few occasions but it never was something that occurred to me," he said. "It was hard enough to adjust after the Olympics but the thought of going full time into boxing was never a runner."

Left

Extending gloved hands skyward in racial protest, U.S. athletes Tommy Smith, centre, and John Carlos stare downward during the playing of the Star Spangled Banner after Smith received the gold and Carlos the bronze for the 200 metre race at the Summer Olympic Games in Mexico City on 16th October 1968. Australian silver medallist Peter Norman is at left.

Sometimes, in boxing, as in any sport, athletes are required to perform deeds for the local media in an attempt to fill a sporting slot on television. Eamon McCusker was no different. In 1968, a local television company requested to film Eamon in training for a boxing feature. As he recalled, the absurdity of the occasion brought him back to earth with a bang.

"The boxing stalwart Albert Uprichard had this idea to have me filmed training and came up with the idea of me chasing a horse across fields," he recalled. "It was a gimmick to drum up some interest in an upcoming fight and I would be shown racing the horse to show how fit I was. Albert was the local Master of the Hounds and the film crew arrived and I was filmed running after him in his hunting gear across a field. So I asked the television producer when this would be on and he said at just before seven the next evening. I was rushing up to the Immaculata in Belfast the next night to train but I called into a real 'spit-and-sawdust' local bar to see myself on the telly. I walked into the bar and the telly was turned down but there was me on the box running after the horse. All the old boys in the bar started commenting on this eejit running after a horse and saying 'he must be mad'. Then all of a sudden I realised that one by one everyone was staring at me, and then at the telly, and everything went silent. I sort of nodded apologetically and to be truthful I was never as glad to get out of that bar and back to the real world."

Chasing horses or not, Eamon McCusker had his last fight in 1969 in the town of Banbridge, where it had all began fifteen years previously.

"My good friend and lifelong sparring partner Bob Peden had hung up his gloves and from then I just found it hard to keep an interest. I fought Paddy Doherty in my last fight and when the final bell sounded I shook his hands and I knew that was it," he said. "It didn't cost me a second thought and I just walked away. The generation of fighters that I had grown up with were disappearing and things had changed. I was great friends with my sparring partner Bob Peden and when he retired I lost interest. I had absolutely no second thoughts about it and it was time to move on."

Eamon McCusker's philosophy on boxing is as insightful as it is intelligent. There is never a boastful comment and he sees everything without rose tinted-glasses.

"If I lost a bout I will always be first to say that a better boxer beat me in the ring," he points out. "The great Dick McTaggart once said that he won every single one of his three hundred bouts, but was robbed by the judges in twenty of those. That showed his humour and I recall that he was a really funny and amusing man outside the ring. The fact is that I always acknowledged if I was beaten in a fight and always looked forward, not back. I never performed away from Ireland and I regret the fact that I lacked the confidence I had at home. I learned a lot in my career and one of the greatest things was respect for others. People with a bad attitude don't go very far in boxing and that's a fact. The nicest people I have come across in life were boxers as respect was mutual across the board. As a boxer, I met Pope Paul VI and saw some of the greatest sights in the world so I can't complain. I could never as a youngster have afforded to have travelled as I did representing my country. I will never forget though entering that stadium in Mexico City as the crowd erupted in the opening ceremony. For a country boy from Banbridge, that was just unbeatable."

Some of us can only dream of such privileges!

Martin Quinn

A Career Lost in the Heat of Battle

In 1969 Martin Quinn was probably the best prospect Ireland had in amateur boxing terms. A visit to the Mexico Olympics in 1968, as a mere eighteen-year-old, had seen him lose on a split decision to the then reigning Olympic champion Josef Grudzien. This was after he had floored the Polish fighter in the third round but, after a bout of over-exuberance on Quinn's behalf – which meant that there was a fight-saving thirty-eight second break in proceedings – Grudzien recovered to win. Quinn returned home to the adulation of the press who had written his chances off, and knuckled down to concentrate on a promising career. That was the highpoint – the low one was yet to come.

On 15th August 1969, Belfast was thrown into violent convulsions. The political tensions that had been bubbling under during that year erupted into communal violence, centred on the area where the Falls, Springfield and Shankill Roads intersected. On that day, Martin Quinn was working as an apprentice barber in the Donegall Street shop of Mickey Donnelly, when his life was changed irrevocably.

By early afternoon, the situation in Belfast had worsened significantly when word reached Marty that his parents' home in Percy Street was under attack. He immediately rushed to the street to find the family home on fire and a situation that was getting seriously out of control. His father and brothers tried in vain to save any belongings that they had, but it was too late as the house was well alight, with the roof having caved in.

On the morning of 16th August, with troops now deployed on the streets of Belfast, Martin Quinn tried to take stock of what had happened. He stood with his parents in what was left of Percy Street and surveyed the smouldering ruins. Everything his parents had lived for was in ashes. In addition to the devastating loss of the family home, Marty Quinn had lost every trophy, medal, certificate, vest, cutting and memento of his boxing career. As he stood in the street, in the only set of clothes he possessed, boxing was the furthest thought from his mind. The heights of Mexico were a distant and irrelevant memory. He has never recovered.

Martin Quinn was born in Newry on 30th November 1949. One of a family of five, to Malachy and Rose, his earliest boxing exploits were carried out in the vest of the Newry Bosco club. By 1961, Quinn had competed for a number of schoolboy titles at the four stones seven pounds class when his family left Newry and moved to Belfast.

"My mother, Rose, worked in the mill at nearby Bessbrook, but that closed down and the whole family left in 1962 and moved to Percy Street," he recalled. "I had fought about ten fights by the time I moved to Belfast and I joined up with the St John Bosco club and continued to box from there."

In 1964 Quinn's potential was spotted by his trainer at the St John Bosco club, George Devlin, who predicted, with uncanny accuracy, that the Newry lad was destined for Olympic success.

"I recall that I was fighting in the Ulster juveniles in Ballymena and I had knocked out a formidable fighter from Ballyshannon called Gallagher," he said. "George said to me in the corner afterwards that when I returned from Mexico in 1968 that I was to bring him a sombrero hat and I thought it was a joke. Suddenly, things just took off for me in the ring and the prospect of an Olympic call-up became a reality and it was something I worked at every day."

In 1965, Quinn won a plethora of juvenile titles, only to lose in the Irish final in Dublin. A year later he won the Ulster and Irish titles and by 1967 had won provincial and national youth titles. In his first year as a senior, the year of the Mexico Olympics, Quinn made an emphatic mark in the Irish featherweight division.

The year started for Quinn with him lifting the Antrim junior featherweight crown, and this was duly followed by the Ulster and Irish titles. At the same time he had been awarded the best boxer award for his performances in Dublin. He followed those achievements within a number of weeks by lifting both Ulster and Irish senior titles and he was fancied for a place in the Olympic team. However, as he recalled, his youth was seen as a hindrance by some.

"Before I was chosen, there were a number of journalists who felt that it was ridiculous to even consider sending me to the Games since I was so young. I knew within myself that I was game for anything, so I had no fear of going to the Games."

The day on which the Irish team for Mexico was announced is one that is well remembered by Quinn.

"I was picked to fight for Ireland at lightweight in May against West Germany; that was on the Friday before the team was to be announced. On the Sunday, I knew that the team would be given out on Radio Éireann so I was on tenterhooks all day in the house. I was lying in bed listening to my transistor when the team was broadcast and when my name was mentioned I just couldn't get over it. I got up, walked downstairs, and announced to the assembled family that I was on my way to Mexico. I then went into the street and told anyone I met that I was in the Irish team and I was just walking on air. It was such a special feeling and everyone was so proud."

At eighteen, the Olympic Games were all that Quinn could have hoped for.

"It was a marvellous sunny day in Mexico City as we entered the stadium for the opening ceremony," he recalled. "We were in our new blazers and there was no doubting that there was a real sense of pride to be representing Ireland. Then the moment came and we entered the arena and I had tears running down my face but I was also laughing with joy at the whole experience. Even today as I think back, the same butterflies are in my stomach at the thought of that ceremony. My heart was literally bouncing and when I looked up there was so much colour and noise, I just thought that there could be no better feeling."

The formalities over and it was a case of down to business. For Martin Quinn, the business of proving the doubters back home wrong was foremost in his mind. In his opening bout, the Newry lad was drawn against the tough Cameroonian fighter Essomba Bernard.

Years later in 2005, a package arrived at Marty Quinn's barbershop in Belfast's Donegall Street. When he opened it, he found a video of the 1968 Olympic Games, which an admirer from Kerry had forwarded. With pride, he slipped on the video and the black and white film of his opening bout was replayed. After two minutes of attacking action, the net result was that Quinn stopped the African with a sweet punch in the first round which had him sprawling between the ropes and the canvas. The crowd were on their feet and the eighteen-year-old was now a runner for honours in the lightweight division.

Quinn now knew no fear. In his next contest, he was drawn against the lightweight Olympic champion in the 1964 Tokyo Games, the Polish legend, Josef Grudzien.

"Eddie Thompson who was an official with the Irish team came in and told me that I was to fight Grudzien and I had no idea who he was and just considered it another bout," he recalled. "I was a happy-go-lucky fighter and began to concentrate on taking on Grudzien. Then some people began to mention how formidable this guy was and how he was the reigning champion and, in hindsight, it was most unhelpful. The doubts started to haunt me and I just began to lose the confidence I had built up."

Doubts and a loss of self-confidence saw Quinn lose on a split decision to the Bulgarian. Yet the fight was not without its moment of drama. The bottom line was that Quinn floored the champion in the third round and through confusion, or maybe a lack of experience, the Bulgarian was let off the hook.

"In the third round, I caught him with a great combination and he was down," he said. "Instead of having my senses about me, I stood over him and the count was delayed while the referee insisted that I went to a neutral corner so that he could begin his count. Maybe it was inexperience on my behalf but that delay was crucial and I feel that I became victim of a prolonged count. I had this guy at my mercy and when the fight was allowed to continue I just went for him and then the bell rang and the chance was gone. Eddie Thompson, who was observing, said that the whole count, instead of taking ten seconds, took almost forty to complete, and that, in essence, allowed Grudzien the time to recover."

The split decision saw Quinn crash out of the Games. Despite this he was still only eighteen, his point had been made at the highest level and the future looked rosy for the trainee barber. The press in Ireland who had dismissed Quinn as too young were forced to eat humble pie. A four-year-old prediction was fulfilled when Quinn arrived back into the St John Bosco club with a sombrero hat for his trainer, Geordie Devlin.

Everything looked to be on course for Quinn as he celebrated his nineteenth birthday in November 1968 but, by 1969, the climate on the streets of Northern Ireland chilled as the political situation stagnated. The eruption of violence in mid-August 1969 came as little surprise and Quinn's family home became a victim of the communal strife. Prior to 15th August, Marty Quinn's life was relatively straightforward. After that date, everything changed for him and changed utterly.

"I remember the day after the fire walking around in a daze around Belfast not knowing what I, or my family, were going to do," he recalled. "I was a young man and I thought I would be able to cope, but it destroyed me and I lost interest in everything. I was literally in a trance and I remember standing with my family looking at what once had been our home when word came through that the troops had been deployed in Belfast. For us, that was too late and if they had have been called in twenty-four hours earlier then my life may never have changed."

In the height of the madness, Quinn remembered one moment of kindness that touched him greatly.

Above

In his day, the man standing was a true cracker!

"I remember coming back to work the next day and a man I knew from the Shankill Road called Sidney McKnight was standing in tears at the top of Donegall Street when he saw me. He was very upset and I felt him put something into the breast pocket of my shirt as he talked to me. When he left I found two crisp five pound notes that he had left there and, as I had been so low, that it gave me a real lift."

The Quinn family was re-housed in temporary accommodation in the Beechmount area of Belfast, but Marty's life was in tatters as everything he had once owned and cherished was gone.

"When I finally got myself together I made the move into the paid ranks and that was a mistake," he said. "The former world middleweight champion of the world, Terry Downes, had showed interest in taking me to London, but, after consulting with my father, I decided to stay in Belfast and joined up with Jimmy McAree. I was not the boxer I had been and in 1970 I was put in against a seasoned professional called Ronnie Clifford in my first bout. He had at least thirteen fights under his belt and the fight was over eight three-minute rounds, which was ridiculous for me as I had never been beyond three rounds. He stopped me in the fifth and the future world champion Jim Watt had been over from Glasgow to watch the fights. I remember Watt came into the dressing room in the Ulster Hall and he was dumbfounded that I was put in against Clifford in my first fight. My next fight was in the Ulster Hall again, but this time I got a points decision over Joe McKee. I was on twenty-five pounds a fight but my heart wasn't in it at all and I was just going through the motions like a zombie."

A defeat to George Salmon in Dublin was followed by a victory over Derek McCarthy in Belfast and that signalled the end of the road for Quinn's career.

"I had met my wife Geraldine at that stage and things were changing," he recalled. "I was still in a state of shock after what had happened in 1969, and, in hindsight, that was what was eating away at me. When I returned from Mexico I was so full of confidence and had my career path all set out in my head. I wanted to be a British champion at some stage and I was confident that if I kept going at the rate I was then I could achieve that. I had my heart set on going to the Olympics in 1972 and then turning professional, but then 1969 happened. My mother died a short time after all the bother and there is no doubt she was heartbroken. Today, I have very little interest in boxing and I don't encourage my two sons to become involved in the sport. That day in 1969 left me heartbroken and all my memories were destroyed and with them went my love for boxing."

Marty Quinn's barbershop in Belfast's Donegall Street contains a scrapbook of his achievements in the ring: none of the cuttings are originals. Hours have been spent by Quinn in the nearby Central Library trying to rescue articles relating to his once-promising career. The fire that raged through his home on 15th August 1969 eventually burned itself out. By 16th August, the burning ambition of Ireland's best amateur prospect was extinguished also.

Eddie Tracey

The Battler from the Broombridge Road

The toughest fight that any boxer could ever comprehend facing is one against a hometown favourite in their own back yard. For Eddie Tracey, the 1968 Olympic Games provided him with such a battle when he met the tough Mexican, Antonio Roldan, in the second round of the featherweight competition.

In his opening fight, the twenty-five-year-old Dubliner had impressed as he saw off, by unanimous decision, the Jamaican Errol West. However, the decision that evening was drowned out by the packed arena chanting 'May-hee-co, May-hee-co,' as their hero, Roldan, entered the hall. The Mexican was considered lucky to see off his opponent from Sudan, Abdel Awad, but the arena erupted as the victory was announced, and the Mexican now had Eddie Tracey in his sights.

The clash of the two men took place at high altitude two days later. Again, the partisan crowd cheered, whooped, screamed and booed as the Irishman frustrated their favourite. The fight went to the judges who, to the delight of the Mexicans, found in favour of Roldan. It was game, set and match to Mexico as Tracey lost to a decision which the Irish press said proved that the Olympic judges lacked any 'intestinal fortitude'. To us lesser mortals, that means 'guts'!

Eddie Tracey was never a man to get down about setbacks like that.

"Never let things like that get to you: it's a case of just getting on with things, and that's been my philosophy in life."

Born in the Broombridge Road area of North Dublin on 5th June 1943, to Edward Snr and Bridget, Eddie Tracey was one of a family of two boys and three girls. His childhood memories are of a happy time which was devoted to sporting activity.

"The Broombridge Road had a habit of producing some great sportsmen in my youth," he said. "We had great footballers in Jimmy Conway, together with Ashley Grimes and Gerry Daly who both played for Manchester United and Ireland. Liam Whelan of Manchester United was a star also when I was growing up, and I remember the shock in the area when word came through that he had been killed in the Munich air crash of 1958."

At an early age, Tracey was enrolled in the local St Finnbarr's school, where his interest in soccer and GAA continued. A devoted follower of the local Bohemians club, Sundays were invariably spent by Tracey at Dalymount Park, where the 'Gypsies' attracted a large following. At the age of eleven, Eddie joined the Avona Boxing Club and soon had acquitted himself well enough to qualify for the Irish schoolboys' finals.

"I remember boxing Jim McCourt from Belfast in the semi-final of the schoolboys' championship in Dublin and I got the decision over him, but I knew he was a bit special even then," he recalled.

Above
An early picture of Eddie in an International vest.

"I saw John Caldwell fight as an amateur also, and he was just amazing for he was known as the 'Wonder Boy' back then."

Tracey transferred to the Arbour Hill Boxing Club and in the space of twelve months, at the turn of the 1960s, he won a clean sweep of juvenile, junior and senior all Ireland titles. That first senior win came at the expense of the experienced Paddy Kenny, who had represented Ireland at the Olympic Games in Rome six months previously. In the semi-final, the young Dubliner had beaten the talented Belfast boxer, Eddie Shaw, who went on to train Barry McGuigan. It was evident that, whilst still relatively young, Tracey could mix it with the best in Ireland.

Accordingly, in June 1961, at seventeen years of age, Tracey was picked to represent his country in the European championships, which were held that year in Belgrade. That Irish team – of which Tracey was the youngest – consisted also of Olly Byrne, Adam McClean, Harry Perry and Andrew Power. Naturally, Tracey, the quietest of the bunch, was not considered to be Ireland's main hope of a medal.

In his opening bout, only his fifth as a senior boxer, Eddie Tracey met the Pole, Piotr Gutman. Five days short of his eighteenth birthday, Tracey put in a creditable performance and the decision was in doubt until the Pole's strength told in the last round. Pleased as Punch by the novice's performance was

Colonel Harry Murphy, manager of the Irish team, who was sure that the experience would work in Tracey's favour in the future.

By this stage of his career, Eddie had joined his father in the family photography business, and boxing was beginning to take a back seat. In 1963 he lost in the Irish final to his Arbour Hill club-mate, Liam Clarke. That loss saw Tracey take almost eighteen months out of the game, but he returned in 1965 to secure his place in the seven-man Irish team for the European championships in East Berlin. The Irish team flew out, via Amsterdam, to the championships, while back home a special half-hour daily radio programme, hosted by Noel Andrews, kept the eager public informed of the boxers' progress.

"East Berlin really shocked me as I had fought previously in West Berlin and could not believe how physically divided the city was," recalled Tracey. "My first bout was against the Hungarian, Lajos Baranyi, and he was a tricky opponent. I lost a narrow decision to the Magyar and he lost in turn to Scotland's Ken Buchanan in the next round. Again, it was hard to accept, but you do eventually and I didn't get too upset about the defeat."

After East Berlin, Tracey took another break from the ring in order to pursue his career in photography. However, the sport of boxing is hard to eradicate from one's system and, with the Mexico Olympics on the horizon, he decided to give the game a further shot.

"I had lived next door to a man called Jim McNamara and he was training for Mexico as a marathon runner," he said. "I joined Jim at the Dunore Harriers Athletics Club and started running and became very fit. I thought to myself that I wasn't getting any younger and Mexico represented my last chance at doing something on the international scene so I went back to the boxing. It gets into your blood boxing does, and there's a love of the competition that keeps you keen."

Tracey duly won his place on the Irish team bound for Mexico and, after four weeks acclimatising to the high altitude, he stepped into the ring to face Errol West. With that fight won easily, the firm favourite of the home crowd, Antonio Roldan, swung a disputed decision over Tracey in the next round.

"Sure, I was down after losing that bout because I was really fit having adapted to the altitude better than most of the other boxers," he said. "You'll always hear boxers say the words; 'robbery', 'terrible' or 'they stole the fight on me', but I have always been philosophical

about those things. You see boxing is not only about the physical side of things, it's also mental and to become too despondent over a defeat will get to you in the end."

Tracey Jnr had the privilege of being accompanied to the Mexico Games by his greatest supporter: his father, Eddie Snr.

"My father always had followed my career and had gone to England and Wales to see me fight," he recalled. "He got a guy in to cover all our photography bookings and then stayed with us for almost three weeks. I thought that it would be easy to arrange accommodation for him out there but everywhere was booked up. Then Eddie Thompson, vice-president of the Irish Board, approached me and asked if my father had been sorted out for somewhere to stay. When I said 'no', he arranged for him to stay in the referees' and judges' quarters in the Olympic Village. That was a real act of kindness and my father never forgot Eddie Thompson until his dying day."

By the time of the 1968 Olympic Games, Eddie Tracey had married Ann and they set up home in Cabra where he continued his career in the photography business.

In 1969 Tracey went to his third European championships, which were held that year in Bucharest. With his experience in three major games, the Arbour Hill fighter, along with fellow clubman, Mick Dowling, was fancied to take at least a bronze medal. His opening contest, against the Swiss fighter, Hans Schellenbaum, saw Tracey outclass his opponent to take a unanimous decision. In the bout, Tracey scored at will and dropped the Swiss boxer in the first, and continue for the next seven minutes to dominate the fight.

However, the crafty and crouching Russian, Sergey Lomakin stood in the next round – the quarterfinal. Whilst the partisan crowd screamed in support of the Irishman, the fight went to the Russian on a points decision. The Russian, a thirty-five-year-old army physical training instructor, proved to be a class above the Arbour Hill man. As usual, Tracey was not downbeat, and he felt that the Russian, and the rest of his team, were miles ahead of Ireland in terms of technique, style and determination.

Just before he departed from the game, Tracey had travelled to London to represent his country, and that particular trip topped everything in his career and is still on a par with the Olympic Games experience.

"The greatest memory, apart from Mexico in 1968, came for me just before I retired from boxing, when I fought for Ireland against England in the Royal Albert Hall," he said. "The Albert Hall is a palace and a great place to box in and if you cannot be inspired by those surroundings then you shouldn't be there. I fought an Englishman by the name of Freddie Williams and the press rated him very, very highly. Indeed, Harry Carpenter from

Left

Left to right: Jim Ryan, Eddie Tracey and Mick Coffey. Victory in the 1968 Irish Senior Final at the National Stadium, 1968

the BBC was chatting to me before the bout and he said to watch myself as the guy Williams was considered to be a bit special. Sure enough, Williams came at me with all guns blazing but I just boxed my normal fight and was a convincing winner on the night. In those days, the Albert Hall was packed with expatriates and they raised the roof when I got the decision. I had never been so proud, and that night ranks as one of the best."

Thereafter, training, boxing and a career in photography became almost impossible for Eddie to combine, and in November 1969, he donned a vest and gloves for the last time.

"It was an Ireland versus France international at the National Stadium and I won my bout and that was the last time I fought," he recalled. "As the final bell sounded, I knew that that was the end and I took of my gloves for the last time."

In the 1990s, with their family of six children now reared, Eddie and Ann Tracey left Dublin and moved to the relative tranquillity of Ballina in Co. Mayo.

"We haven't looked back since we moved to the west coast of Ireland, and we are very happy here."

On the state of Irish boxing today, Tracey admits that he doesn't follow the amateur game at all.

"I haven't been to the National Stadium to see the amateurs in many years." he said. "It's a totally different scene and I would say, with all the protection fighters get now, that it's more like fencing now. I have absolutely no difficulty in recommending boxing to any young person today, as all the checks and balances are there that were not when I was growing up."

He freely admits that the greatest Irish amateur he saw was Jim McCourt of Belfast, but, in the professional stakes, nobody could ever have touched Sugar Ray Robinson.

"He was magic and the greatest all-rounder there ever was," he said. "He was a pleasure to watch and there was no-one – in my view – that could ever touch him."

As it is, Eddie Tracey, veteran of three European championships, one Olympic Games and Irish internationals too numerous to mention, is a happy man in retirement. His son once asked him whether he should give the noble art a try: Eddie Tracey was sure in his response.

"I said: 'Son, by all means give boxing a try but if you fancy any other sport, I'm sure that you'll be good at it'."

His son John is an accomplished golfer while his other son Edward Jnr is a club pro. Proof if ever there was that sporting skill and ability are inherent in one's genes.

For Eddie Tracey, boxing glory may now be a generation

Mick Dowling

"Please, Don't Mention Split Decisions"

The Marble County of Kilkenny, in sporting terms, is best known as a breeding ground for masters of the ancient game of hurling. The Cats, in their famous black and amber, have traditionally been a standard feature in Croke Park on All Ireland finals' day each September, and the Liam McCarthy Cup has found a second home resting beside the River Nore. In boxing terms, however, the Kilkenny equivalent of Eddie Keher, DJ Carey or Henry Shefflin is a man by the name of Mick Dowling. The Castlecomer native was a giant in the amateur bantamweight division in the late 1960s and early 1970s.

Two bronze medals at European Boxing Championships, coupled with two appearances for his country at Olympic Games, were a true reflection of his ability. Dowling also holds the record for the most titles claimed at the same weight in Irish amateur boxing history. Add to this the fact that he was undefeated in Ireland from 1968 until he retired in 1976, and you will agree that it's not a bad record for a guy who came to Dublin in 1962 to train to be a waiter at the Gresham Hotel.

Born in 1946, Mick Dowling followed the standard pursuits of a Kilkenny native where hurling and athletics became his main interests. On leaving school, the bright lights of Dublin soon beckoned and the teenager duly accepted a chance of work in one of Ireland's most prestigious hotels.

"I 'emigrated' from Castlecomer at the age of sixteen to begin a job as an apprentice waiter in the Gresham Hotel in O'Connell Street," said Mick. "The Gresham then was the most exclusive hotel in Dublin and I was staying with my sister up there. I had done a bit of boxing in Kilkenny with the Castlecomer Club but nothing too serious. I was better known as a hurler and athlete back then, so boxing was in no way my top sport."

Boxing may not have been top of Mick Dowling's priorities as he learned the intricacies of silver servicing and place setting. Athletics still was his main interest and, as he recalled, it was disappointment, coupled with determination, which saw him return to boxing again.

"I remember one year that I had finished sixth in the Leinster cross-country championships, so I was determined to win the race in the succeeding year. The next year was a total disaster for me as I finished well down the field in about tenth spot and I was just inconsolable. My brother suggested that I turn to boxing, as he felt that it could give me that added edge in athletics. So I joined up with the Arbour Hill Boxing Club in March 1965 and that's where it all began."

By October of 1967, Dowling had been crowned the Irish junior bantamweight champion and he was picked for a senior international, ahead of Paddy Maguire, who had stopped Dowling in the Irish senior final.

"Paddy and his trainer Ned McCormick were, rightly, annoyed about me getting the call-up, as he was the man to beat in those days and was reigning senior champion. Paddy Maguire was the only man ever to stop me inside the distance and I can say without doubt that he and Terry Hanna from Belfast were the two toughest men I ever fought. However, I fought a box-off with Paddy seven months later and I beat him on that occasion."

Dowling was now in prime position for a call-up to the Irish team bound for the Mexico Olympics: this was assured by winning the Irish senior bantamweight title in 1968. Mexico was an experience beyond all expectations, as he explained.

"Mexico was just fabulous as it was all new to us; the culture, the food, the people, everything was amazing."

In October 1968, the front pages of the Irish papers were dominated by the growing discontent on the streets of the North. However, the back pages were reporting the carnival of sport taking place in Mexico City. In the eye of the competitive storm was bantamweight Mick Dowling.

His first opponent in the Games was the tricky East German, Bernard Juterzenka, and in an uneven encounter, Dowling dispatched him in with ease. Tremendous right hooks, from the Arbour Hill fighter, which floored his opponent twice, saw the fight stopped in the first round – a fabulous debut for Dowling on the world's highest stage.

"Recently, a guy from Kerry, Mart O'Shea sent me up a video of that fight, and when I see the punch that put the East German on the floor I still take a sharp intake of breath as it was just so perfect," recalled Dowling.

The next round of the Games pitted Dowling against the Australian John Rakowski. Early in the second round, Dowling floored the Australian with a vicious right hand. Thereafter, the result was a formality and, after the Australian had been warned twice for the use of his head, referee Ronald Schwartz led Rakowski to the corner and Dowling was through to the quarterfinals on a disqualification.

With Dowling just nine minutes away from at least a bronze medal, he was drawn against the Japanese boxer Eiji Morioka. The fight was hard-fought and went to the judges, who found the encounter in favour of Dowling's opponent. Two formal warnings during the contest cost the Irishman the fight, and a bronze medal.

"Once I got the second warning that killed off any chance I had of taking the decision," recalled Dowling. "The fight itself was pretty even but I cannot complain, given the warnings, over the decision."

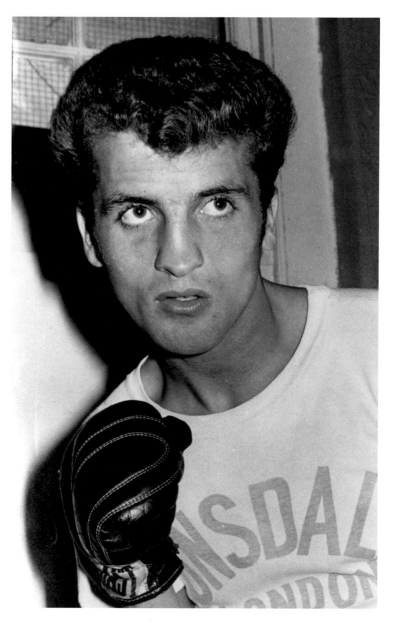

Above

Mick Dowling pictured in 1967 wearing training gloves

From within grasping distance of a medal in Mexico, Dowling returned to the relatively mundane life of the Gresham Hotel. A year later, as reigning Irish champion, he was picked to go to the European Boxing Championships in Bucharest. Dowling collapsed with an influenza virus on the eve of the Games but luckily recovered in time for his first bout. Dr Sean O' Flanagan, the Irish medical advisor, gave Dowling the all clear and he duly entered the ring to take on his first-round opponent, the fair-haired Russian Igor Kulagin, whom he beat on points.

The third day of June 1969, however, went down as a bad day at the office for the Irish contingent. Team captain Jim McCourt crashed out of the championships on points, along with the Banbridge fighter Eamon McCusker. Brendan McCarthy's campaign ended in the second round of his bout with the Olympic silver medallist from Poland, Artur Olech.

Hopes of an Irish medal now rested with Dowling, Frankie Downes and Eddie Tracey. In his quarterfinal bout, the Kilkenny man was drawn to meet the talented East German Reinhard Schulz. Dowling put in what was considered to be his best performance in a green vest as he bounced around the ring to out-box his German opponent. He was awarded a unanimous decision as he completely dominated the fight from start to finish. Assured of a medal, his semi-final opponent was to be Frenchman Aldo Cosentino: Dowling's confidence was rising with each bout.

Both Tracey and Downes were put out of the competition at the quarterfinal stage and, in hindsight, strange as it may seem, apart from the bronze medal, Dowling had another prize awaiting him. Tradition in Irish boxing had meant that only boxers who had won a medal at major games were permitted to keep the tracksuit supplied to them by the IABA. The Irish team manager in Bucharest was Colonel Jim Devine and after Dowling's win in the quarterfinal, he announced to Mick, and the assembled media, that his exploits had won him the right to keep the Irish tracksuit.

"Mick, you were great out there tonight and as a souvenir you can keep your Ireland track suit," said Devine. In the modern age of corporate sponsorship it seems strange to think that keeping a tracksuit was considered such an honour.

Regardless, the semi-final was lost by Dowling on a four-one split decision. The phrase 'split-decision' occurs many times when describing the career of Mick Dowling and he always associates those two words with defeats in major games. His defeat to Cosentino was another decision that could have gone either way, but it was not to be.

Roll on the next significant championships and Dowling once again represented his country, at the European Championships in

Madrid in June 1971. Under Benny Carabini and Colonel Devine, the Irish team which went to those Championships came home with an excellent return of three bronze medals, with Dowling's name again among those honours. Things had not started smoothly for the Irish team in Madrid, as an administrative mix-up saw the new blazers ordered for the Championships delayed in Dublin. However, they arrived by airfreight just in time for the opening ceremony and the Irish team, resplendent in their green jackets, avoided the indignity of turning out like 'Dolly Mixtures'.

Dowling's opening round opponent was the tough Greek, Adhansios Houliares. After seconds of the bout, the Kilkenny man dropped his opponent with a sweet combination to the head and chest. Undeterred, the Greek fought back but Dowling was comfortable in the final two rounds and many eyebrows were raised when he was awarded the bout only on a three-two decision. Whilst Dowling, Brendan McCarthy and Neil McLaughlin were making great progress, both Charlie Nash and Paddy Doherty crashed out of the Championships.

Dowling's quarterfinal opponent was to be the hometown boy, Jose Luis Otero, and 5,000 Madrilènos packed the arena to cheer him on. In front of the partisan Spanish crowd, the Arbour Hill fighter kept his cool to win the bout convincingly and assure himself of at least a further bronze medal. Dowling's supreme accuracy and use of the left jab swung the fight in his favour. His uppercuts and cross shots had the Spaniard rattled; the arena accepted the decision with dignity as Dowling's hand was raised. In front of the Irish Ambassador to Spain, Dennis Gallagher, and Transport Minister, Brian Lenihan, Ireland was now assured three bronze medals, as Dowling joined McCarthy and McLaughlin in the semi-finals.

However, by 18th June, the Irish contingent had to be content with just the three bronze medals, as all three semi-finalists were defeated. Dowling's defeat to the Russian Alexander Melnikov was considered to be the most contentious.

"He never hit me with anything during that fight," recalled Dowling. "It was the perception then that you had to put a Russian on the canvas to beat him and it was a hard decision to accept."

One sign of progress did arise from the performance of the Irish team at the Championships when it was decreed by Colonel Jim Devine that each member was permitted to keep their tracksuit. So, for the IABA, the search for new tracksuits began as the Olympic Games in Munich in 1972 peered over the horizon.

In September 1972 the now-veteran Dowling again went to the Olympic Games with his country. Those words 'split-decision' were to come back to haunt him as he fought his way to a quarterfinal battle with the Cuban, Orlando Martinez.

87

Above

Irish Golden Gloves Champions on tour in the USA in 1971. Members of the team include Gerry Storey (*far left*), Jim McCourt in the patterned shorts, Charlie Nash, and Mick Dowling (*fifth from left*) sporting a black eye. Neil McLaughlin is in the front row on the far right wearing shorts

In his opening bout, Dowling defeated convincingly the Swedish representative, Ove Lundby, on a four-one verdict. Now only three rounds away from the bronze medal, the draw was the hardest possible as Martinez' name came out alongside Dowling's. The fight was nine minutes of total action and when the split decision was called in favour of the Cuban, Dowling was down, devastated and out. Another split decision and a case of what could have been.

Dowling remembers well the terrible event which marred those games. On the morning of 5th September, as the Irish team awoke in the Olympic Village, they knew something had gone seriously wrong. The kidnapping and killing of eleven Israeli athletes by the Black September group in the village was big news all over the world.

The news began to filter through in the morning that something bad had happened in the Israeli quarters and it got worse as the day went on," recalled Downing. "The part of the village affected was cordoned off and it really did put a downer on the whole event and atmosphere surrounding the Games."

The Olympic Games in Munich was to be Mick Dowling's swansong on the international competitive games' front. He established a sports shop in Terenure and continued to defend his Irish bantamweight title with vigour until 1975. On his retirement, he continued to involve himself as coach in the Mount Tallant and Drimnagh clubs. His athletics career continued to flourish and, at sixty years of age, he still has the fitness and build he had in 1975. One sideline that has seen the name of Mick Dowling remain familiar across Ireland is his punditry for RTÉ. On meeting Mick, it is evident through his articulacy and knowledge, that he was a natural for the media.

"It started when I was asked to do a bit of punditry on the radio and then I moved on to do the televised Olympics for RTÉ. Barcelona in 1992 was my own personal highlight and I enjoy the work in the media as analysing boxing has always come easy to me."

If you are interested in athletics and wish to purchase some gear, Mick Dowling is currently the man to see for some sound advice. His south Dublin shop is considered to be a Mecca for running enthusiasts. Look closely on the walls of the shop as behind the shoes and vests you will find the odd picture of Mick in his boxing prime. Indeed, if you met Mick Dowling for the first time, you would be amazed to know that he was one of Ireland's best-ever boxers.

"I've been here in Terenure for a very long time and I am very happy with my life and the business I've built up," he said. "I am still involved in sport with my business, and if people ask me what the highlight of my career was, then I would say that my time in boxing was littered with highlights. I lived a dream for at least a decade and those events are special to me. However, sometimes I can hear the words 'split decision' in my head and it brings me back to the major games I appeared in. But there's no point in looking back."

On meeting Mick Dowling, one thing becomes evident: he is still the absolute competitor. If he had stayed in Castlecomer in the 1960s, he would, in all probability have a plethora of All Ireland hurling medals to his name. If he had stayed on in the Gresham Hotel, he may well have been General Manager by now. Instead, history has recorded with pride his achievements in Irish sport. However, what might he have achieved if it were not for 'split decisions'?

Neil McLaughlin

"I only got into boxing by mistake"

Many Irish amateur boxers would agree with the statement that it is just as difficult to claim a medal at the European boxing championships, as at an Olympic Games. The fact is that a favourable draw at the Olympics can see a boxer progress relatively smoothly until a shot at a medal becomes a realistic possibility. However, in the European championship, especially prior to the fall of the Berlin Wall, the draw was littered with formidable Russians, Poles, Romanians, Turks and East Germans, where the class was telling from the off. Ireland failed to secure any gold medals at these games since Gear O'Colmain's heavyweight triumph in 1947, until Paul Griffin's triumph at featherweight in 1991. In the intervening period, a plethora of mostly bronze medals were testament to many hard luck stories and the country's expectations remained mediocre as the championships came around.

One year in the early 1970s did become notable as the country claimed a trio of bronze medals. The seasoned class of Mick Dowling and Brendan McCarthy fought gamely to ensure that two of those medals were bound for Dublin's fair city. While, at flyweight, a Derry fighter by the name of Neil McLaughlin ensured that a third accolade went north.

A year later in Munich, McLaughlin emulated his Madrid heroics by storming through the flyweight division at the Olympic Games. Two victories saw him within touching distance of a bronze medal. However, a defeat in the quarterfinal to the eventual silver medallist, the Ugandan Leo Rwabwogo, ended that particular dream. His boxing achievements were highly commendable for a man who, in his youth, had set his sights on becoming a gymnast. In Derry today Neil McLaughlin's achievements in Madrid and Munich are still remembered fondly.

Neil McLaughlin was born on 10th May 1948 in the now-redeveloped Bogside area of Derry City. His early days were spent attending the local gymnastics club where a love of that particular sport developed.

"I really only got into boxing by mistake," he recalled. "I loved gymnastics and was all set to try and go on and take it very seriously when I had a bit of a falling out with the teacher at the club, so I decided to leave the sport behind. I was at a loose end and somebody suggested that I go up to the St Eugene's boxing club in the city and give the fight game a try. Well, the next thing I know is that I am in the ring sparring under the watchful eye of the trainer Patsy Havern and I began to realise that boxing came naturally to me."

That natural talent soon became apparent across the North West as McLaughlin's career in the amateur ranks saw him lift numerous schoolboy honours. Wins in the Donegal and Derry district championships saw him progress and make a name for himself in Ulster. Before long, provincial titles in the junior and senior divisions followed. As he explained, his progress in those intermediate years was rapid and the poise and balance learnt through gymnastics had proved to be of immense benefit.

"I was really shaping up well and the club were putting me in to spar with lads well above my class," he said. "I was just getting better and better and, whether it was my balance or style that was helping me, I am sure that the grounding I received as a gymnast was a great help."

The natural route to Irish titles followed and the green vest at international level was attained by McLaughlin in late 1969. A debut for his country against Scotland in Dundee established his credentials as a flyweight of note and as the 1970s dawned, preparations for a trip to the European championships in Madrid in 1971 became a priority.

Standing in McLaughlin's way in the Irish flyweight division in 1971 was the Belfast boxer Davy Larmour. Their clash for honours in that year's final was the key to the trip to Madrid. In February, the two fighters had stood toe-to-toe in the Ulster Hall where McLaughlin had been awarded the decision unanimously on points to lift the Ulster title. The rematch in Dublin, two days before the team for Madrid was to be announced, provided Larmour with the chance of sweet revenge.

Larmour was a seasoned campaigner who had claimed a bronze medal for Northern Ireland in the 1970 Commonwealth Games in Edinburgh and was well capable of reversing February's decision. The fight was a classic which McLaughlin won by a split decision, with many in the National Stadium of the view that the Derry man had been most unfortunate to shade. There were slow handclaps and booing echoing around the arena when the decision was called. Larmour had been given two warnings for ducking too low in the first round and this had, most likely, swayed the judges in McLaughlin's favour. The decision, regardless of the intricacies of the bout, secured the flyweight nomination for McLaughlin and he was duly picked as the flyweight representative for Madrid.

Madrid was a world away from the austerity of Derry in 1971. The Troubles had just begun on the streets of the city and the chance to represent Ireland was a welcome diversion for McLaughlin.

"Times were bad back home and it was a very big event to be at," he recalled. "I had done my homework well and been tutored in the international fight scene for Ireland. There is no way that I was overawed in any sense and that I feel worked in my favour."

The Games took place in June 1971. In his opening bout, McLaughlin was awarded a points' decision over the Bulgarian

Dimiter Milev, in a bout that saw the Derryman in fine form against a fast moving opponent. The Irish team as a whole impressed the observers with their style and, whilst the countries on the far side of the Iron Curtain impressed also, the Irish were tipped for at least one gold medal.

In his quarterfinal fight, the Derry hope was paired with the dangerous Turkish boxer, Mustafa Ozben. A slow start was overcome in the second and third rounds when McLaughlin unleashed a fearsome barrage of left hooks that opened the Turk's eye, and saw him safely into the semi finals, and, most importantly, gain a medal for his troubles.

However, waiting in the next round was a real class act in the Spaniard Juan Rodrigues. As McLaughlin recalled he was up against the odds, but one incident before the fight unsettled his composure.

"As I was preparing for the fight the Spaniards made an objection as I was not wearing bandages under my gloves. I had never worn bandages as they felt uncomfortable to me, so we consulted the rulebook to get clarification. The rulebook stated that the bandages were not a necessity, but rather than argue the point we agreed to wear bandages. Regardless of that, I was well beaten and the Spaniard went on to take the gold medal and he proved himself as a great boxer in later years. He was strong and muscular and beat me fairly but I have to say that getting that bronze medal gave me an awful lot of pleasure."

Those Games in Madrid were considered a success for Irish boxing, as McLaughlin's medal was added to on finals' night by bronze for both Mick Dowling and Brendan McCarthy.

McLaughlin returned to Derry to his day job as a tea blender but things were worsening considerably in the City as the Troubles took hold. For boxers and other athletes, the ability to pursue their careers was tested to the full.

"I recall that I was training in our club which was situated within Derry's Walls and each night was an ordeal to get there and back," he recalled. "There was a permanent army checkpoint to get through and my kitbag each night was searched coming to and going from the club. It was a real strain at times and I felt pretty annoyed about the hassle but it was just part and parcel of the times and after a while you just came to accept it. Sometimes though I began to question whether it was worth it all in the end and things on the streets were desperate."

Right

Neil McLaughlin, knocking out Henry Schmitt, USA Golden Gloves Champion in 1971

Events in Northern Ireland and Derry in particular, became very severe as 1972 dawned. The event known as Bloody Sunday on 30th January that year set the agenda for future years. Regardless, McLaughlin retained his national flyweight crown and secured his spot on the Irish Olympic team bound for Munich. Joining McLaughlin was his fellow Derryman Charlie Nash.

In McLaughlin's first bout, the Derryman defeated the Sudanese boxer Abaker Mohamed on a unanimous decision. In his next bout, he knocked out the Egyptian Mohamed Selim in two rounds. In the quarterfinal, his luck did not hold as

Rwabwogo of Uganda stopped the Derry man in two rounds to end the Olympic dream.

On his return to Derry, Neil McLaughlin's love of boxing waned and with his home city now the centre of the growing violence, he decided to take stock and walk away from the amateur game.

"To be honest I knew that my heart and soul was not committed to boxing and, when a boxer cannot muster up the enthusiasm he once had, it was time to walk away," he said.

That was the way things stayed as the twenty-four-year-old continued with the task raising a family. However, the yearning to return to the ring was a constant factor in McLaughlin's lean years and by late 1975, he decided to accept an offer to go professional.

"Gerry Hassett was looking after Charlie Nash at the time and he approached me with the prospect of a few bouts as a professional. I was not sure but thought it over and decided that I had nothing to lose so I decided to give it a second go."

On the evening of 26th January 1976, McLaughlin stepped into the ring after a break of almost two years to resume his career, this time as a professional. His opponent that evening in Glasgow was George Sutton. Whilst McLaughlin acquitted himself amicably in the bout, he ended up on the wrong end of a points' decision. It was a less-than-auspicious start to a career, which would soon become standard.

"I make no bones about my professional career and the truth is that I was just a journeyman, plain and simple," he said.

His next two fights against Tony Kerr in Glasgow saw McLaughlin record a win and a defeat. Three bouts with the legendary Welshman Johnny Owen followed and, while the pair drew at the Templemore Sports Complex in Derry, Owen won their last two encounters convincingly on points.

McLaughlin's tour of the under cards continued and his next two bouts saw him draw and then lose to London's Dave Smith. A return to Derry in July 1977 saw him lift the Northern Ireland area bantamweight crown with a stoppage of Terry Hanna in the fifth round. However, in October, any aspirations of hope were ended abruptly when the darling of the East End of London, Charlie Magri, knocked McLaughlin out in the second round of their clash at the Royal Albert Hall.

Nine months of inaction were ended in June 1978 when McLaughlin defeated Ian Murray in Derry. Yet, a defeat to Gary Davidson at the Wembley Conference Centre soon left the Derryman back at square one in the fight game. History has a habit of repeating itself and McLaughlin's next fight saw him paired in Belfast against his old nemesis from bygone days, Davy Larmour. That bout in October 1978 saw the Bogside battler put

his Northern Ireland title on the line against his old adversary. Larmour was awarded the decision that evening, and that disputed defeat at the National Stadium seven years previously was truly avenged. For Neil McLaughlin, at thirty years of age, the fight game was not being kind.

Undeterred, he went on to fight a further fifteen bouts over the next four years and the journeyman tag stuck. A fourth meeting with Johnny Owen ended in defeat in September 1979, while a shot at the British Empire title in Nigeria against Ray Amoo saw McLaughlin unlucky to come away on the wrong end of a disputed decision.

In June 1982, Neil McLaughlin was stopped by the hard-hitting Welshman Ivor Jones at the Royal Albert Hall. That defeat was to prove the end of his career and he returned to Derry to continue his life away from the boxing game. McLaughlin's professional career saw him lose twenty of his twenty-eight bouts: the spark that had ignited a successful amateur career in Ireland was never to return.

McLaughlin has retained the love of the sport and the discipline it brings: "As I said, I was just a journeyman and there was no way that glory was going to come to me. At the time, I was in it for the money but it is a truly hard sport and I have no regrets looking back.

"I have a grandson now who is boxing mad, and while his mum is not happy at the situation I give him all the encouragement I can. I have seen a lot in my time and hopefully everything I have learned I can use to advise him. I have had the privilege to have seen and met some great fighters in my time and I cannot rate highly enough some of those boxers. Their dedication and skill was a tribute to them and sometimes a lot of observers don't appreciate that sacrifice. I enjoyed every minute of my career and when I think of the time I spent in Madrid in the European Games it gives me so much pride. Sure, I have had low points and felt on many occasions that there was no point in going on. As it is though, I don't have, and never will have, any regrets for it was marvellous."

John Rodgers

"Very Pleased to Meet You, Mr Castro!"

The beauty about amateur boxing is that so-called 'ordinary' young men can find themselves sharing moments with world leaders and, in this particular case, a truly historic figure. In August 1974 Ireland sent a two-man team to the inaugural World Boxing Championships which were held in Havana, Cuba. For Davy Larmour from the Shankill Road in Belfast, and John Rodgers from Lisburn, the trip to the citadel of Communism in the Caribbean Sea was a chance to savour an experience of a lifetime.

On one memorable afternoon, as the two Irish representatives relaxed outside the boxing arena, a number of state cars pulled up. A flurry of security men alighted and gathered around the main car in the cortege. Eventually, a familiar face with an even more familiar cigar, the bearded figure of Fidel Castro, stepped out of the car and headed towards the arena.

On his way in he paused to exchange a few pleasantries with the two Irish boxers. The Cuban leader might well have expressed his solidarity with the proletariat in their struggle against hated Capitalist oppressors. Then again, he may not. The fact was that Fidel spoke swiftly in his native Spanish tongue to the two dazzled sportsmen, caught like rabbits in a headlight. There, in the company of two quiet and unassuming boxers, stood one of the earth's most powerful individuals. Now John Rodgers could not wait to get back to Lisburn to tell everyone about this story.

"Castro was a formidable man and had great presence," recalled Rodgers. "He was in full military battle dress and carrying his own gun in a very prominent holster. I remember that he refused to speak any English and spoke at all times through his interpreter. There we were, two lads from back home, meeting one of the most famous men in the world. He wished us well, shook our hands, and left us stunned as he and his bodyguards left to go into the arena."

Meeting Castro in Cuba was one of the highlights of John Rodgers' career. However, a trip to the 1972 Olympic Games in Munich was an experience that he ranks as something that will never be bettered.

John Rodgers was born in Lisburn in March 1947. Sitting proudly on the banks of the River Lagan, ten miles outside Belfast, Lisburn was elevated, along with Newry, to city status in 2002. In 1947 the town was coming to terms with the aftermath of the war. The Rodgers family lived on the Longstone Road and John was one of five sons and three daughters to Rose and Johnny Rodgers.

The Lisburn Boxing Club was where ten-year-old Rodgers learnt his love of the sport, and established a lifetime's friendship with his trainer, Frank Prenter. As John recalled, his early days as a competitive boxer had plenty of setbacks.

"I seemed to always get to finals only to be beaten in my schoolboy days," he said. "Eventually, I won my first Ulster and Irish senior titles in 1965 and then represented Ireland in a European Under-21 competition in Poland."

By 1970, with two Irish senior titles to his name, Rodgers was picked for the Northern Ireland team that travelled to Edinburgh for the Commonwealth Games. In the opening round, Rodgers was drawn against the England's top welterweight, Terry Waller. Whilst the Englishman was the reigning ABA champion, he had been stopped in each of his previous two internationals. It was therefore feasible that the Lisburn boxer possessed the ability to win the bout.

Rodgers entered the ring in Edinburgh on the same night that colleagues Gerry Jordan and Mickey Tohill opened their Games, while Paul Carson and Bob Espie were to follow later that evening. Rodgers' opening round was scrappy, with the Englishman adjudged to have shaded it. The second, however, belonged to Rodgers and the fighters were level-pegging going into the final round. Waller chose his punches well in the last, and put in a final spurt which saw him shade the contest. The fight itself was close and the scoring reflected this fact. Two of the five judges found in favour of the Londoner, whilst three scored it as a dead-heat. The Lisburn man was eliminated.

It was an accident of history that John Rodgers happened to be making a name for himself whilst the top Irish boxer in his division was then near-legendary Jim McCourt. The Immaculata pugilist had won a bronze at the Tokyo Olympics, and followed that with a gold at the Commonwealth Games in 1966. He was considered to be unstoppable within the British Isles.

The fact that McCourt was the number-one welterweight in Ireland meant that he was the man to beat if Rodgers was to progress at international level. Bouts between the two became keenly contested and one meeting in the Ulster Hall is still remembered, but for all the wrong reasons.

"Jim McCourt and I had some great fights, especially in the Ulster Hall and the Stadium," recalled Rodgers. "We met in the Ulster Hall in the senior final in 1971, and it was a real classic. My style was all action, two-handed, and I needed to be supremely fit. That night I took the fight to Jim and was really keyed up for the battle. Well, it went to a split decision and Jim got it in the end, but an awful lot of people in the Ulster Hall thought I should have won. Well, words were exchanged between boxers and corners, and we both left the ring unhappy. On the way out, the Lisburn contingent bumped into the Immaculata lads and the bad grace continued. The end result was that there was a bit of 'handbags at fifty paces' and I got a cut eye for my efforts. Afterwards I went to the Lagan Valley Hospital to get seen to, and the doctor asked me how the cut had happened. I said that I had been boxing in the Ulster Hall that evening and he said to me: 'Are you Rodgers the boxer?' I said 'Yes, why?' He said: 'Well, I saw your fight on the television before I left the house and didn't notice a cut eye.' So I admitted that there had been a bit of 'afters', but to be truthful Jim McCourt and I have been great friends ever since that night."

Jim McCourt subsequently had a disagreement with the Irish Amateur Boxing Board over the issue of collective squad training. That cost him his place at the Munich Olympics and opened up Rodgers' route to the highest stage of all.

"I remember I picked up the paper one morning in 1972 and read that I was on the Irish team for the Olympics," he recalled. "I was in tears and went up to my mother's house with the paper, and she was just overjoyed for me. I was going to the greatest show on earth and had been a late selection for the team.

"My first bout in the Games saw me beat the Dane, Ib Boetcher, after he had been disqualified in the third round. I was living the dream but then my name came out of the hat in the quarterfinal along with the Russian Anatoly Khokhlov and I knew I was up against it."

Rodgers was on the wrong side of a unanimous decision against the Russian, and his Olympic dream was at an end.

Above

John Rodgers holding photographs of his boxing career

Christchurch was the venue for the 1974 Commonwealth Games and Rodgers was determined to claim his place on the podium on that occasion. Lady Luck shone on both Rodgers and Gordon Ferris, and they received byes in the draws. This meant that both boxers stood only one fight away from at least a bronze medal since they were straight into the quarterfinals.

Rodgers was paired to meet the Australian welterweight champion, Robert Dauer. The fight with Dauer did not last very long and the Australian was counted out thirty-one seconds into the bout. Rodgers circled the ring twice, took aim and landed with a perfect left hand on Dauer's chin.

Rodgers must have broken some form of record, in that he had performed for only fifteen seconds to secure a medal in a major games. The first person into the ring to congratulate Rodgers was Davy Larmour, who had won through to his semi-final prior to the Lisburn man. Both Rodgers and Larmour were later joined by Enniskillen's Gordon Ferris in the semi-finals securing, at least, three bronze medals.

The semi-final opponent for Rodgers was to prove to be a tough customer. Welshman Errol McKenzie avoided Rodgers' left hand for the full three rounds to outbox the Lisburn man. The Welshman kept the fight at long-range and kept Rodgers at a distance throughout. In the last round, Rodgers took some punishment in the corner and a four-one defeat was considered to be a fair reflection of the bout.

In August 1974, the aforementioned trip to Cuba, which included the memorable meeting with Fidel Castro, took place. The inaugural games in Havana were a world away from the trouble-torn streets of Northern Ireland, but for Rodgers and Davy Larmour it was an eye-opening experience.

"I remember the grinding poverty that we saw in Havana back then. The American embargo on the island was in full flow and I was shocked by the conditions. My first bout was against the Spaniard Antonio Saez and I came through that comfortably enough to win to set up a bout with Reginald Forde of Guyana. Well, he hit me with the head and I retaliated likewise, but, as they say in life, I broke the eleventh commandment – 'don't get caught' – and I was disqualified."

With the experience of Cuba behind him, John's boxing career waned as he concentrated on raising his family. However, he recalls boxing for an Ireland Golden Gloves team in Madison Square Garden in New York.

"The Garden was just fantastic and along with Soldier Field in Chicago they must rank as my most memorable venues."

In May 1976 John Rodgers fought his last fight for Ireland, in an international against Hungary at the National Stadium. John Rodgers has since then been associated with the Lisburn Boxing Club. His friendship forged in the earliest days with club trainer Frank Prenter has remained solid and each night John's wife, Marion, prepares dinner for Frank.

On his greatest memories, Rodgers recalls the trips with pride but always remembers sparring with John Caldwell in the Immaculata club as a highlight.

"It was a privilege to spar Caldwell as I learned so much from him in the ring. He was the best and there was nobody could have touched him in my view. On my low-points, I always got depressed when I lost a fight that I was sure I had won. I have enjoyed my time in boxing and the times I had will never be bettered. It is the greatest sport for young lads to get involved in, and I am so glad I made the decision as a boy to join the Lisburn Boxing Club."

Davy Larmour

Sugar Ray Robinson and the Shankill Road

From the mean abode of the Shankill Road came a man by the name of David Larmour. Born the day after April Fools' in 1949, Davy became the darling of Belfast and beyond as he claimed gold and bronze medals in successive Commonwealth Games, and represented Ireland at the 1976 Montreal Olympics. His highlight as a professional came in March 1983, when he took the British bantamweight title by beating fellow Belfastman Hugh Russell. A fabulous achievement for a man who had nurtured the dream of holding the coveted Lonsdale Belt from the moment he had first worn boxing gloves.

Davy Larmour can pinpoint the exact day he fell in love with boxing. It was one Saturday afternoon in early September 1957, when he witnessed *America's Fight of the Week* on BBC television. A fight that took place before his young eyes, in less-than-glorious black and white, on a twelve-inch television.

"I was just a kid and the *Lone Ranger* had just finished when the boxing came on the telly," he recalled. "I was about to go out to play when the presenter announced 'And now, from Yankee Stadium in New York City, it's *America's Fight of the Week*'."

Larmour watched dumbfounded as the master of ceremonies, Johnny Addie, master of cerimonies, introduced Carmen Basilio to a rapturous crowd of forty thousand. No sooner had he arrived than Addie announced the name of the champion, the one…the only…Sugar Ray Robinson. For Larmour, it was instant opium.

"The bell rang and these two guys just went for each other from the off," he remembered. "They were so muscular and with the style, speed, sweat and grease it was just an awesome sight. The fight just got faster and harder and my father had to tell me to calm down as I was now jumping up and down. Anyhow, when the fight was over, Robinson had been defeated and I turned around to my father and asked him to buy me a pair of gloves. I was totally and irreversibly hooked."

Larmour had the breeding to make it in the fight game. He had three uncles – Frankie, Jackie and Danny Briers – who had made names for themselves in the game. Indeed, Jackie had won a professional flyweight title in his prime. However, Davy's first request to join a local club ended in bitter disappointment.

"I went to the local boxing club and I was only about three feet high," he said. "I was in love with the place. It was something out of *Oliver Twist* and I approached the trainer Jimmy Hamilton and told him I wanted to box. Jimmy looked at me standing there with my new boxing gloves and he asked me where my vest, slippers and towel were. He then chased me home and told me to ask my mother to get me some gear and only then could I join the club. I ran home in tears that night and threw my gloves under the stairs and that was me finished with boxing."

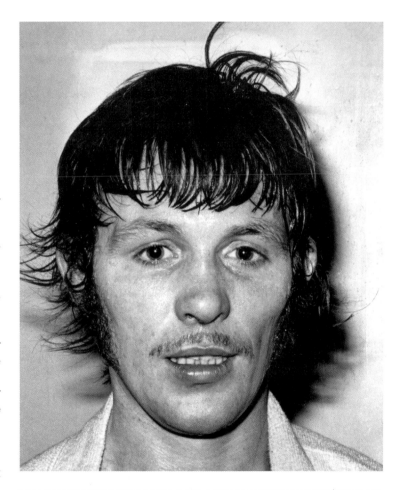

Or so young Davy thought. Three weeks later, his mother came up with the necessary equipment and a career in boxing was underway. Larmour learned the hard way and in his first juvenile championship bout, he was stopped by Paddy Moore.

"I remember that fight as it was the first time I had ever worn a gum shield, which was made out of rubber, and it made me sick," he said. "It was not until my third year of trying that I won the Ulster and Irish titles at seven stones, seven pounds."

Back at school, fourteen-year-old Davy was becoming a star due to his success. On the Shankill Road, his name became the talk of the shops and pubs as he went on to further national honours as a junior boxer. However, as he entered the senior ranks, Larmour became somewhat of a 'bridesmaid' as he formed a habit of losing in finals.

In 1970, his career was afforded a boost as he was picked as Northern's Ireland flyweight at the Edinburgh Commonwealth Games. A brave effort in the Games was ended as Larmour lost out in his semi-final to the classy Ugandan fighter Leo Rwabwogo. The Ugandan was in turn beaten by Dave Needham of England in the final and Larmour was content with a bronze but as he later recalled, there was very little hype about his achievement on the streets of the Shankill.

Above

A young Davy Larmour pictured around 1970.

"To me it was just another medal and, whilst some people acknowledged me, it was a very low-key return for me."

Successive defeats in both the Ulster and Irish senior flyweight finals in 1971 and 1972 seemed to reinforce Larmour's tag as a nearly man back home. A defeat to Derry's Neil McLaughlin in 1972 saw Larmour left at home as the Bogside man made the trip to the Munich Olympics. In 1973, his luck turned and he claimed his first national flyweight title: he went on to retain it in the three succeeding years. An international call-up was achieved in 1973, but in a most peculiar manner.

"I was working at Ballymena's Michelin factory one day when I was told that there was someone at the gate to see me," he said. "I thought it weird as nobody in Ballymena knew me but I went to the gate and there waiting for me was a priest. It was Father Darragh who was involved with the All Saints club in Ballymena and he said that the call had come from Dublin for me to box against Romania that night. I hadn't even time to think and he left me on the train at Ballymena so I could get to Belfast. I just about made it to the National Stadium on time and there I was in the green vest fighting for Ireland in an international."

The Commonwealth Games in Christchurch in 1974 saw Larmour victorious in the flyweight division. His victory over the Indian, Chandra Narayanan, to claim the gold, sparked off a wild celebration on the Shankill.

"We arrived home in the middle of the night and the taxi took me home to Leopold Street at the time when the Troubles were really bad. I was totally dumbfounded when I saw the crowds waiting for me as I had been on the other side of the world and unsure how the reaction would be. It was fantastic and I posed from the bedroom window for photographs, but at the same time I was exhausted and could have just gone to bed."

In 1974, Larmour represented Ireland at the European championships in Poland, where he lost out on a bronze medal to England's future world champion, Charlie Magri. That same year, a trip to Cuba for the world boxing games saw Larmour fall in love with the island – he still holds an ambition to return.

By 1976, with his fourth successive Irish title in the bag, Larmour got the nod for the squad to travel to Montreal for the Olympic Games. In the opening two rounds of the competition, the Shankill man was afforded walkovers. This left him with a tough quarterfinal against the American, Leo Randolph to

Left

Davy Larmour pictured during a brutal British title eliminator bout at the Ulster Hall with Hugh Russell. He lost on this occasion but got his revenge six months later.

contemplate. The fight in the Olympic arena was close and the American shaded the decision on points. Randolph went on to defeat the Cuban, Ramon Duvalon, in the final and Larmour's chance of glory was missed.

"The Olympics were on a different level to anything I had ever encountered," he said. "I found that things were competitive to the extent that a lot of the friendliness disappeared. I definitely didn't enjoy the experience due to the things that were done by others to get the edge over opponents. I will, however, never forget meeting Sugar Ray Leonard as he was a pleasure to know and the Americans just loved him."

By this stage, Davy had left his job as a gardener with the Belfast City Council and was working in the Harland and Wolff shipyard in the east of the City. Having attended all the significant games which an amateur could aspire to, the paid ranks now beckoned.

"I was twenty-seven years old and had had taken just about enough of the boxing," he recalled. "I was married and losing money through it so I decided that it was time to get my life in order. But I was still training and boxing had still got a hold of me and then the urge to become a professional was still there. Then Gerry Hassett offered me a chance to turn professional so before I knew it I was in Derry fighting a guy called Jimmy Bott and getting paid for it. I stopped him in the first round and it was, in hindsight, the worst result I could have had as with my amateur record nobody wanted to come up against me. To be truthful, I was still working in the shipyard and the extra money was the reason I turned professional."

Larmour's reputation saw him without a fight for seven months and, when he returned, he suffered two defeats. The first, after an invitation at short-notice to fight John Feeney; the second, to George Sutton. In his fifth fight, the Welsh Wizard, Johnny Owen, stopped Larmour and the Belfast man began to have self-doubt about his ability.

"I fought Owen after getting two days' notice and just hadn't the fitness for the fight so he stopped me in the seventh round," he said. "I was not getting a run of victories and the fact was I was not having the confidence I had as an amateur due to the lack of regular fights," he said. "I was at the wrong end of the age bracket and thought my chance of glory was behind me. I did beat Neil McLaughlin for the Northern Ireland title but in British terms it wasn't happening. Gerry Hassett started putting a few bills together in the Ulster Hall and I was beginning to get up the ratings in Britain but I just couldn't get the fights I wanted."

However, as the trouble decreased across the North, big time boxing returned when local promoter, Barney Eastwood, put his faith in a Clones lad named Barry McGuigan and the local

Above: Davy Larmour pictured with his Commonwealth medals: bronze from 1970 and gold from 1974.
Left: Blood streams down the face of Davy Lamour but he outpointed Maina of Kenya in their quarter-finals flyweight boxing bout in the Commonwealth Games at the Murrayfield Ice Rink.

1962. Suitably the King's Hall was to be the venue with Barry McGuigan pencilled in to top the bill. However, McGuigan's fight was cancelled but the crowds turned out to pack the arena for the eagerly anticipated fight. Twelve bruising rounds were fought out between the two protagonists. Larmour dropped the champion in the fifth round and got the decision after twelve close rounds. At thirty-three years of age, David Larmour had finally reached the pinnacle of his career as the Lonsdale Belt was placed around his waist.

"When I was a kid the Lonsdale Belt was the ultimate – the only thing that was attainable – and it was a really special honour to get it after so many years," he said. "To me it was a toss-up whether I was going to retire as champion at that stage or whether I was to fight on. In an interview I was asked what the next step was for the oldest champion in the bantamweight division ever. I said that I was going to have a think about things and then the prospect of a defence against John Feeney came up at the King's Hall."

On 16th November 1983, Barry McGuigan claimed the European featherweight championship at the King's Hall in Belfast by stopping, with a flurry of vicious body shots, the challenger, Valerio Nati. The main supporting bout that night saw Davy Larmour throw his last punches in the fight game in vain against John Feeney. The Lonsdale Belt left Belfast after Larmour was stopped.

"All I recall from that night is that Feeney caught me with a cracking left hook and the referee stopped the fight," he recalled. "I wasn't too disillusioned although I tried my best and was a week off my thirty-fourth birthday and I knew the sell-by date was up."

So that was that for the Shankill Road man. The dream had been attained but no fortune accompanied it.

"When I fought Hugh Russell for the British title I was given a thousand pounds," he recalled. "But I wanted that Lonsdale Belt so much that I would have fought for nothing that night. Even back then, a thousand pounds was peanuts. After the tax man took his bit and my expenses came out, I was left with no great amount. I made great friends in boxing but, alas, there was no crock of gold."

David Larmour is a highly educated individual. He has qualified as a counsellor and has retired to the Co. Down seaside resort of Millisle. In his living room, books on politics and history outweigh his medals and trophies. A life spent learning to survive in the hardest areas has given way to a love of study. He is articulate, highly philosophical and a pleasure to deal with. For the man who dreamed the dream in front of a black and white television in the late 1950s, boxing – and life – has left him happy and for the ageing generation on Belfast's Shankill Road, he has

fight scene was reborn. In addition to McGuigan, Eastwood had signed up the 1980 Olympic bronze medallist Hugh Russell. The New Lodge Road man soared through the British bantamweight division and a collision course with Larmour was on the cards. Training in the Eastwood Gym in Castle Street alongside McGuigan and Russell was Davy Larmour. When the opportunity to spar 'The Clones Cyclone' was offered, the Shankill Road man jumped at the chance.

"I sparred with Barry McGuigan on many occasions and, to be truthful, I was learning a lot more from being in the ring with him than he was with me," said Davy. "Then I fought and lost to Hugh in a final eliminator for the British title and he then went on to win that crown by a disqualification in January 1983. I fought on the under card that night and it was announced that I would be Hugh's opponent in his first defence of that title."

That fight, on 2nd March 1983, was the first all-Belfast

Gerry Hamill

A Boxing Beacon in the Seven Towers

There is nobody who could argue that Gerry Hamill during his career didn't go there, see that and buy the tee-shirt. Over sixty outings in an Irish international vest, seven Ulster and two Irish senior titles, two trips to the Commonwealth Games – at which he won a gold medal in 1978 – and one to the Olympics in Montreal in 1976, told the tale of his career. Now installed as trainer at the All Saints Boxing Club in Ballymena, together with fellow former international Tony McAvoy, Gerry Hamill is imparting his experience in the ring to future generations in the Co. Antrim town. A dedication to the sport of boxing is inherent within his genes.

Born to Joe and Kitty Hamill in the Cullintree Road area of Belfast in 1955, Gerry was one of a family of ten children. The local Immaculata Boxing Club was doing a roaring trade in turning out champions at this stage and the older Hamill boys were to the fore at the club.

In 1962, when Gerry was seven years of age, his second cousin, Charlie Rice, went to the Commonwealth Games in Perth, Australia, and was disqualified in his semi-final bout against the New Zealander, Wally Coe. That decision, which was greeted with uproar in the arena, saw the Belfast boxer denied his bronze medal and it was only after a prolonged campaign, waged by coach Gerry Storey and others over many years, that he was rightfully awarded the medal.

Two years later, in 1964, with the Immaculata basking in the glory of Jim McCourt's bronze medal at the Tokyo Olympics, Gerry joined the 'Mac' and a career that would see him travel the world was underway.

"As a kid at the Immaculata, I was seeing all these guys who were excellent boxers such as Jim McCourt, Barney Wilson, Spike McCormick and my own favourite, Paddy Moore, so it was only natural that a lad would be inspired," he said. "I remember Spike McCormick losing narrowly to Ken Buchanan, who I regarded as one of the best ever, so there was always class and skill to look up to."

By the age of eleven, Gerry's family had moved to the outskirts of Glengormley, however, the young prospect had, in purely boxing terms, made a more important personal move.

"It just happened that I drifted away from the Immaculata and ended up with Gerry Storey in the Holy Family club," he recalled. "Their gym used to have sparring sessions on a Sunday morning and I began to feel at home there and that is where I stayed. I never looked back as a juvenile and won four Down and Connor titles, together with four Ulster and All Ireland championships."

By 1973, Hamill was maturing as a boxer and a clean sweep of Antrim, Ulster and Irish junior and senior titles seemed to be

106

on course until he met Derry's Damien McDermott in the Irish senior final.

"I was on a roll that year but lost out to Damien and it was a devastating experience, but one which was to stand by me in future years. At the time I was playing Gaelic football and soccer and, having played a game in the week of the Irish final, I could feel that my legs were not holding out in the ring. I was playing soccer with Cliftonville and one day Dr McGarry from the club said that I could not keep up all the sports and would have to choose which one I wanted to do.

"That occurred about the time I was picked to go to New Zealand for the Commonwealth Games and I knew then that boxing was the one sport that could deliver everything I wanted. Christchurch and the Games were a dream for me and at nineteen I was now totally dedicated to boxing and loving every minute of it."

The exuberance of youth was to see Hamill eliminated in his second bout in Christchurch when he was disqualified in his clash with the Kenyan, Samuel Mbunga.

"The team that went to those Games was a great mix of youth and experience and I looked up to, and learnt so much from guys like Davy Larmour and John Rodgers."

By 1975, Gerry had moved up to lightweight and, whilst he won the Ulster title, he was to lose to Charlie Nash of Derry in the National final. However, a trip to the "culture shock" that was the Soviet Union for the European Under-21 championships was a further accolade in Hamill's growing status in the ring. The Hamill family had by then moved to Ballymena and, whilst Gerry was still a member of the Holy Family in Belfast, he began also to use the facilities of the local All Saints club for training.

The Montreal Olympic year of 1976 saw Hamill victorious in both Ulster and Irish senior finals and a trip to Canada was assured. Lady Luck was not with him however as, of the thirty-five entrants in the lightweight division, Gerry was paired in one of two preliminary bouts with the Yugoslav, Ace Rusevski.

The fight was close but Rusevski was victorious on a four-one verdict and Hamill's Games were ended prematurely. The Yugoslav went on to win a bronze medal and was considered unlucky to lose in his semi-final to the eventual gold medallist Howard Davis of the United States.

"I, as a trainer, always tell my boys to listen to me in the corner as it's my job to advise them how best to handle their opponent," said Gerry. "In 1976, I made the mistake of not listening to Gerry Storey as he had told me how exactly to handle Rusevski. I was fighting the wrong fight and not keeping him at the end of my left hand at distance and that was to cost

Above

Gerry Hamill pictured around 1978

me in the end. The most important thing I tell my lads today is to listen to your corner and I know that all too well."

Undeterred by the experience of Montreal, Hamill won Irish and Ulster lightweight titles in 1977. A year later he again won the Ulster title and was chosen to join Northern Ireland's team for the Commonwealth Games in Edmonton.

Hamill breezed through the lightweight division and saw of the challenge of Zambian Teddy Makofi in the semi-final. In the final, he was considered lucky to sway a split decision over Kenya's Patrick Waweru. In hindsight, Hamill is sure that the gold medal was deserved and is the highlight of his impressive career.

"I have the video of the fight and I felt that I was entitled to win the gold," he said. "One sure sign was that Gerry Storey in my corner, who would let you know his honest opinion on your fight, was confident that I had won. What happened next is just a blur in my memory as after my hand was raised I just was so happy and can recall nothing of the medal ceremony."

Tired and exhausted, the team travelled home and Gerry received great welcomes in both Belfast and at the family home in Ballymena. After the heights of Edmonton, Gerry took time away from the ring and settled into a new home in Ballymena with his wife Jean Anne.

By 1980, Gerry had retained his Ulster title with a victory over Holy Trinity's David Irving at the Ulster Hall. However, a devastating fire destroyed the interior of his Ballymena home and all thoughts of travelling to the Moscow Olympics became secondary for Gerry.

"The fire was just a catastrophe for us and boxing just took a back seat," he said. "I lost a lot of boxing mementos and the most important thing for me was to get the house back in order and get on with life.

"Eddie Thompson was overseeing Ireland's preparations for the Olympic Games at that time and he contacted me to say that I had been picked in a squad to meet Scotland. I said to Eddie, given all that had happened, that I really wasn't up to boxing at that stage and I couldn't face it. He said that if I did not box against Scotland that I was out of the reckoning for the Olympics and that was that for me and I told him to forget it and I have never put a glove on to fight since."

Eight months after the fire, the Hamill family moved from their repaired home to another part of Ballymena but the draw towards boxing for Hamill was still strong and he soon took a number of coaching courses and fell in with the All Saints club.

The All Saints' most famous representative was, of course, the world-famous Ballymena actor Liam Neeson. An international prospect in the early 1960s who won many titles with the club, Neeson still visits regularly and keeps a keen interest in the sport.

Today, the club that first put onto a stage the undoubted talent of Liam Neeson, is thriving with Gerry Hamill at the helm. Recently, Gerry's cousins, the Hamill brothers – Dermot and Thomas – have represented the club at Commonwealth Games and it is something that gives Gerry significant pride.

"Sure, it's time-consuming but there is a lot of pleasure in seeing lads progress and show their ability. It's hard also to tell lads that, for their own good, they should not pursue boxing further, but that is my job also. Sometimes I see what it means to boys to go into a ring and show their ability and win a contest. Their joy is real and I get great happiness to think that I in some way contributed towards that.

"The thing about boxing is that you will be found out quite easily in the ring if you are not giving it your total dedication. I have seen that from the corner and it is something that could get someone hurt. Boxing today is all about fitness and mental preparation and my job is to ensure that my lads have that edge in the ring."

Despite his love of the sport, Gerry's family had mixed feelings about his career. While his mother was a feature at most of his Ulster and Ireland outings, his father Joe was less enthusiastic about his son's boxing.

"Mum went to all my fights of note but my father never saw me box after the age of fifteen," said Gerry. "By that age he felt that I had nothing left to prove in the ring and he felt that the further my career went, the more likelihood there was of me getting hurt. He was born and reared in Sailortown in Belfast and he had seen the way that the fighters of old had ended up, so maybe that is what behind his view. He was set against me going professional and I recall he confronted one man in a bar one night who suggested I should. That made him angry and he told the man straight that if he thought I should turn professional, why wouldn't he ask his own two sons to do the same?"

Today, Gerry Hamill has his own pork wholesale business operating out of Ballymena. He was Northern Ireland's third boxing gold medallist at the Commonwealth Games – an event that is still top of the memories chart. His trained and skilful eye – developed through many years with his coach Gerry Storey – stands him well as the All Saints in Ballymena goes from strength to strength. Boxing is – and always has been – a way of life for Gerry Hamill. The game in Ireland will benefit from his dedication in future years.

Philip Sutcliffe

"Muhammad Ali – Have You a Problem?"

Whenever in life you come across your all-time hero in person, it's most unusual that such a meeting would end up in an argument. However, for Philip Sutcliffe, that is precisely what happened when he bumped into Muhammad Ali in Chicago in 1978. As Philip explained, maybe it was nerves, or just being overwhelmed by the occasion, but he and 'The Greatest' just did not hit it off on their first meeting.

"I was part of an Irish team out in America, and Ali came along to talk to us – and for me this man was just the most famous person in the world," said Sutcliffe. "I just idolised him as a sportsman and I had followed his career from the start, and to see him in the flesh was just amazing. I was a light-flyweight at the time and he seemed to be like a giant as we all posed for photographs. Then he called me over to sit on his knee like a 'nice little Leprechaun'. Well, I just snapped and told him, literally, where to go. There were a few choice words used by me but I just don't know what happened as something just snapped. Anyhow, it was soon smoothed over, but it was the whole thought that Ali could have said that to me that hurt. It wasn't his fault as that was all part of the showman he was. Today, though, I still think he was the greatest fighter and sportsman ever lived, and it's funny to think that you could wait a lifetime to meet your hero, only to fall out with him."

Maybe the above-mentioned incident was evidence of Sutcliffe's bravery – bravery he brought to the boxing ring in every bout he fought. Philip Sutcliffe is a true son of Dublin. Born in 1959, he was by seven years of age a fully-fledged member of the Drimnagh Boxing Club. As a schoolboy he prospered by taking Dublin, Leinster and Irish titles before an injury curtailed his early promise.

"I fell off a swing when I was about eleven when I broke my shoulder so I didn't pack boxing in, boxing packed me in for a while so to speak," he recalled. "That was a bit of a setback for me and I couldn't defend my titles in the all-Ireland championships that year."

With the injury on the mend, Sutcliffe's career was soon back on course but as he recalled, there were quite a few other classy boxers in the hunt for national honours at that time.

"The main man to beat back then was a guy called Jimmy Coughlan, who was from the Transport Boxing Club in Dublin. He was the best thing around in Ireland and he beat me twice I recall. He also beat Barry McGuigan, Mick Holmes and Hughie Russell in the Irish championships, so he was quite a boxer in his day. There was great competition around back then and we all met in the various championships. I remember though losing to Barry McGuigan and being gutted, as I know I won the fight. If you see him, mention that to him, would you?"

Below

Philip Sutcliffe in tracksuit at front on far right, just before his disagreement with 'The Greatest'. Gerry Hamill is also pictured in the back row wearing a tracksuit

Sutcliffe landed his first Irish senior title at the National Stadium in 1977 in the light-flyweight division. His opponent that night was the up-and-coming Ulster champion, Jimmy Carson. A call-up to box for Ireland in Hungary soon followed and, as Sutcliffe recalled, it was a very new experience.

"I was only seventeen at the time and it was only the second occasion that I had ever been out of Ireland. I remember that we were based way out in the mountains in a training camp, and I was by far the youngest, so I was quite overwhelmed by the whole thing."

While the trip to Hungary may have been only Sutcliffe's second time out of Ireland, his first foreign excursion had been to the ABA finals in London a few weeks earlier, where he saw at first hand the English light flyweight champion, Paul Fletcher. That glimpse of the talented Liverpudlian had been to prepare the Dublin lad for the forthcoming European Senior Championships in Halle in East Germany. An event in which the Englishman was tipped for gold.

Sutcliffe was chosen by Ireland for the championships in the light-flyweight division and his comparative youth was ridiculed by the-then English coach Kevin Hickey. Maybe, in hindsight, Hickey's criticism of Sutcliffe was over-the-top. Perhaps there was an element of fear as it was evident his protégé, Fletcher, would have to go toe-to-toe with the talented Dubliner.

Hickey expressed the view that Sutcliffe was too young to be at the championships and the Irish selectors should have left him at home. He added that the Dubliner's inexperience would tell against him and he had no chance. With the predictions of the Englishman ringing in his ears, Sutcliffe relished the draw in the second series which, appropriately, saw him pitted against Paul Fletcher.

The bout took place on 1st June 1977, in front of four thousand spectators in the boxing arena. Sutcliffe put in a wonderful display to see off the ABA champion by a unanimous points decision. He not only exacted revenge for any slight on his ability, but he got a five-minute standing ovation for his efforts as he left the ring.

Sutcliffe had disposed of Fletcher in only his fifth senior fight. He was the centre of attention to the assembled press and media in the changing rooms afterwards. Fletcher had been forced to take two standing counts during the contest as Sutcliffe's two-handed style proved too much for the Englishman to deal with. Irish team manager Frank Bannon, never one to understate matters, said that Sutcliffe had literally "boxed the head off Fletcher".

History will recall that the Republic of Ireland soccer team lost their chance to qualify for the 1978 World Cup by losing to

Bulgaria the night that Sutcliffe beat Fletcher. However, another Eastern European test awaited Ireland's finest as Sutcliffe was pitted against the excellent Pole, Henryk Srednicki, in the semi-final. Gerry Storey, Ireland's coach at the Championships, was aware that the Pole was a formidable ask for Sutcliffe. With an advantage of an additional 150 contests at senior level, Srednicki who had the build of a featherweight, was an odds-on favourite.

Sutcliffe's advice for that fight had been to box the Pole 'side-on' in order to avoid the long reach of his opponent. It was not to be, as the Pole proved to have the measure of Sutcliffe and the Italian referee stopped the bout with three seconds remaining in the third round. Sutcliffe did catch Srednicki with a sweet right hand to force him to take a standing count. However, Sutcliffe took three counts in the fight and he was to be content with a bronze medal. Ireland was justly proud of its latest hero.

Sutcliffe was now the darling of the National Stadium and the City of Dublin took him to its hearts. He regained Irish senior titles and in 1979, he was again picked to represent Ireland in the European Championships. This time the Dubliner was chosen to fight in the bantamweight division. His Irish team mates that year were Hugh Russell, Mick Holmes and PJ Davitt. Sutcliffe carried an ankle injury into the Championships, but was still tipped as Ireland's best chance of a medal. He was drawn to meet the fancied Frenchman Kamel Djadda in his first bout.

On the day that Margaret Thatcher was elected as Prime Minister of Great Britain, Sutcliffe turned on the style to outclass his Gallic opponent. A four-one split decision that was tarnished however by the scoring of the English judge, who gave the fight to Djadda. Regardless, the tipsters were noting Sutcliffe's progress, and his technique and work rate made him a certainty for a bronze medal at least.

In his next bout, Sutcliffe outclassed the Yugoslavian fighter Zvonko Milicevic with a near-excellent performance. His relief at getting a unanimous decision was apparent to all in the arena as he displayed his joy in the ring. He had out-foxed and outclassed his opponent by what was probably his best performance in a green vest. Irish coach Benny Carabini was glowing in his praise of the Dubliner, and said that if he could keep his composure in the ring then the gold would be coming back to Ireland.

Alas, it was not to be and Sutcliffe crashed out in the semi-final to the Russian Stefan Forster. During the contest Sutcliffe was forced to take three counts, and lost on a unanimous decision. Critically, Sutcliffe broke a bone in his right hand and fought most of the bout in extreme pain. A second bronze medal was scant consolation and, whilst he was only the second Irish boxer to win medals either side of the Iron Curtain, he decided to retire from boxing. At nineteen years old, it was a rash decision

After much cajoling and soul-searching, Sutcliffe returned to the game after his hand had healed. By 1980 he was on his way with the Irish team to the Moscow Olympics as the country's bantamweight representative. In his opening bout, he was to come across the little-known Mexican, Daniel Zaragoza. Although losing on a unanimous points' decision, Sutcliffe had just been beaten by a man who would go on to claim world professional bantamweight crowns on three separate occasions.

"It was my goal in life to go to the Olympics from when I was a kid, and the hand problem was still giving me a lot of problems," he recalled. "I had lost the Irish final in 1980 to Ritchie Foster but my reputation was such that I got the nod to go. I saw the video of my fight with Zaragoza recently and I still don't know how I came through the bout when I think of the pain that my hand was in."

Returning to Ireland, Sutcliffe worked in numerous jobs, as he learnt that even being an Irish Olympian did not guarantee him an easy life. In 1982 Sutcliffe joined the Irish Army and was based at the Clancy Barracks in Kilmainham. On his reasons for joining the military, he is sure in his response.

"I had always wanted to join the army but not to be a mere soldier, rather to re-educate myself and get involved in the physical training side of things. I had retired again from the sport but I was involved in all the sporting activities and my company sergeant, Tony Hutchinson, helped me out greatly. I was the coach of the boxing team and we had great success in the world military games, with Michael Kelly and Henry Coyle both winning gold medals and James Phillips and Tommy Sheehan winning bronze medals on two occasions each. You have to remember that some of the hardest men fought in these games, with Russians, Koreans and Americans all competing."

In 1985 Sutcliffe volunteered for a tour of duty in the Lebanon, and it was an experience that has left a deep mark on the Dubliner.

"It was a real bad time over there when I went out. One of the lads on my company was killed while I was stationed in the Lebanon and I think Ireland lost five soldiers in all during my time there."

Sutcliffe had signed up for the Irish Army for initially a three-year period. Twenty-four years later, in October 2006, Corporal Philip Sutcliffe ended his military career.

"I enjoyed my time in the army and I was given a lot of respect for what I had achieved in boxing. It was just a time for me to change and I decided to move on."

Today, Sutcliffe runs the Crumlin Boxing Club in the west side of Dublin. He broke his links with the Drimnagh Boxing Club in 1992 after a period of twenty-six years to take the reins in Crumlin, a decision he admits was difficult to make.

"In Drimnagh, I had started as a lad and done everything from sweeping the floor to competing in internationals, so leaving was a hard thing to do. Paddy Whelan approached me one night to come and look after the Crumlin club. The world was at my feet as boxing was thriving in Drimnagh, as Michael Carruth had just won the Olympics in Barcelona. But I thought it was time to move as this is what I would call a working club and I am happy with that. I see kids come in here and make progress in their boxing and, indeed, in life in what is a hard area to grow up in. I want to see the kids that hang outside this club coming inside and none of them will be treated any differently. I have parents coming up to me and thanking the club for how we have changed their sons with the discipline that boxing has given them. That is what this club has to offer the kids – and we are by no means soft with them – and there are over one hundred local lads members."

Trips to Spain and Australia for the youngsters of Crumlin are part of the rewards for the work that is put in by Sutcliffe and others. One of the shining lights of the club is one Philip Sutcliffe Junior, and he will do his father proud in future years. On his simplest pleasure in the sport, Sutcliffe Senior is certain of the answer.

"We have competitive boxing here once a week and sometimes you see a kid in action, who two weeks earlier could not tie his laces, throw a perfect left hand. That is pure pleasure and that is why I am still involved in boxing."

For a man who once offered Muhammad Ali a fight, those are words that come from the heart.

Paddy Maguire

Ploughing a Lonely Furrow

In the 1970s, when Northern Ireland was enduring the darkest days of its Troubles, professional boxing suffered its own technical knock out, as the game died a sudden death. Bars, restaurants, cinemas and all forms of nightlife ground to a halt as the streets of the major towns and cities hibernated in the face of the turmoil. It would have been considered folly for any promoter to invest money into a game that had become another casualty of the violence, and many promising careers suffered as a result.

One Belfastman, however, did decide to plough a lone furrow in the paid ranks, but found that the only way to secure decent competition was to travel across the Irish Sea and take his chances in England. Paddy Maguire was that man. A fighter who claimed the British bantamweight title in 1975, and then went on to draw controversially with Daniel Trioulaire, for the European championship. This result was considered to be one of the greatest miscarriages of boxing justice in the 1970s, that robbed Maguire of further glory.

Left

Paddy Maguire meets 'The Greatest' in Wembley Arena, 1975

Paddy Maguire was born in Belfast's Kashmir Road on 26th September 1948. He fought one bout for the Immaculata club in the Down and Connor boys' championships before moving to the Star Boxing Club where his career as an amateur soon flourished. Later he joined up with the Hollerith Club in Devonshire Street and made a name for himself as an all-action fighter who put immense and unrelenting pressure on his opponents.

By 1966 Maguire had secured the Ulster senior bantamweight crown and in Dublin, in the Irish senior final, he came up against the formidable Mick Dowling. Maguire beat Dowling that night when he stopped the Kilkenny-born fighter in the second round and was the only fighter to stop Dowling during his career. Now crowned as Ulster and Irish champion Maguire was confident that he would be included in the Northern Ireland Empire Games squad who were to compete in Jamaica in August 1966.

Sure enough, after much procrastination and indecision, the Ulster Boxing Council selected Maguire for the Games, but as a featherweight – two divisions above his natural fighting weight. Having to punch literally above his natural weight, Maguire was not fancied to go far in the Empire Games. Experienced featherweights such as Denis Swami of India, Hugh Baxter of Scotland and the favoured Welshman Tommy Duncan, were just four of the thirty-two entrants who stood in his way.

"The press thought that England's Kenny Cooper was the best thing to come along since penicillin and they had awarded him the gold medal before the Games began. However, Hugh Baxter of Scotland beat him in the ABA Finals. Baxter thought that he would beat me easily in Jamaica but I boxed the ears off him. I was flying through the competition and next up was the Duncan from Wales and prior to the contest I had been told that Duncan would, in Belfast terminology; 'eat me alive in the ring'. I replied to the person who had said that that nobody would eat me alive as I was the hungriest fighter at the Games, and it would be the other way around and Duncan was well-beaten.

"In the final I lost to the crack Kenyan fighter Philip Waruinge, who said that I was the only boxer that gave him a decent fight at the Games. The thing about the final was that I had gone out in the sun without a shirt the day before and my back was roasted off me. This was Jamaica in high summer and I was very silly to have gone out in such heat, but we were only kids from Ireland and knew no better. I have seen the footage of the final and the one thing you will notice is that I kept going forward as to have rubbed against the ropes would have been agony for me. As it was, I was very proud of the achievement, but I often wonder how it would have turned out if I had not had a touch of mild sunstroke going into the ring."

Paddy returned to Belfast a hero and his career went from strength to strength. However, the times were changing and for many Irish lads in the late 1960s, the lure of good money in London proved to be very enticing. Boxing began to lose its appeal for Maguire.

"After Jamaica, I had a fair few fights for Ulster and Ireland and I recall one of the hardest things I had to do was go into a box-off against my good friend Paddy Graham to represent Ulster in a match against London," he recalled. "Money was always needed so I decided to leave boxing altogether and was working in London at the time doing a bit of labouring. There was a crowd of us at the time pulling down the old London Bridge which the American guy had bought thinking it was Tower Bridge. I remember that we were selling bits of rubble from the Bridge on the side to tourists for a dollar a go, so it was quite rewarding. Then I met up with Eddie Herron in London, who asked me to come and do a bit of training at his club just to keep fit. I moved up to Birmingham with Frank Sullivan and they paid my expenses to go back home so that I could enter the Irish seniors, but it was the chance of getting home that attracted me rather than the boxing. When I got home I thought about the professional game and realised that I was skilled enough to give it a go and one thing just led to another."

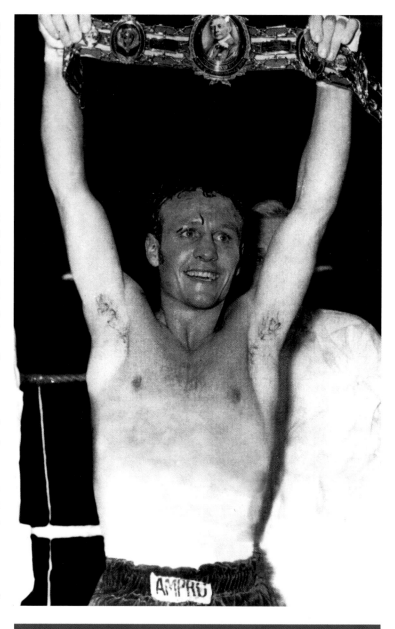

Above

Paddy Maguire after winning the British title against Dave Needham in October 1975

Paddy Maguire's first professional fight took place at the Ulster Hall on 4th March 1969, when he out-pointed Manchester's Bernard Nicholls over six rounds. Within a month, he had scored a victory over Gerry McBride at the same venue. However, Maguire returned to labouring in London and did not fight again until February 1970, when he knocked out Liverpool's Joey Lando.

By the time of Maguire's third fight, the Troubles had escalated. The Kashmir Road, where Paddy's parents lived had seen the worst of the disorder in 1969 and the army were now installed on the streets as an uneasy calm took hold. The fact was that professional boxing in the city was struggling to pay for itself and Maguire was well aware of that fact.

Paddy went on to fight five more times in Belfast's Ulster Hall in the space of a year. The Glaswegian Al Hutcheon was dispatched in three rounds in March 1970, while the French contender Kamara Diop lasted less than a round one month later. The rugged southpaw Glyn Davies from Merthyr did not make the fifth round in October, while the Spaniard Dionisio Bisbal was stopped in the seventh round.

Paddy Maguire fought his last fight in Belfast in January 1971, when the Welsh Area Bantamweight Champion, Colin Miles, was seen off in a comfortable points' decision. Little did he know at that stage that he was going to have to continue his career as an exile, but the situation on the streets was chaotic to say the least.

"I felt that it was really a case that I was going to have to move at that time if I was to get anywhere, so I was offered a number of fights in London where I was based in the Lambeth Boxing Club," he recalled. "Nobody was prepared to come to Belfast to fight due to all the bad publicity at the time, and I teamed up with Frank Duffet and started getting noticed over in England. I remember I got a great following from the Irish fight fans over there and they took me to their heart and turned up each time I boxed. But the fact was that I was now fighting guys in their own back yards where the abuse could be bitter and the decisions strange, but that is what I had to do."

Paddy's first taste of the professional fight scene in London ended in bitter disappointment when, in May 1971, when he lost on points to the future European Champion, Bob Allotey. The fight took place in Mayfair, where the Ghanaian-born, naturalised-Spaniard shaded the decision over eight rounds. Seven months later, after juggling a boxing career and many jobs, Maguire fought his first fight in the Royal Albert Hall and stopped the Nigerian Karim Young in the fourth round. Three further victories in London in early 1972 saw Maguire offered a fight on a bill back home in Ireland that has attained legendary status.

On 19th July 1972 Paddy Maguire fought on the under card of one of the most extraordinary sporting occasions that Ireland had ever witnessed. The Muhammad Ali road show invaded Dublin, as the legend was paired to fight Al 'Blue' Lewis at Croke Park on the city's North Side. It was for Ali just another bout to tide him over while he prepared to try to regain his world crown, which he had lost in 1971 to Joe Frasier. The blarney and shillelagh was rolled out as Ali was feted by the then-Taoiseach, Jack Lynch. He even tried his hand at hurling under the watchful eye of Kilkenny's Eddie Keher.

A crowd of 35,000 turned up on a balmy evening in Dublin to see Ali. Paddy Maguire beat the Frenchman Guy Caudron on points in one of the opening bouts. Maguire has fond memories of the occasion and feels privileged to have spent much time with Ali during that momentous week. The rest of the bill featured such notables as Joe Bugner and John Conteh, but Maguire will never forget coming into close contact with the World's greatest sporting legend.

"Muhammad Ali was without doubt the greatest and had time for everyone involved on the bill," he recalled. "He had something special and it was just in his ability to do things out of the ordinary was always a joy to watch. I remember once he stood up during one of the press conferences when he saw a flyweight walk in and his eyes widened in mock fear and he then blew on him as if that was all he needed to knock him over. That was his style and he was always a showman with that bit extra over everybody else.

"Ali took an interest in me during that week and years later when I met him again I was astonished when he said 'Hi Paddy, how are you?' as he never forgot who I was. I got chatting to him about boxing and we were talking about the fight he had had with George Foreman, and I asked him how he took so many powerful left hooks without going over. He told me that one of the punches by Foreman made his toes curl upwards and his hair straighten outwards, but his will was that strong that he just knew that he could not be beaten. That quote from Ali has stayed with me ever since as an example of how determination and will can see you through anything."

After the heights of Croke Park, Maguire saw off the promising talent of Ben Saleh Abdesselem at the Empire Pool in Wembley and a points' decision over Barry Sponagle at the Albert Hall set up a crack at the British title.

The bantamweight title fight was scheduled for the Royal Albert Hall in March 1973. Johnny Clarke was to be the toughest opponent in Maguire's career to date, as a prior record of thirty-seven fights with victories in all but four of his outings proved. Clarke had fought Alan Rudkin twice for the bantamweight crown and had lost both times. Apart from a draw in his opening bout, a defeat to Dundee's John Kellie in a British title eliminator was his only other reversal. Coupled with the fact that the fight was to take place in the Albert Hall, which would be full of partisan Clarke fans, Maguire was up against the odds.

The fight was a true classic which went the full fifteen rounds. Maguire, fighting in his seventeenth fight, was all action for the full duration and was dismayed when the decision was called in Clarke's favour.

"I am convinced that I won that fight easily but it was literally in Clarke's back yard so the pressure was on to swing a decision towards the local lad," he recalled. "If that fight had have been in Belfast or Dublin there would have been absolutely no doubt about the decision, but it was just one of those things as I was the outsider."

After the setback of the defeat to Clarke, Maguire did not box for a further ten months, when he knocked out in one round the Blackpool-based Frank Taberner at the Royal Albert Hall. Two victories on points over Antonio Tenza and Achene Saifi set up a further crack at the British title, which at that stage had been vacated by Johnny Clarke. The opponent for that bout was to be the Nottingham-based former Commonwealth flyweight gold medal winner, Dave Needham. As was usual for Paddy, he was forced to undertake the fight in his opponent's 'back yard', and the Ice Rink in Nottingham was chosen for the bout on 12th December 1974.

This fight is remembered as one of Paddy Maguire's career low points.

"That was the most partisan and intimidating atmosphere that I ever fought in," he recalls. "It was the time of the Birmingham pub bombings and tensions were at an all-time high, so you can imagine as someone from Belfast how I was received, especially as I was fighting the local hero. In the ring that night, I heard some terrible things being shouted at me and it was a frightening experience. I knew that I was up against it and felt that the referee would have stopped the contest even if my nose had started to bleed."

Needham had been undefeated in twenty-two contests when he fought Maguire and was awarded the title after fifteen bruising rounds. For Paddy Maguire, it was now a case of starting to climb to the top again.

"After the Needham fight, I was prepared to fight anywhere, and then Mickey Duff came along and offered to get me a few good pay days. I went to America and fought in Australia, where I was beaten in a Commonwealth title bout by Paul Ferreri, but I got some good pay packets for those bouts."

On his return, Paddy got the rematch he really wanted with Needham, but this time the bout was fixed for the World Sporting

Above

Paddy Maguire pictured with his mother, May Maguire, in 1975

Club in Mayfair, where Maguire would have a more vociferous support. History will recall that Paddy Maguire became British bantamweight champion on 20th October 1975 when he stopped Needham in the fourteenth round of their fight. At the age of twenty-seven, he had secured the title after six hard years of battling. Now that he was champion, Paddy harboured an ambition to return to Belfast to defend the title in the Ulster Hall, where his career began.

In the pursuit of further glory, Maguire set his sights on acquiring the European bantamweight crown. As usual, Maguire was forced to travel and took on the French titleholder Daniel Trioulaire on his home patch in Cluzes, France. Trioulaire had never boxed outside of his native France, and had won the title the previous year with a victory over Bob Allotey. In late 1975 he was awarded a dubious draw, to deny Dave Needham the European title: the scene was now set for a defence against Maguire in early 1976.

For the second time in five months, Trioulaire was afforded a draw as Maguire came within a whisker of taking the champion. The decision was hotly disputed and neutrals were certain that an injustice had taken place. With the British title still to his name, Maguire embarked on a number of non-title bouts which saw him undefeated in seven. However, in April 1977, he lost on points at Wembley Arena to Heleno Ferreira, a defeat that was to signal the waning of his career.

His next fight took place a month later in the majestic surroundings of the Olympic Stadium in Los Angeles, where he lost to Alberto Sandoval. By this stage, Paddy Maguire was beginning to have serious problems with cuts to his eyes. The British Boxing Board of Control arranged for a specialist Harley Street doctor to examine his left eye, to establish whether his career could continue. As Maguire explained, the necessity to keep boxing led to him being somewhat less than candid with the doctor.

"I had the appointment in Harley Street, and there was myself and Alan Minter being treated by the same doctor. When the Doctor asked me to show him the damaged eye, I pointed to my right eye instead and he looked at it and said there was no problem and that I could box on."

Despite this approval from his doctor, his next fight against the thirty-seven-year-old Italian Franco Zurlo, for the European title, was stopped due to eye damage. Time was running out and on 29th November 1977, Paddy Maguire put his British title on the line against the promising Welsh contender, Johnny Owen.

By this stage, Paddy Maguire's best fighting days were behind him. Johnny Owen was a class act and was expected to outbox Maguire, with the Belfast man's only hope coming in

a display of power punching that would grind Owen down. The fight was to prove to be the last of Paddy Maguire's career, as Owen gave a self-confident display of youthful ambition. It was unfortunately, damage to Maguire's eye that forced the referee Sid Natham to call a halt to the fight in the eleventh round. It was a sad day for Maguire as he announced his retirement from the ring immediately after the bout.

Johnny Owen went on to prove his greatness by winning a Lonsdale Belt, the Commonwealth and European title. In September 1980 he went on to box for the world bantamweight crown against the champion, Lupe Pintor. The contest was evenly matched, with many having Owen well ahead, until the twelfth round when the Mexican knocked the British champion to the canvas. Owen never recovered and he died on 4th November. His loss was felt deeply by all associated with the sport and Paddy Maguire was no exception.

"Johnny Owen was a fabulous fighter and I feel privileged that he of all fighters took my title off me. He was such a loss to the sport and would have been a great champion as he was ahead in the Pintor fight until he got hurt."

For the man who had made a living in the fight game in London and beyond, there was little alternative but to return with his family to Belfast as the 1970s ended. He continued to involve himself in the sport. In 1983 he was in the corner of Shankill Road man Davy Larmour as he won the British flyweight title over his rival, Hugh Russell. A victory that was – for Maguire – a very sweet experience. He feels that boxing today is not the game that he was involved in, and believes that he would have achieved more if he could have stayed in Belfast.

"I look at the Northern Ireland amateur boxing squad that went to the Manchester Commonwealth Games in 2002," he said. "They were taken to train in Cuba before those Games when in 1966 when we went to Jamaica and were taken to acclimatise at Paisley Park, just off the West Circular Road in Belfast. There are men today in Ireland who have got great experience in the amateur ranks but that is being overlooked. I had to go through a lot of hardship in England to make a career in boxing and many times I felt like just walking away from it through sheer loneliness. But I always thought of what Ali said about having the will to survive, no matter what, and I think of the support I always got from my wife, kids, mother and father that kept me going. I have had some moments of great pride such as in Jamaica and after winning the British title, and they are great memories. I fought in Australia, Los Angeles, Wembley Arena and Croke Park among other places so I can't complain. Boxing gave me everything and taught me so much about life and for that I have a lot to be thankful for."

Charlie Nash

"Charlie, Charlie, Charlie, King of the Ring"

The historic City of Derry has enjoyed a proud and illustrious boxing history and has produced many skilled fighters over the decades. Boxers such as Billy and Jimmy (both known as 'Spider') Kelly, Neil McLaughlin and, more recently, John Duddy, have represented the city with pride in arenas throughout the world. The sport is alive and thrives in the city today.

However, one fighter, above all, captured the imagination of the Derry and Irish sporting public for an all-too-brief period during the late 1970s and early 1980s. His story is one of success in the face of political and social adversity: a fighter who overcame the odds to scale the heights of world boxing, whilst the society in which he lived was turning in on itself. Charlie Nash is the name of the man who beat those odds and remains a legend in his native city.

To appreciate what made Nash such a boxer, it is necessary to understand the political and social context of Derry in the 1960s. In that period, Northern Ireland was enduring a period of growing political tension and upheaval. The city had become a cauldron of dissent as the ongoing campaign for civil rights grew in intensity. On 5th October 1968 the city made world headlines, when images of a march from the Waterside area to the city centre being broken up by police were beamed across the globe. The signs were ominous as the end of the 1960s loomed.

In August 1969, Derry was again thrust upon the world stage as the Battle of the Bogside erupted and was captured by the assembled media. Images of pitched battles between police and the Bogside residents showed the city at its worst. Eventually, troops were called in to stop the fighting and the scene was set for thirty years of conflict. It was truly a depressing era with gun battles and rioting occurring on a daily basis. Derry became a war zone as normal life ground to a halt. This was the context in which Charlie Nash was setting out to make a career in boxing.

However, as the new decade dawned, not all was doom and gloom in the city. A couple of episodes in March of 1970 provided the citizens of a well-deserved respite from the trouble and an excuse to celebrate. On the evening of Friday, 20th March, Derry was thrown into celebration when news came through from Dublin that local lad Charlie Nash had claimed the city's first-ever Irish senior boxing title. Immediately, preparations were made in Nash's hometown to welcome back their all-conquering

Left

Victorious after beating Francesco Leon at the Burlington Hotel in Dublin, 1980.

hero. That Saturday afternoon, he was duly paraded through the city and acclaimed by the thousands who had gathered there to greet him.

Just as the people of Derry were welcoming home Nash, that very evening, a local schoolgirl named Rosemary Browne, better known to the world as Dana, from the Rossville Street flats, upstaged the boxing hero by winning the Eurovision Song Contest in Amsterdam. Her performance of the song 'All Kinds of Everything' secured Ireland's first ever victory in the contest and upstaged established names such as Mary Hopkin and Julio Iglesias to win. Within the space of a weekend, Derry had acquired two new heroes.

Two days after Nash's reception, a massive homecoming for Dana was organised and the city was well and truly on an emotional high. The never-to-be-forgotten scenes as Dana sang from the window of her home in the flats to the gathered multitudes, is ingrained in the minds of all who witnessed it. For both Dana and Charlie Nash, despite the looming spectre of the Troubles, the 1970s were to be an era full of promise.

Charlie Nash was born into a family of thirteen children in 1951. He grew up in the city's newly-built Creggan estate and it was there, at the age of eleven, that he took his first steps in a successful boxing career.

"I joined the St Mary's club in Creggan in 1962 and I recall that I experienced quite a few set backs and defeats in the early days before I began to come into my own. I just had a love for the game and a determination inside me to keep going, despite

Above

Striking a pose before the 1972 Olympics in Munich

those defeats," he said. "Eventually I won the Derry and Donegal district boys' title and this led on to me winning in 1966 the Ulster Junior Championships at the age of fifteen. I moved up the ranks and won the Ulster senior title in 1969 and then went on to claim my first Irish international vest in 1970, just after I had won that Irish senior title in Dublin. It was such an honour to wear the green vest and to represent Ireland against the best boxers in the world and I had become a reluctant star in Derry."

Charlie Nash was now becoming a boxer of note. In one of his first international bouts at lightweight, he stopped the Scotsman John Gillan, who had been a silver medallist at that year's Commonwealth Games held in Edinburgh. However, whilst he was making a name as an international, that victory over the Scot gave Nash particular satisfaction, since he had been overlooked – in his view unfairly – for a place in the Northern Ireland team at those Games.

"That win over Gillan gave me great satisfaction as I did not go to the 1970 Commonwealth Games, due to the fact that I had to take part in an organised box-off in Belfast for that right," he said. "I was Ulster champion at the time and should have been the natural choice but the authorities insisted on the match and I was made to fight Paul Carson for the right to represent Northern Ireland in Edinburgh. I lost that fight due – in my view – to a clash of heads in which I came off worst and I lost out on the chance to go to the Games and Carson was picked. To be truthful, I was very bitter at the way the whole thing had been handled, but I just accepted it and got on with it. However, at the

Games Carson lost to the Scot John Gillan, so I felt somewhat vindicated when I stopped Gillan in an international in Dublin later on in the year."

Whilst Derry was thrown into convulsions by the Troubles in the early Seventies, Nash tried to concentrate on his boxing career. However, his life was visited with tragedy on the black day of 30th January 1972 – Bloody Sunday. Nash was devastated when his nineteen-year-old brother William was one of fourteen people shot dead by Paratroopers in the aftermath of a civil rights march. William was shot in the chest near a barricade as the city erupted on a day which left an indelible mark.

The situation across Northern Ireland worsened significantly after Bloody Sunday. Violence engulfed Derry and Belfast and the cities became ghettoised with the creation of no-go zones. Nash struggled to contend with the loss of his brother and engrossed himself in boxing to find comfort. Later that year, as Irish champion, Nash was selected to go to Munich as part of the Irish Olympic boxing squad. He did well and was just one fight away from a bronze medal when he was defeated on a technical knock out by the eventual gold medal winner, Jan Szczepanski of Poland. Further amateur success and international appearances for his country left Nash by 1975 with the realisation that he had to make a decision on his boxing future to make.

"It really became hard as my wife and I had our first child but I was losing money through being away from work all the time with boxing, so I decided that I would retire from the amateur game," he said. "I was a printer by trade and had to think about

at the time. Then a guy called Gerry Hassett contacted me and suggested that I turn professional. In my view I had very little option as the money seemed to be better than what I was earning. He organised my first fight, which was against Ray Ross of Ardglass, for the Irish lightweight title. It just goes to show you how poor the professional game was in Ireland when I was fighting the champion in my first bout."

Nash duly won that bout on points and his career took off in the lightweight division. In 1977, he won a British lightweight title eliminator against Joey Singleton in Birmingham. A crack at the then-British champion, Glasgow's Jim Watt, was now on the cards.

Born in Glasgow's East End in 1948, Jim Watt was to prove to be the bane of Charlie Nash's career. Watt's career had been transformed in 1976, when he joined up with the London-based manager Terry Lawless and, thereafter, he went from strength to strength. With his loyal and vociferous Glaswegian support, together with the added advantage of fighting in his beloved Kelvin Hall, Watt was a tough opponent and had proved his undoubted class. For Nash, the biggest problem initially was to clinch a deal for a showdown with Watt. As Nash explained, arranging the fight with Watt was not as straightforward as he had anticipated.

"The fight went out to purse and the money offered by the promoters was very small," he said. "Then I met with up with the promoter Jack Solomons and he offered to look after the bout, but Watt was reluctant to come to Derry. I felt that he was trying to avoid meeting me for purely boxing reasons and I used this to my advantage as I ridiculed his reluctance to come to Derry."

Eventually Nash was forced to go through the courts and to the British Boxing Board of Control in an attempt to secure a bout with the elusive Watt. However, it was all for nothing as Watt relinquished his British title and went on to fight for the European title, which he won with a victory over Perico Fernandez in February 1978.

Nash eventually won the British title vacated by Watt in 1978 when he defeated Johnny Claydon in Derry. That fight at the Templemore Sports Centre was stopped in the twelfth round as the referee had Nash so far ahead on points. His next step on the boxing ladder would inevitably lead to talk of a bout with Watt for the European title.

"Again the purse went out and it was to be the biggest ever European title fight, but Watt was unhappy with the prospect of coming to Derry and I was convinced that he was still avoiding me," said Nash.

Eventually, Watt relinquished the European title and Nash claimed the vacant crown with a unanimous point's victory over Andrew Holyk. Nash followed this win with a successful defence of the title in Copenhagen against the legendary Scot and former world champion, Ken Buchanan.

In April 1979, in Glasgow's Kelvin Hall, Jim Watt claimed the World lightweight title by defeating Colombian Alfredo Pitalua in front of an ecstatic crowd. A clash between Watt and Nash now became inevitable.

Prior to finalising of the details of the clash with Watt, Nash's manager, Jack Solomons, sadly passed away leaving the Derry man ineligible for the bout since he was manager-less. It was at this stage that the London-based boxing promoter Mickey Duff approached Nash and offered to look after his affairs. Nash was happy initially to join Duff as he explained.

"The bottom line was that Duff was offering to make me money and get me the fights I wanted. This clash with Jim Watt was what I wanted at that stage and he organised it. I had been after this fight for a very long time and Duff was in a position to provide it for me when others had failed to do so. I just went with him to secure the Watt fight and anything after that would be a bonus."

The clash with Watt for the World Boxing Championship title took place at the Kelvin Hall in March 1980 and Ireland came to a standstill in anticipation of a Nash victory. With a win over Watt's nemesis, Ken Buchanan, under his belt, Nash was in confident mood going into the bout. The Kelvin Hall was packed to the rafters as Derry's finest entered the cauldron of local favourite Watt. Despite catching Watt and flooring him in the first round, the Scot regained his composure to overwhelm Nash. By the fourth round, the Derry fighter had been floored four times and the fight was stopped.

In more ways than one, the bout was a brutal experience, as Nash recalled: "I remember that fight so well as I had my tactics worked out perfectly, I thought," he said. "I was really up for it and in the opening round I caught him with a combination that floored him and at that stage I thought I had it in the bag. He was hanging on for dear life but he then opened my eye, which proved to be my downfall. At the end of the third round, the referee approached my corner and said that the cut would not hold up much longer and he was going to stop the contest. My tactics went straight out the window but I gave it all I had but I was caught a few times, and my sight began to go and my teeth had come through my lip at this stage. He dropped me a couple of times and the fight was stopped in the fourth and that was that."

While the defeat to Watt was a set back to Nash, he returned to boxing and in December 1980 he retained his European title with a victory in Dublin's Burlington Hotel over Francesco Leon.

Above

Coaching at the Ring Club, Derry

"That win gave me probably the greatest pleasure in my career," said Nash. "A lot of people had written me off but I had prepared well and was delighted when I won on a unanimous decision."

Things, however, did not go smoothly for Nash in his next bout, which was a defence of his European title at Dublin's Dalymount Park. During the fight he was put on the canvas on three occasions, the last of which he did not get up from to continue.

"Mickey Duff had arranged a bout with an Italian guy called Joey Gibilisco, who was renowned as a puncher," said Nash. "It was held on May 10th 1981, but I recall that the night was freezing and I just could not settle. He caught me with a great punch and I was knocked out. After that I felt that I was on the way out."

Coincidentally, as one Irishman's career was waning at Dalymount Park that cold evening, a certain Barry McGuigan made his professional debut on the under card. The sport in the 1980s was set for a fabulous decade – however, without Charlie Nash.

After his defeat in Dalymount Park, Nash was released by Duff from his contract. He struggled to attain anything near the heights of the late 1970s and fought a further four times, winning two and losing two. His last fight took place in Cologne, Germany on 4th March 1983, almost three years after his bout with Watt. Nash lost to Rene Weller on a technical knock out in the fifth round. That was the end of his career, which had spanned almost eight years and ended with a record of thirty fights with twenty-five wins and five defeats.

At the age of thirty-two, Nash was faced with the prospect of continuing to support his family after devoting so long to a career that had in no way left him financially secure. After his retirement from boxing, Charlie worked in the insurance business for over twenty years but retired recently due to ill-health. Today he is still involved in boxing and keeps an interest in the budding pugilists at Derry's Ring Boxing Club.

On his proudest moments, winning the British and European titles are mentioned, but reclaiming the European title after the Watt defeat was the bout that gave him the greatest satisfaction in hindsight.

Charlie Nash sees the stars of tomorrow coming through the Ring club. Asked for words of inspiration that he could give to them for their careers, he shows great wisdom and respect for those who helped him in his life.

"I always have my mother and father to thank for keeping me dedicated and for that I am grateful – they set me a wonderful example of what hard work can achieve," he said. "They sacrificed a lot for me and our family when times were very hard and for that I am eternally grateful. To the lads I would say to always enjoy your boxing when you're young; you will never experience a sport like it to give you satisfaction. Boxing will teach you everything you need to survive in life, and I believe to this day that it is a fantastic sport to be involved in."

Today, Charlie Nash can still be found passing on advice to youngsters at the Ring Boxing Club in Derry. He is dedicated to the sport and gets the greatest satisfaction in seeing his proteges step up to the mark. For the man who had Jim Watt at his mercy within the first round of their world title bout, all he has left are the memories and the thoughts of what could have been. Derry has come through a lot of strife in the last generation. Charlie Nash was a beacon of hope for many in that city during the bad years. He is still as dedicated as the day he left boxing and returned to Derry for good. With Charlie Nash's knowledge and wisdom, it is probable that the Ring Boxing Club will produce in abundance boxers stamped with the influence of his undoubted calibre.

Kenny Beattie

Leader of the Magnificent Seven

Kenny Beattie, a skilled southpaw from the Shore Road in Belfast, was a member of the 'Magnificent Seven' – but not, needless to say, in any acting sense. In 1960, the classic western of that name depicted the exploits of seven gunslingers sent to defend a small Mexican village against a gang of outlaws. In 1978 Northern Ireland sent seven of its most talented pugilists to make their presence felt at the Edmonton Commonwealth Games. Seven artisans, under the watchful eye of shrewd coach Gerry Storey, who made a marked impression in the Canadian city. When the dust had settled by 13th August, justice had been done in the ring and the Magnificent Seven flew off into the sunset.

Barry McGuigan was the most famous member of the merry band which travelled to Canada that August. Add into the mix, names such as Hugh Russell, Kenny Webb, Jimmy Carson, Gerry Hamill, Tony McAvoy and Kenny Beattie and the squad became a very formidable bunch. Immediately dubbed the 'Magnificent Seven' in the local press, by the closing ceremony of the Games, the boxers had achieved two golds, one silver and one bronze medal. Kenny Beattie, the silver medallist in the welterweight division, led the Northern Ireland team around the Clarke Stadium in the closing ceremony. For a man from the White City club in Belfast, with the Northern Ireland flag

in his hand, it was an unforgettable experience. Beattie would have made it a triple gold for the boxers, but for one small but significant detail: the person who beat the Shore Road man was a classy Jamaican fighter by the name of Mike McCallum; a true legend in the making.

Born in the Mount Vernon district of Belfast in 1956, to Jackie and Florence Beattie, Kenny was first to taste boxing success in the White City club in the now redeveloped area of Belfast known as Sailortown. It was a habit of losing unofficial bouts to his younger brother George, in the living room of their two-bedroom house, that made Beattie initially consider the fight game as a healthy option.

"Our living room was very small and we lived in a two-up, two-down, house I recall," said Beattie. "My father used to put the corner of the armchair against the settee and that formed an artificial boxing ring where George, my younger brother, and I would fight the bit out on most Sunday afternoons. George was at the boxing club and was beating me easily, so I thought that I'd take the game seriously, initially for the sake of family pride."

With Beattie soon a fully-fledged member of the boxing club, parity in the boxing stakes was soon restored in the family home. He went on to make his mark in the boys' and juvenile championships in both Ulster and Ireland. By 1977 Kenny had claimed the Ulster senior welterweight crown and went on to Dublin to win the first of his four Irish titles. In 1978, as Ulster champion, Beattie was a natural choice for the Northern Ireland team with Gerry Storey as trainer setting the squad on track for glory at the Edmonton Games.

"Gerry Storey and the Ulster Council had everything planned out for us that year with the Commonwealth Games taking place," he said. "They had a number of representative matches against formidable opposition laid on for us in an attempt to gel the team together. We fought East Germany in the Shankill Working Men's Club and we stayed in the Slieve Donard hotel in Newcastle in an attempt to get things right ahead of the Games. The squad training was held in the Stella Maris club in Belfast and we did our sprints in the afternoon on a golf course near Downpatrick.

"I'm not a great believer in squad training but looking back it was a great thing for us and everything went like a dream. We did all our preparation and then Gerry gave us the week off and by the time we got together again we had all peaked at the right time."

Prior to the commencement of the Games, the Ulster team put in a bit of competitive sparring in Canada against the Australian representatives. In each case the Ulster fighters took on an opponent one weight above their own and, without exception, the Australians were beaten soundly. Master tactician and coach Gerry Storey ensured that his seven fighters went into their first round bouts on a virtual high.

The opening ceremony of the games took place on Thursday, 3rd August. The seventy strong Northern Ireland team was warmly received in the packed arena, which was filled with its fair share of Ulster exiles. The team's bowlers, cyclists, swimmers and runners all got down to business as the boxers awaited their draws.

The first of the seven boxers to enter the competition was the Larne featherweight, Kenny Webb. His bout against the Canadian, Guy Bout, was a thrilling affair until he was caught by a sucker punch in the third round from which he never regained his composure. With three seconds left of the bout, Webb was led to his corner by the referee and the Ulster team were off to a poor start.

The luck of the Irish also deserted the light-flyweight Jimmy Carson when he was out-pointed by the Indian fighter Birender Thapa. The fact was, however, that Carson had been awarded a draw, with four of the judges split evenly between each of the protagonists. Mr Foo (trust me: that was his name) from Malaysia, the fifth judge, had called the contest a draw, only to award his casting vote to the Indian for his perceived "greater aggression".

Thankfully, the bad run came to an end as Barry McGuigan, Gerry Hamill, Hugh Russell and Kenny Beattie all came through their opening bouts with a clean bill of health. Beattie saw off the challenge of Samuel Whymms of the Bahamas by a four-one majority and he was composed and assured throughout his bout. The Belfast southpaw was drawn in the quarterfinal against the Ghanaian Moro Tahiru, with at least a bronze in the bag should he overcome that particular hurdle. After a poor fight, the Shore Road man was declared the victor.

"I thought my fight with Whymms was a scrappy fight and I was not happy with my performance," said Beattie. "But to get a win in your first fight gives you that extra little bit of confidence and that grew as the Games progressed."

Alas, it was not to be the case for the senior member of the team, Ballymena's Tony McAvoy. In his opening fight, he hit the canvas in the third round of his bout with the Western Samoan, Ropati Vipo Samu. Whilst he was considered to have been well ahead, he was counted out and after taking a shot in the last round of the fight. So, after the opening exchanges, it was a case of three down, four to go, for the Northern Ireland boxers.

The next round saw Beattie floor his opponent Tahiru in the opening twenty seconds of the contest. Whilst the Ghanaian possessed a dangerous uppercut, the Shore Road man kept moving, and twice in the third round had his opponent sprawling on the ropes. The result, a four-one decision in favour of Beattie, did not reflect the superiority that he had enjoyed. Safely through also were McGuigan, Russell and Hamill: for the Ulster boxers a quadruple gold medal haul became a possibility.

The party continued into the semi-finals for Beattie as his Welsh opponent Tony Freal was beaten convincingly on points. In the second round the referee stopped the bout to have a look at a cut on Beattie's eye, but it was determined to be a minor nick. The judges scored the fight unanimously in the Belfastman's favour and the crack at the gold was on the cards.

"I though that the fight against Freal was the biggest one to get over, and the sense of relief at getting to the final was great," he recalled. "Now I felt I could relax a bit and just concentrate on the final."

Both McGuigan and Hamill made the finals also, while Hugh Russell was counted out when the Canadian favourite, Ian Clyde, caught him with a sweet right hand. The New Lodge Road boy's dream was over, but Ulster still had hopes of a trio of gold medals.

Awaiting Beattie in the final was the formidable Jamaican, Mike McCallum, who would go on to become a world champion

at three different weights. However, future legend or not, Beattie was ready.

"I did not know who McCallum was but he was the hot favourite for sure," said Beattie. "The day before the fight I got word that he was the class act who had been to the Olympic Games and that got to me a bit. I lost the fight for sure, but I regret that I didn't follow the orders that Gerry Storey had given me beforehand. He told me to box McCallum and not to get too involved, but I went head-hunting, as he had been cut in the eye in his previous fight. He was a class act alright and he went on to prove that as a paid fighter."

Beattie got probably the short straw when it came to the finals as his two compatriots went on to claim victories and glory. Barry McGuigan and Gerry Hamill took gold and, on both occasions, they were considered lucky to do so. McGuigan was forced to take three standing counts in his bout with the hot favourite and hard-hitting Tumat Sugolik. While he battled bravely, the seventeen-year-old Monaghan boxer took a lot of punishment. However, he fought on gamely to swing the decision on a split vote.

Meanwhile, in the lightweight final, boos of derision greeted the decision that saw Ballymena's Gerry Hamill take gold. The Kenyan Patrick Waweru was considered to have been a handy winner over the Ballymena butcher, but when the luck was with the Irish, they were proving hard to beat. A protest at the decision from the Kenyan's corner saw the arithmetic re-checked by the judges. But there had been no mistake, and the Northern Ireland team had claimed its second gold.

The net result for the Magnificent Seven, regardless of the idiosyncrasies of the judges, stood at two golds, one silver and one bronze medal. Quite an achievement, when one considers that the rest of the Northern Ireland Commonwealth Games team could muster only an additional bronze to add to the boxers' total.

At the closing ceremony, Kenny Beattie was chosen to carry the flag in the arena. A privilege that rounded off a fabulous experience for the Shore Road man. When they returned home to Aldergrove airport two days later, a mass of well-wishers was spotted from the air awaiting the heroes. As Kenny recalled, the 'mass of well-wishers' consisted mostly of the members of the extended Beattie clan, who had decamped en-masse from their base in Shore Crescent.

"It was great to see everybody again, for the main thing is that you are completely unaware how things are being perceived back home. It must have been a very big event, but of course we knew very little until we were coming into the airport and someone spotted the crowds and banners."

The magnificent seven boxers all went their own ways after the games. Two future British champions emerged in McGuigan and Russell: Barry of course went on and claimed a European and World title. Kenny Webb from Larne has sadly passed away, while Tony McAvoy and Gerry Hamill are still involved with boxing in the Ballymena All Saints club. Jimmy Carson is alive and well in his native city of Belfast.

Kenny Beattie returned to the White City club but never acquired the appetite for the professional ranks. In a strange twist of fate, Beattie was to meet up with his old foe, Mike McCallum, while attending a Lennox Lewis title defence in London.

"I was over for a Lewis fight and Barney Eastwood was there and he called McCallum over and asked him if he knew who I was," he recalled. "Mike was all over me and he asked me how much money I had made as a professional. He was staggered when he found out that I had stayed an amateur. But he is a real nice guy and never forgot me, which was nice."

Beattie continued with his amateur career and returned to the Commonwealth Games in Brisbane in 1982. That year he was captain of the boxing team, and he explained that this accolade added to the pressure on his shoulders.

"I really felt that I could not concentrate totally on my boxing due to the added responsibility of being captain. In addition, I had over-trained prior to the Games and when I arrived I knew that I was not right within myself. I lost in the opening bout and that was it for me."

Kenny Beattie left his career behind to concentrate on his career as a fitness coach. He still works out regularly and retains the physique that he had as a boxer. Time has not dimmed the memories or the enjoyment of his amateur career. However, top of the memories are the six weeks in the high summer of 1978, when Kenny Beattie *et al* rode their luck in Canada as the Magnificent Seven.

Left

Kenny Beattie in action at the 1978 Commonwealth Games final in Edmonton, Canada

Hugh Russell

"A Snapshot of Greatness"

In Irish boxing history, the date 29th July 1980 has some significance. On that day, the Irish medals famine, in Olympics terms, came to an end as Hugh Russell defeated the Korean fighter, Yo-Ryon Sik, to secure a bronze medal at the Moscow Games. The Belfast flyweight had emulated the achievement of Jim McCourt in Tokyo sixteen years previously and had his sights set on becoming Ireland's first boxing gold medallist.

In Moscow, the gold medal proved beyond Russell's grasp as he lost in the semi-final to the eventual champion, the Bulgarian, Peter Lesov. With a Commonwealth and Olympic medal to his name he went to the European Championships, but failed in his attempt of collecting a hat-trick of major medals at boxing games.

Russell became the sixth boxer to achieve a medal for Ireland at the Olympic Games and he went on to carve out a very successful professional career. In the King's Hall, in February 1985, he won outright the coveted Lonsdale Belt by defeating Charlie Brown in the twelfth round of their contest. Only four

Irishmen have this accolade to their name; Freddie Gilroy, Sam Storey, Hugh Russell and Neil Sinclair. Russell has this gold belt as a permanent memento of his career, and it has pride of place in his vast collection. Quite an achievement in quite a life, which all began in Belfast in December 1959.

Hugh Russell is now a renowned and respected photographer working for the *Irish News* in Belfast's Donegall Street. He has witnessed at first hand political and social history through his lenses. In 1985 Russell recorded the signing of the Anglo-Irish Agreement. In 1989 he was in the press pack outside the Old Bailey as the Guildford Four were released. Two years later he was on hand to see the Birmingham Six set free. A love of photography has blended with a love of boxing for Russell. The boxing had been in his veins from an early age, while an abundance of roubles in Moscow set Russell off on a love of photography.

"When we were in Moscow in 1980, I bought my first-ever camera," he recalled. "The thing about Russia back then was that everybody changed their money on the street as the rate was better than anywhere else. Being in the Olympic village made it hard to spend any money as everything was free anyway to the athletes. At the end of the Games, I had an awful lot of spare money and you could not bring Russian money back with you. So I spied this large Zenith camera and bought it and that started me on the photography."

That trip to Moscow put the name of Hugh Russell in the limelight across Britain and Ireland. Joining him in the Irish boxing squad were Phil Sutcliffe, Gerry Hawkins, Sean Doyle, Martin Brereton, Patrick Davitt and Barry McGuigan. As the other boxers fell one by one, Russell was setting his own pace in the flyweight division.

In his first bout, the New Lodge man beat unanimously Samir Khiniab from Iraq. His next opponent, Emmanuel Mlundwa from Tanzania, was seen off in a similar fashion. In the quarterfinal, Russell rode his luck somewhat to neat his Korean opponent on a split decision, and he, and Ireland, was assured at least a bronze medal. The semi-final bout ended in a clear-cut win for the Bulgarian, Lesov. Regardless, and blissfully unaware, Russell was now a hero back home in Ireland.

"The thing about the Olympics is that you are cocooned in the village and you are living in an unreal perfect world," he recalled. "Everyone is so healthy that it is surreal and almost as if the rest of the world doesn't exist. I remember seeing Ovett and Coe race in the 1500 metres and I had no idea that this was massive back home. But the Olympic village is such a strange place that I remember meeting the guy known as 'Yifter the Shifter' who had taken the 5000 and 10,000 [metres] gold medals and I hadn't a clue who he was.

"I am told that in the New Lodge area that there was a lot of rioting going on at the time of the Games and as soon as my fights came on the television, the streets cleared for fifteen minutes, and afterwards the rioting started again. Looking back it was the oddest feeling to come home. The street was decorated with a massive banner saying 'Welcome Home Bronzy'. There was a guy who lived near me called Artie Osborne who worked in the local undertakers and he had the sign made out of coffin lining. Maybe now, looking back, I can only appreciate the achievement and with age the Olympic bronze will probably become my proudest moment."

Fast forward now to December 1981. It's the Ulster Hall in Belfast's Bedford Street, and Barry McGuigan is topping the bill against Peter Eubank. That August, Eubank had been awarded a disputed decision against the Clones Cyclone in Brighton. Retribution is in the air. As the capacity crowd files into the hall, Hugh Russell steps into the ring to start his professional career against a journeyman called Jim Harvey.

Along with another local fighter, Danny McAllister, Russell had joined the Eastwood stable and was fancied to make his mark. Sure enough, the bout was stopped in the fifth round and

title. Russell's victory was noted by the knowledgeable Belfast crowd, who would soon be on their feet as McGuigan exacted revenge over his Brighton nemesis.

"To be truthful, one of the nicest people I have ever come across in my life was my trainer Eddie Shaw," remembered Russell. "Barney Eastwood was more than good to me also and everything I was ever promised by him I got. I was an ordinary lad from Belfast but I could not have asked for more from my management."

Just over four weeks later, Russell fought in London where he got a six-rounds points decision over Mike Wilkes. Within three months he had won a further five bouts and was moving steadily up the British bantamweight division.

In June that year, Russell returned to the World Sporting Club in Mayfair. His bout against Stuart Shaw took place immediately after stable-mate Barry McGuigan's fight with Young Ali had ended in tragedy. The African fighter never regained consciousness after he had been knocked out. Russell, who is a now a chief inspector on the British Boxing Board of Control, remembers that night well. In his present role, he is often called upon to defend the sport.

"It was hard to come into the ring after what had happened that night in London, and there was a real sense that something had gone badly wrong. In my position on the Board, I am called upon to on many occasions to defend the sport, but the fact is that there has always been an urge in humans to fight and sometimes in boxing things do go wrong. The problem is that if people are truthful and say that they want to ban boxing as it is dangerous, then I would say that it would be near impossible to do so. Sporting injuries are a fact of life and we in the Board do our utmost to ensure that boxing is regulated to the highest standards. I know that there is unlicensed boxing going on in Ireland and this can lead to all sorts of unfortunate incidents. It's a fact of life and if boxing was banned then it would just emerge in some different, more dangerous form."

Four months after his victory over Shaw in London, Russell was paired in the Ulster Hall in a final eliminator for the British title against his fellow Belfast fighter, Davy Larmour. A bruising encountered ensued in front of a packed arena which Russell won on a points decision. A crack at John Feeney's British title was assured and the date was fixed for 25th January 1983.

The Russell versus Feeney fight will go down in history as the last ever British title fight to be scheduled for fifteen rounds. However, it only went twelve as Feeney was disqualified for persistent use of his head and Russell, in his twelfth fight, was

"As a professional, the Lonsdale Belt was what I had set out to win, and it was a great feeling to get the title," remembered Russell.

Unbeaten Russell, now only two defences away from winning the Lonsdale Belt outright, was faced with the prospect of defending the title. In late 1982 a promise had been given by his manager Barney Eastwood that, should Russell win the British title, his first defence would be a rematch against Davy Larmour.

The scene was set for that March for a double-header with McGuigan scheduled to fight for the featherweight title and Russell and Larmour to battle at bantamweight. McGuigan's bout was cancelled and the main event became the battle of Belfast's bantamweights. Any question marks over the ability of Russell and Larmour to fill the south Belfast arena were answered on the night, when the public turned out in force for the fight. As Russell recalled, nobody was surprised.

"You have to remember that there were very few other attractions in Belfast at that time. The Troubles were ongoing and the prospect of two local lads slugging it out was a sure winner. People bought into the whole thing and our profile was very high at the time."

The fight that ensued was a classic. Larmour had his homework done on Russell and reversed his defeat from the previous October to take the title. Russell had been champion for thirty-six days.

Russell was now back as a contender and he made the decision to drop a weight and try his chances in the British flyweight division. That October, he began his ascent of that division by beating Julio Guerro on points in the Ulster Hall. On 16th November, Larmour relinquished his bantamweight crown at the King's Hall, while Russell recorded a points victory over Gabriel Kuphey to set up a crack at the flyweight title.

The champion, Kelvin Smart, came to Belfast in January 1984 and was stopped by 'Little Red' in the seventh round of their bout. Russell had now won his second British title and the future was looking bright.

"That was a hard fight and there was a time during the fight when both of us lost the head, but it was a vital part of the fight for both of us and I just got stronger as the fight went on."

In November 1984, Russell took his second step in his quest for the Lonsdale Belt. The Welshman Danny Williams was stopped and the scene was set for a defence against Charlie Brown for the right to claim the belt outright.

That night in front of the packed King's Hall, anticipating the world title eliminator between Barry McGuigan and Juan Laporte, Russell delivered the goods. In the twelfth round he stopped his opponent and the belt was his – this time for good!

Lord Lonsdale's belt is made partly from gold and porcelain. For aspiring boxers in Britain it is the be-all-and-end-all in boxing terms. In 1985, three notches on the belt meant that a boxer could hold on to the belt as a permanent trophy of his achievements. At the height of his career, Russell retired. In hindsight, he has no regrets. In June 1985 the Eastwood stable enjoyed their highlight, when Barry McGuigan claimed the world featherweight crown from the legend, Eusebio Pedroza. Russell was not on that bill and was a mere spectator. When I mention that a Lonsdale Belt was sold at auction for almost £60,000 in the not too distant past, Russell winks and whispers:

"Please, don't tell my wife that. My view was that I was only going to have a limited career and the Lonsdale Belt was the height as far as I was concerned. The European champion then was an Italian who was reluctant to fight outside Italy, while the world champion I wanted was a Mexican. I was then working in the *Irish News* and I had to make my mind up as to my future. I was having problems making the flyweight division, and as an athlete there is only so much punishment a body can take. Back then it was sweat and guts and technology and, unlike now, science never was considered in boxing. Just look at Amir Khan today and you can see how the game has changed. He got to an Olympic final and everyone was bending over backwards to offer him the best deal as a professional. When I went to the Commonwealth Games in 1978, I was paid off at the Belfast docks as I was to do a number of weeks in collective training. A lot of sacrifices were made by me in boxing but I have no regrets at all."

For a generation of people, Hugh Russell has grown in stature as a well-known photographer. As time goes by his achievements in the ring will diminish in the eyes of the public. Olympic, Commonwealth and British titles will fade with time, but not in the mind of Hugh Russell. As he points out, time has made the memories of the ring sweeter and, in future years, it is likely that those thoughts will get even sweeter.

"Hindsight is a great thing but I look back and think that the Olympic medal was the best feeling. If you had've asked me five years ago, I may have said the Lonsdale Belt was my greatest memory. But time does that to a person and things fall into place only long after an event. But as I said, I left boxing at the right time and I have never looked back."

Gerry Hawkins

Shining Light of the Holy Trinity

The Holy Trinity boxing club and the Hawkins family in particular are synonymous with Irish boxing and have left an indelible imprint on the sport on this island. Of the six brothers born to Thomas and Bridie Hawkins, light-flyweight, Gerry, known as 'Diddler', shone brightest of the talented clan as an amateur for both club and country. He went to two Olympic Games, together with three European Championships and a Commonwealth Games in Australia in 1982. Packing a devastating punch in each hand, Diddler was a skilful boxer who mixed it with the best and gave everything for Irish boxing.

Born in the Belfast's Shore Road bungalows in 1961, Gerry Hawkins was the second youngest of six brothers. However, not all was favoured towards the males in the household as four sisters were added in turn to the Hawkins family mix. By 1963, the family had moved across town to west Belfast where they settled in the Turf Lodge district and that is where the story of the Holy Trinity club begins.

As Gerry recalled, his inspirational mother Bridie was a guiding force in the establishment of the club.

"My mother was a very special person and she along with the local priest, Father McWilliams, was instrumental in helping to get the boxing going. It all started in an old wooden hut which stood where the new club now stands and it gave the kids of the area something to do in the evenings. My mother did everything for the club and I can remember her stitching our vests and shorts so that we were all well turned out. All my brothers were at one stage involved in the club and when my chance came in the early 1970s, I was ready to give the game a go."

Gerry's early days at the club saw him find a valuable sparring partner in the form of his slightly older and accomplished brother Peter, who would, in turn, become his greatest fan. Even in those early days, the success that was to become the Holy Trinity hallmark was evident with a string of cracking young boxers including David Irving, Damien Fryers, Mark Rea, Mick Mooney and Hugh Reynolds.

While the Hawkins clan were at the helm of the organisation others were also hugely instrumental in making that success happen. The Holy Trinity, one of the leading club sides in Europe, would not have functioned for the past thirty-five years without the immense contribution of the family's life-long friend and Holy

Trinity's 'Mr Fix-it', Desi McPhillips. Veteran coach Jim McNeilly was another key man in the Trinity triumphs. Big Jim and Geordie Harper were in the vanguard of a stream of dedicated, willing and able coaches and helpers down the years – unselfish men who gave their time voluntarily to help the Trinity kids in pursuit of their sporting dreams.

Gerry won the Ulster four stones' boys' championship in 1972 and went on to Dublin to claim the Irish title. However being small and not able to gain weight led to some novel dodges to make the competitions in those days.

"The Irish board brought in a rule soon after that the lightest weight a boy could fight at was six stones but I just could not put on any weight," he recalled. "I remember that I had to have my hands stuffed with fifty pence pieces as I went on the scales in order to make the weight and in turn I was up against lads who were a stone heavier than me."

In 1974 Gerry Hawkins went on to claim the Irish six stone title, while a stone lighter than the other fighters and was awarded the best boxer of the tournament. That high standard continued unabated and in 1980, with the Olympic Games in Moscow on the horizon, the decision was taken to enter the Ulster Senior Championships.

The golden boy of Irish light-flyweight boxing that year was considered to be the Holy Family's Hugh Russell. In the final, Russell faced a comparative novice in Hawkins and, while not overawed by Russell's reputation, the Turf Lodge man gave Russell plenty to think about, only to lose on points. Undeterred, Hawkins decided to go for National honours in Dublin and two weeks' later the rematch with Russell took place in front of a capacity crowd at the National Stadium.

They say that revenge is sweet and Hawkins exacted his retribution spectacularly on Russell that night by knocking him out in the first round. Displaying remarkable confidence, the Holy Trinity man toppled Russell with a string of looping rights and continued his onslaught until the hot favourite Russell was counted out. National honours were assured for Hawkins and the Olympic dream was back on track.

After the heroics of the Irish Championships, Hawkins was picked for the Irish team that went to the European Junior Championships, which were held in Rimini in June 1980. While Barry McGuigan and Martin Brereton took bronze medals for Ireland, the Holy Trinity fighter was eliminated in his first bout.

However, his mind was set on securing a place in the Irish team which was to go the Olympic Games.

After the delights of Rimini, Hawkins duly got the nod for the light-flyweight berth on the Irish team for Moscow. Hugh Russell moved up a weight and went as flyweight and was to take bronze for Ireland at the Games.

"To go to the Olympic Games is every boxer's dream," said Hawkins. "Turf Lodge is a very close-knit community and it was big news when I was picked. Everyone was pleased for me and wanted to wish me well everywhere I went. But it was great for the younger kids in the club to have someone to look up to and try to emulate."

At the Games, Gerry was afforded a bye in the opening round and was then drawn to meet Ismail Moustafov from Bulgaria. But the Belfast boy was given a sharp lesson by the Bulgarian who won the bout unanimously. At the end of the third round, it was a bloodied Hawkins who left the ring defeated, but not disheartened, since youth was on his side. Defeat to the aforementioned Moustafov was nothing for Hawkins to get down about. The Bulgarian went on to claim a bronze in Moscow, the gold at Seoul in 1988, while he was also twice European champion and, in 1982, he won the World Championship. In addition, he was voted the best Bulgarian boxer of the Twentieth Century by panel of that country's journalists.

"In hindsight, I was very keyed up for that fight and rushed at him, only to be caught by some clever and hard shots," recalled Hawkins. "But when I think of what Moustafov went on to achieve then I realise that I had taken one of the greatest fighters in the world.

"Another great memory I have of Moscow is of rooming with PJ Davitt, who died tragically a number of years back. He was a really great guy."

While the Olympic adventure was at an end, one of Hawkins proudest moments as a boxer was to come in October 1980. As part of its centenary celebrations, the Amateur Boxing Association of England organised a prestigious Multi-Nations Games at the Wembley Arena. The event was a showcase for the best talent in boxing and Hawkins excelled to take a gold medal at light-flyweight. In the final against England's Nigel Potter, Hawkins boxed with raw energy to win convincingly and was to receive great adulation for his achievement.

"Earlier that night at Wembley, Barry McGuigan had been on the end of a very poor decision against Scotland's Ian McLeod so I felt I had something to prove going into the ring," said Gerry. "I was young and bursting with pride and to take the gold medal that night was magic."

Ireland's Gerry Hawkins (*right*) misses with a right uppercut as Hungary's Rozsa (*left*) covers up at Wembley

That Saturday, the *Irish Independent* named Hawkins its 'Irish Sport Star of the Week' for his achievement in London. Gerry's only regret was that his feat was not part of the highlights package that evening on the BBC's *Sportsnight* programme.

"I had been interviewed by Harry Carpenter and was sure that everyone back home would see me win as the BBC had shown my semi-final win over a tough Hungarian. But they must have been short of time and my bout never got on the show, but at least I had the gold medal to show everyone back home."

In May 1981, Gerry was picked for the Irish team that travelled to Tampere in Finland for the European Championships. In his quarter-final bout, he was drawn to meet the unfancied Frenchman, Alain Jumineaux. The contest was close to call but Hawkins was awarded the decision by a three to two majority. A semi-final clash with the East German Dietmar Geilich ended in defeat, but Gerry had given a fabulous display and was considered to have been unlucky.

Some of the Irish press pack present vented their frustration at the decision afforded to Hawkins with words such as 'robbery' and 'disgrace' mentioned in dispatches. However, the European Championships were renowned for political voting and Hawkins was left with the bitter taste of defeat that Fred Tiedt, Jim McCourt and Mick Dowling had experienced before at previous Games.

An unsuccessful trip to the 1982 Commonwealth Games in Brisbane with the Northern Ireland team was followed in 1983 by an appearance in Sofia at the European Championships. In his quarter-final bout, Hawkins lost on a split decision to the Russian Beybut Eszhanov and the feat of taking bronze in 1981 was not to be repeated. With the Holy Trinity man considered to be untouchable back in Ireland, he was a natural selection for the 1984 Olympic Games in Los Angeles.

As Gerry Hawkins later recalled, the American experience was one that ranks as the highlight of his career.

"Los Angeles was just fabulous and everything about it was special. It was totally different to Moscow and we were away for four weeks in total."

In the preliminary round, Hawkins was drawn against the Italian, Salvatore Todisco. The contest was dominated by the Italian and he was awarded a unanimous decision over the Belfast fighter. As in Moscow, Hawkins was to lose to a class act as Todisco went on to the final but a hand injury prevented him from competing and Paul Gonzales of the United States was awarded a walkover.

"Sometimes I meet people and when they hear I went to the Olympics they are surprised to hear that I was eliminated in the opening round both times," said Gerry. "That may be so but when you consider the class of the boxers that beat me it is a consolation in many ways. I would never have swapped the experience for the world though."

Gerry Hawkins' rise to prominence came at the time when professional boxing in the North was on the crest of a wave. Former amateur team-mates Barry McGuigan and Hugh Russell were packing the Ulster and King's Halls in Belfast, but for Hawkins the paid ranks were not to be.

"There was talk back then of some form of contract being offered but things did not happen and I never really pursued it," he said. "I was happy travelling the world and the rewards I got from boxing were immense. I was always dedicated to the game and it was a great release, especially when you consider that times were difficult in Belfast. A lot of things were happening on the streets, but I was dedicated to my sport. Looking back, the Holy Trinity was – and is – a great facility for the kids of the area and remains today a great institution.

"I had the best of times through boxing and saw a good deal of the world and would say to anyone to have a go at it. Sure, sometimes with injury and bad defeats to contend with you can feel a bit down. But the rewards are immense and with dedication you can get there. I made some great friendships in boxing and the sport provides an alternative to the negative culture that some kids can be led into. I know that there is great talent coming through in Ireland and if we can nurture that then I cannot see why the country will not get Olympic success in the future."

Today, Gerry Hawkins works with his brother Michael in a successful family business on Belfast's Andersonstown Road. Michael's own achievements, both as an amateur and professional coach, are well documented. In addition, Ireland's brightest professional star Bernard Dunne is trained by another Hawkins brother, Harry, while Thomas is the secretary of the Holy Trinity club and the Sports Editor of *The Irish News* in Belfast. The youngest of the brothers, Joe, also boxed in the green and white Trinity colours and has been an excellent administrator for the Holy Trinity complex.

The Hawkins family's contribution to boxing would fill a book on its own. Gerry's individual achievements mark him out as one of Ireland's top amateur competitors. The world of Irish boxing has not heard the last of the Hawkins Family – nor the champions of the Holy Trinity club.

Kieran Joyce

A Rebel with a Cause

The Rebel County of Cork has produced its fair share of gifted sportsmen over the years. In GAA terms alone, the names of its great footballers and hurlers could fill many books. In soccer, the name Roy Keane is synonymous with the rebel spirit for which the county is famous. However, when it comes to the 'noble art' of boxing, the best thing to come out of Cork is twice-Olympian and European bronze medallist, Kieran Joyce. His battling style of controlled aggression made him renowned as a tough fighter across the world and one of Ireland's amateur greats.

Born in the north side of Cork city in 1964, Kieran was one of twelve children raised by Brian and Elizabeth Joyce. Times were not easy on the tough streets of Cork as the Joyce family sought to carve out a living overseeing their coal delivery business. Kieran and his brother Gordon joined the Sunnyside Boxing Club and under the guidance of Albie Murphy both their careers took off.

"I think I was about ten when I started boxing," remembered Kieran. "I felt that I was destined to be a boxer, as I seemed to be a natural at it and it came easily to me early on. I had a good right hand and soon I was progressing through the competitions winning titles at junior and juvenile levels."

At eighteen, Joyce won his first Irish senior title at the National Stadium. In 1983 he was rewarded with a trip to the European Championships in Varna, Bulgaria. The Irish team that accompanied Joyce consisted of Gerry Hawkins from Belfast, Tommy Corr from Coalisland and Army private, Tony De Loughrey.

In his opening contest, Joyce was handed a tough baptism with the prospect of a clash with the Hungarian, Tibor Molnar. Despite his raw youth, the Sunnyside man swarmed all over the Magyar and won with a display of undaunted aggression. Molnar's best form of defence during the bout seemed to be in holding the exuberant Irishman, and for this tactic he received a public warning. The onslaught from Joyce was relentless and he was worthy of the unanimous decision at the end.

Three days into the Championships, Joyce found himself as Ireland's sole survivor as the rest of the team was eliminated. Joyce was handed a tricky draw against the Norwegian representative, Kristen Reagan, and, at eighteen, the Corkman was considered to be in for a tough fight. The fight against Reagan was too close to call. However, the judges awarded Joyce the verdict on a split vote. Joyce attacked doggedly throughout the bout and his greater aggression was crucial in the victory. Twice during the contest the referee warned the Scandinavian for holding but Joyce did take punishment from his opponent. A slight cut eye sustained by Joyce did not deter him, and his victory raised no complaints from the Norwegian contingent.

The Corkman had now won a place in the semi-final and for all his endeavours ended up with a draw against the Russian, Piotr Galkin. Galkin was a twenty-five-year-old Red Army private with a record of over two hundred senior fights. Ireland had traditionally had a poor record against Russians in such championships, with political voting by other Eastern-Bloc countries having been prevalent.

Joyce entered the ring with the sole aim of becoming Ireland's first European Championship finalist since Terry Milligan had achieved that feat in 1953. The fight saw the Corkman display the valour for which he would become renowned. In the opening round, he gave Galkin a bloody nose as the contest ebbed and flowed. In the second, Joyce was cautioned as he led with the head but as both fighters left their stools for the last, Joyce was considered to be slightly ahead. In the final round, the experience and craft of the Russian came to the fore as he measured his shots to great effect. Joyce was caught throughout, but he continued to fight bravely. In the end, three of the five judges found for Galkin, while the Finnish judge gave it to Joyce and the Italian viewed it a draw. A bronze medal was on its way to Cork. For Joyce, the experience had been a learning experience from start to finish.

"I got more out of going to Bulgaria than I could have imagined," recalled Joyce. "Just to see how the Russians, the Poles, the Hungarians and the East Germans approached boxing and the routines they undertook in training was food for thought. I spent my spare time seeking sparring partners from those countries, so I received a valuable education as well as the competition."

A year later, Kieran Joyce was picked for the Irish team which travelled to the Olympic Games in Los Angeles. The Corkman was afforded a bye in the opening round of the welterweight division, and was paired with Basil Boniface in his first contest. Accordingly, Joyce performed a demolition job on the helpless Boniface in an arena which included his mother and father, together with Dr Pat O' Callaghan, who had won a gold medal for Ireland in the Olympic hammer event in 1932.

Displaying bundles of nervous energy, Joyce gave his opponent three standing counts. Halfway into the second round, the referee led the brave Seychelles representative to his corner. The slick barrages of punches thrown by Joyce in the bout were truly impressive, but it was evident that his opponent was out of his depth at an Olympic Games. A better class of opposition awaited in the third round.

John Tracey became Ireland's star of the Los Angeles Games as he battled to claim a silver medal in the marathon. That feat came on the last day of competition, but he had disappointed

earlier in his attempt to claim a medal in the 10,000 metres final. On the same day of that final, Joyce entered the ring to face a tricky Finn by the name of Joni Nyman. It was to prove to be a disappointing day for Joyce, and he had no complaints as the Finn's hand was raised in victory.

A caution for Joyce in the second round saw the fight swing in favour of the Finn. Nyman pulled away in the third with shots and combinations that caught the eyes of the judges. A disappointed Joyce was heard to say to team trainer Paddy Muldowney that he had let himself and the team down. However, his all-battling style was absorbed by the Finn, who was a worthy winner.

By the Seoul Olympic Games of 1988, Joyce had enjoyed a long unbeaten run in Ireland and moved up to the light-middleweight division. Seven boxers were included in the Irish team and Joyce was joined by Wayne McCullough, Michael Carruth, John Lowey, Joe Lawlor, Paul Fitzgerald and Billy Walsh. Some questions were posed about Joyce's ability to keep to the weight and his tendency to adopt 'uncompromising methods' which had seen him fall foul of judges in the past.

The doubts regarding Joyce's ability to keep to the weight were proved right, as it was decided in Seoul to enter him in that division. The draw pitted the Corkman against Filipo Palako Vaka of Tonga in what was to be his first bout as a middleweight. As in Los Angeles four years previously, the opening bout saw Joyce outclass his opponent; the fight was stopped in the first round by the referee.

Joyce's next opponent was the Ugandan fighter, Franco Wanyama, a renowned puncher. The results for Irish boxing that night were considered to be an unmitigated disaster as Joyce, Wayne McCullough, Michael Carruth and John Lowey were all eliminated. For Joyce, it was a particularly galling experience as he lost on a narrow split decision after he was given a questionable count in the final round. The Corkman gave it his all in the bout and dished out considerable punishment to the African when he caught him on the ropes. Whilst the Ugandan scored with clean shots to Joyce's head, the Irishman was ahead going into the last round. Seconds before the finish, with the fight in the balance, the Peruvian referee gave Joyce a standing count to the dismay of the Irish contingent. As the result was called, it became evident that the count had cost Joyce the fight and he went out on a three-two split decision.

"That decision killed me, as I was sure that I had won the bout," recalled Joyce. "I went to the corner after the bell and you just know, as do your corner, whether you have done enough to win the fight, and we were happy. The last person a fighter can fool is himself and when the decision was called I was devastated. Maybe, in hindsight, I was over prepared for Seoul and was too fit, and as a boxer that will do you no good. The fact is though that, whatever you do in the ring is left to the judges' opinion, and there will always be some strange decisions, but that's boxing."

Today, with the highlights of his career now distant memories, Joyce is very philosophical on the sport of boxing. He is the head coach at the Sunnyside club in Cork city and gives his young charges the same dedication that he gave his own career.

"When I look back on my career, I cannot thank my parents enough for what they did for me," he says. "I remember my father getting up in the darkness of the early morning and him driving his car behind me, with full lights on, so that I could do my roadwork in safety. It was not easy for my parents as they had twelve of a family, but they did so much for me and were always there. My father travelled to all my fights and was very proud of my achievements; he was brilliant."

The dedication that Joyce has given to the Sunnyside Club has paid dividends as he has seen two of his boxers, Paul Buttimer and Michael Roche, follow in his footsteps to represent Ireland at Olympics Games. On his own career, he is philosophical:

"When I was at my peak I would have loved to have had the knowledge about nutrition and dehydration that I know now, I think I could have been Olympic champion. I fought against Russians, Cubans, Americans, Germans and I never felt they were fitter or stronger. I was always working at my weight and that was a disadvantage.

"Today I would concentrate on my dehydration a lot more, eat certain foods at the right time. I was very disciplined with my training and eating habits. The knowledge I have now in this myself I pass onto my boxers to make sure they don't go through what I had to. Knowledge, time, experience is power.

"Every lad that goes to represent this club is told that he is an ambassador for the club and, most importantly, himself as an individual," Joyce said. "I always got a great pride in wearing a green vest and, even today, my vests take pride of place in the trophy cabinet. To me, the fact that international boxers are restricted to wearing either red or blue vests is not the same. I recall putting the green vest on before a fight and the sense of pride it gave you was great in terms of confidence also. It's the same as the Ireland versus England rugby game in Croke Park in 2007, as those boys were truly inspired in their green shirts. I teach my boys the importance of representing their country with pride. Everywhere I went to in my sixty internationals, I felt that being Irish broke down many barriers and gave us preferential treatment."

In February 2007, Kieran Joyce, together with Gerry Storey and Billy Walsh, was honoured by the Irish Amateur Boxing Association at the senior finals in the National Stadium in Dublin. He was a tough fighter whose fitness, skill and sheer battling ability saw him represent Ireland as a formidable boxer. His dedication to the sport is unquestionable and remains so. The city of Cork, Ireland and Kieran Joyce can be justly proud of his achievements. He is arguably the greatest boxing ambassador to come out of Ireland's famous Rebel County of Cork.

Sam Storey

Excellence in the Family Tradition

Sam Storey is articulate. Sam Storey is a straight talker. Sam Storey knows his mind and is not afraid to speak it. He owns outright a Lonsdale Belt, is a former Olympian, and took silver at Commonwealth level. He has no mean record for he fought both Steve Collins and Chris Eubank for professional honours. However, he is an enigma in a sport where the scars of battle are all too often evident to observe. Incidentally, he is also the son of Gerry Storey, but he never needed to rely on his father's name to prove his class in a boxing ring.

The fact is that if you met Sam Storey in the street, you would never guess that he had ever donned gloves or stepped over a rope into a ring. Today, the former British super middleweight champion uses his experiences in boxing as a motivational speaker. He influences audiences through his talks to change negative mindsets and replace them with positive thinking. From the power of the fists to the power of psychology, Sam Storey tells it as it is.

Left

Taking a breather during training

Born to Gerry and Belle Storey in the New Lodge district in 1963, the expectation that Sam would end up in a boxing ring may have been a racing certainty. Yet, he freely admits that boxing was not a first love.

"I never was – and to be truthful am still not – in love with the sport of boxing," he said. "I was more of a football fan in my youth and the boxing was just a hobby back then. One day trying to juggle both sports caught up with me when I stayed after school playing football until six o' clock. When I got back to the house Dad was not too happy as I had a quarterfinal bout in the Ulster juvenile championships later that evening. The net result was that I was beaten due to the fact that I had used up all my energy earlier playing football. It was a sore lesson, but I always take positives from defeat and knew where I had gone wrong."

Storey's philosophy on taking positives from negatives was to stand by him in his career and his record as an amateur is exemplary. By the early 1980s, he was carving a niche for himself as a future Olympian. A trip to the European junior championships in East Germany in 1983 was followed by a silver medal at the Commonwealth championships in Belfast, where he lost to the ABA champion, Rod Douglas.

As with many prospects, the biggest obstacle to their progress is a rival of class and distinction within their own weight

Sam Storey pictured with Irish President Mary McAleese and his Lonsdale Belt at the Holy Family Club

and country. For Sam Storey, Ireland's top amateur at the time was the 1982 world championship bronze medallist, Tommy Corr from Tyrone. For Storey, Corr was the man to overcome if he was to realise his Olympic dream in Los Angeles in 1984.

The Storey and Corr battles in the Ulster Hall during that period were classic encounters. In 1982, the first of the encounters took place in the Ulster Hall at the senior finals. Corr took honours over Storey in Belfast that year and was Ireland's top light middleweight.

In Munich in May, Corr was beaten in the semi-final in the world championships by the eventual gold medallist, the Russian, Alexander Koshkin. In real terms, it would take a monumental effort by Storey to shift Corr from the top spot.

"The rivalry with Tommy Corr was really big back then," recalled Storey. "I remember being in the changing rooms in the Ulster Hall and I could hear the crowd chanting our names well before the bouts. The atmosphere was electric every time we met and they were always hard and close bouts."

The two protagonists met again in the 1983 Ulster senior final and this time Storey showed his class and was triumphant. However, in the Irish seniors one month later Sam was forced to withdraw due to a serious throat infection. However, Sam Storey was now the man in the driving seat for Los Angeles, in the running for the following year's Olympic Games.

"To lose in the Ulster final to Tommy in 1982 only doubled my determination to beat him and that paid off the following year. I recall that soon after I won the Irish junior title I was picked to fight for Ireland in a senior match with Scotland where I came up against the formidable Davy Milligan, who was the ABA champion. He was a very cocky guy and when I beat him I felt that I had nothing to fear and was certainly not out of my depth in the senior division."

In 1984, Storey took both Ulster and Irish titles and claimed the light-middleweight berth on the Olympic team. Corr moved up a weight and was included as the middleweight, despite having lost the Irish senior final to Sam's brother Gerry. The Los Angeles Olympics for Storey, whilst an honour and privilege, was tinged somewhat by the fact that his father Gerry had been overlooked for the position of team coach. However, an injury sustained in training five weeks before the Games almost put his own position in jeopardy.

"I recall I was sparring Kieran Joyce before the Games and the gloves I was using were not the best," he said. "One thing led to another and I caught my thumb and it was badly swollen. The fact was that from five weeks before the Games until I stepped into the ring, I had not put a glove on due to the injury. This was all hushed in the papers and, in hindsight, I should have been sent home. Eventually, I made the Games but I always recall missing the opening ceremony as the officials did not want me exerting myself in the heat as I was due into the ring the following day. When I spoke to my Dad back home he was very disappointed that I didn't make the opening, and he should know how important they were, given that he had been to three Olympics.

"I was drawn to meet the Italian, Romolo Casamonica, who was the reigning World Champion, who had been put out of the previous year's European championships by the gold medallist, Valeri Laptyev. I wasn't right psychologically, the thumb injury had been playing on my mind and the fact that I had not been training properly was all weighing against me. The first two rounds saw me taking the fight to the Italian and I was in front. By the time I came out for the last, I was completely exhausted and he stopped me with thirty seconds to go."

Despite being down over the Olympic experience, Storey redoubled his efforts in the amateur game and went on to represent Ireland at the 1985 European championships. In his opening bout against the Hungarian Zoltan Fuzesy, he ended up on the wrong end of a unanimous decision. At the end of the bout, Storey made a very important decision.

"I remember going to the corner and looked at my dad and said: 'That's it, I think it's about time I turned professional.'"

On 3rd December 1985, Sam Storey stepped through the ropes of the Ulster Hall to make his professional debut. Ironically, a bout of Shingles prior to the fight did not stop him knocking-out Nigel Shingles after five rounds. In his fifth fight, Storey won the vacant Irish middleweight title by defeating Rocky McGran on points at the King's Hall. That crown was to be relinquished to Steve Collins – whom Storey had beaten as an amateur – in Boston less than a year later and Storey set his sights on the British title.

Four straight wins followed and in September 1989, the super middleweight title was claimed with a points' victory over Tony Burke in Belfast. Two months later, Storey stopped Noel Magee in

the first defence of that title and a fight to take the Lonsdale Belt outright was scheduled with James Cook in Belfast for October 1990. Cook was a tough fighter with a renowned uppercut who would go on to claim the EBU European championship. He used his hook to great effect and stopped Storey in the tenth round after he had knocked him to the canvas on two occasions.

Once again, using his philosophy of taking positives from negatives, Storey resumed his quest for glory. In Berlin in May 1990, he was considered to be very unlucky to go down to a split decision to Ali Saidi. Despite that setback, within nine months, Storey had recorded three successive victories which were to put him in contention for a further crack at the British title.

Meanwhile, Brighton's very own Christopher Livingstone Eubank was making a name for himself as the WBO super middleweight title holder. In August 1994, a crack at Eubank's world title was secured by Storey. The fight, which took place in the International Arena in Cardiff, saw a valiant Storey forced to retire in the seventh round. Subsequently, it was discovered that he had suffered a fractured ankle. Storey had proved his ability at the highest level when some journalists had written him off completely.

That performance against Eubank was to assist Storey in getting a crack at the British super middleweight crown. A fight in Bethnal Green against Ali Forbes went the distance and Storey, six years after he had first become champion, was declared the victor and holder by right of the Lonsdale Belt. Four such belts have come to Irish shores, three of the winners – Sam Storey, Hugh Russell and Neil Sinclair – having come out of the Holy Family stable.

Storey then challenged Henry Wharton for his Commonwealth and European belts, but suffered a fourth round stoppage. Two fights were to follow; a victory over Jake Kilrain and a defeat against David 'Jedi' Starie for the vacant British title which Storey had relinquished.

Storey retired in April 1997 with a record of twenty-five wins and six defeats. By the time he was on the wane, Steve Collins had acquired Chris Eubank's world crown, but an all-Irish title fight, as promised, was never to be realised.

"I just could not make the weight any more and it was taking it out of me trying to get there," he recalled. "I just knew it was time to move on as my interests outside the ring were growing."

Today, Sam Storey uses his experiences to inspire others in many fields. A Lonsdale Belt may be a significant achievement, but it is only the icing on a career that has been personified by excellence and pride in the ring.

Left

Belfast's Sam Storey (right) on his way to regaining the British Super middleweight title from Ali Forbes at York Hall, Bethnal Green

Barry McGuigan

"He's got him with the Right!"

Prior to 1978, the market town of Clones in Co. Monaghan was best known as the home of the annual Ulster Gaelic football final. Each July, the town came to a virtual standstill as thousands of spectators poured in from across the province to witness the best players in Ulster football slug it for the Anglo-Celt Cup at the picturesque St Tiernach's Park. On such occasions, the shops, bars and restaurants in and around the town's central Diamond did a roaring trade. The second Sunday in July was indeed the highlight of the year in Clones.

However, from 1978 until the late 1980s, Gaelic football as the number one sport in Clones was eclipsed by boxing, as a local lad named Barry McGuigan began to put the town on the world map. His career became the talking point in streets, shops and bars as he established his credentials as one of the greatest boxers produced by this island. For the town that would become known as 'Barrytown', a legend was in the making.

Finnbarr 'Barry' McGuigan, the son of Pat and Katie, was born into a family of five boys and three girls on 28th February

1961. Prior to assuming the mantle of fame, another member of Barry's family had already come to international prominence when young McGuigan was a mere seven years old. For one night in April 1968, Clones was the talk of Monaghan, Ireland and Europe, as Barry's father represented Ireland on the stage at the Royal Albert Hall in the 1968 Eurovision Song Contest.

Pat McGuigan (or McGeegan, as he was became known through a misspelling of his name on a promotional poster) finished in a creditable third place at the contest with his rendition of 'Chance of a Lifetime' – and Ireland was truly delighted. McGuigan Snr was placed behind the evergreen Cliff Richard, who had been hot favourite with the catchy 'Congratulations', while the contest was won by the truly memorable 'La La La' by the Spanish entrant, Massiel. In a dress rehearsal for the celebrations, which Clones would host two decades hence, Pat McGuigan's return to the town on 8th April 1968 was a night to remember.

For a decade though that was it in terms of excitement in Clones. In the 1970s the Troubles in the North cut the town's hinterland of Co. Fermanagh off as roads were cratered and blocked. Clones seemed to become just another 'Border Town'. However, this border town had a difference – Pat McGuigan's son was beginning to learn his ring craft.

Boxing was in Barry McGuigan's blood from an early age. After an initial grounding in the sport in the nearby club in Wattlebridge, he soon settled at the Smithboro boxing club, approximately five miles from Clones. Under the keen eye of trainer Frank Mulligan, McGuigan progressed rapidly through the ranks and, by 1976, had claimed his first Irish junior title, when he defeated Martin Brereton. In February 1978, Barry McGuigan came of age when he won the Ulster senior bantamweight crown by beating Enniskillen's Kenny Bruce at the Ulster Hall.

The Ulster Hall is an elegant building situated in Bedford Street, just behind Belfast's City Hall. In addition to hosting the cream of the entertainment world, the Hall had witnessed many fraught political meetings since it was opened in 1862. However, politics apart, it was to play an important part in the making of the McGuigan legend. As a venue for boxing it is believed to be unsurpassed anywhere in Ireland, as its perfect acoustics and intimate atmosphere have transformed to legend even the most mundane of bouts. The Ulster senior finals are the highlight of the Northern boxing scene and many careers have taken off on the strength of a sparkling performance in front of a knowledgeable audience.

As Barry recalled, the Ulster Hall was his favourite boxing venue due to the closeness of the crowd to the ring and the feeling that generated.

"As a place to box, the Hall is fabulous as the people on the balcony are almost leaning into the ring," he said. "You can hear everything from the back of the Hall to the ringside and they are a very knowledgeable and appreciative crowd. The Belfast crowd are a very fair bunch and they applaud skilled fighters when they see them and accept decisions, even if it is against a local lad."

McGuigan pinpoints the victory in the Ulster Senior Championships as something that accelerated his career and led to many memorable times in a period of uncertainty across the North.

"I remember not long after winning the Ulster title I was picked to represent an Ulster select against a German select in Belfast," he said. "It was the most surreal experience I had ever encountered as the fights were held in a working men's club on the Shankill Road and times were really depressing. It was the height of the Troubles and Belfast was a ghost town, but it was an incredible night and I recall that the band Clubsound was doing the cabaret at the show and they were fantastic. I had only just turned seventeen and was pitted against a classy guy called Koch who went on make a name for himself by winning the world amateur light welterweight championship. There was a magical atmosphere in the club as during my fight I put this guy under tremendous pressure to get the decision over him the in the end."

McGuigan gained his first green vest when he represented his country in an Under-19 international in Drogheda later that spring. However, his amateur career soon suffered a setback when he was not picked to represent Ireland in the European Junior Championships, which were held in Dublin that year.

"I lost out to a guy called Hugh Holmes, whom I had beaten in the Irish championships, for the bantamweight choice in those games and it really cut me up badly," he said. "I was hurt inside and felt really hard done by and when Holmes went on to claim a silver medal in Dublin it was worse, as I felt that I could have claimed the gold if I had have been picked."

While the 1978 European championships were a disappointment for Barry McGuigan, the anomalies of Ireland's North-South divide, in geographical and political terms, provided a chance to shine on a greater stage. In August 1978, the eleventh Commonwealth games were held in Edmonton in the Canadian province of Alberta. The Northern Ireland side that went to those games consisted of the cream of Ulster's champions and the Clones boy was on the way to fame.

"It was a fabulous experience from start to finish and I'll never forget the Games for the spirit within the team was marvellous," he said. "We were under the guidance of Gerry Storey and we stayed in the Stella Maris hostel in Belfast prior to the games to get the collective training done. I'll not say that it was the most exclusive of surroundings, but we were very well looked after. The team gelled together. It was my first experience of collective training and we worked out in Newcastle, Co. Down, and I remember that we did sprints and boxed three times a day, which left me so fit. Once in Edmonton, we stayed beside the Northern Ireland bowlers and we became really friendly as they could not do enough for us. The thing about major games is that everyone is looking out for everyone else in their team and as someone progresses the good will and expectations grow which leads to a great spirit. The boxers that year were a real exceptional bunch and the rest of the Irish team were fantastic in the way they encouraged us all the way."

The boxing squad that represented Northern Ireland that year was indeed an exceptional collection of fighters. Barry McGuigan took gold in the welterweight division, as did Ballymena's Gerry Hamill in the lightweight class. Silver medals were claimed by

Right

Eusebio Pedrozo is stopped in his tracks in London, 8th June 1985

Kenny Beattie, while Hugh Russell from the New Lodge area in Belfast claimed a bronze.

McGuigan's progress through the bantamweight competition was fairly straightforward and he was paired in the final to meet the dangerous and well-built Papua New Guinea fighter, Tumat Sugolik. Sugolik had powered his way to the final by knocking out all who stood in his way. As McGuigan explained, Gerry Storey, as trainer, had made sure that McGuigan had not seen the muscular fighter and he was surprised when his opponent climbed into the ring.

"I remember I was getting changed for the fight and I noticed this guy in the corner and could not believe his build; I thought he was a couple of divisions above bantamweight and felt that I was lucky not to have to have fought him. When I climbed into the ring and saw that this person I had seen in the changing room was to be my opponent I had no time to let it sink in and just had to get on with it. I suppose it was reverse psychology by Gerry Storey not to let me see this guy who had been knocking out everyone in front of him, and it worked in my favour in the end."

McGuigan survived and outfought the Papua New Guinea fighter to get the decision, but recalls that he found himself on the end of one of his haymakers, a punch that still makes him wince to this day.

"He caught me during the fight and I thought honestly that my head was going to come off my shoulders," he said. "He was a crude and heavy-handed fighter and he packed some punch and it was the hardest one I had taken in my career to date."

Adorned with the gold medal, McGuigan's tears on the podium in Edmonton as the strains of 'The Derry Air' echoed through the arena, caught the imagination of the people back home. The image of an inconsolable seventeen-year-old first put the name and the face of the Clones lad into the hearts of the Irish public. On how he felt at that moment, Barry is convinced that the tears were an expression of the frustration he had felt over not being picked for the European games earlier in the year.

"I suppose I had an awful lot of things pent up inside me and that was the release I needed," he said. "I was still deeply emotional about being overlooked for the European championships and that moment was really special to me. The whole thing was fabulous: a fabulous experience and with 'Danny Boy' playing it all becomes a bit emotional. The tears just came as I stood there and I felt so proud to have done so well, but in my heart I knew that all the hard work had been all for something. But it wasn't the first time that I had been cut up in those games as I had been upset and in tears when Tony

McEvoy was eliminated earlier in the Games. Tony looked after us at the games like a father and he was a great inspiration but I remember that night I shed tears for him."

Those particular games produced a plethora of exceptional fighters and McGuigan recalls one encounter with a future world champion with pride.

"Mike McCallum, who became a world champion in 1984 by defeating Sean Mannion to win the world junior middleweight title, was representing Jamaica and he had beaten our own Kenny Beattie to claim gold at lightweight," he said. "I remember meeting him at a get-together after the finals and I will never forget what he said to me. He looked at me and said 'I'll see you at the top son' and I'll never forget that. In the featherweight class the great Azumah Nelson won the gold, so it was quite a games in boxing terms."

On returning to Ireland, McGuigan continued to flourish in his amateur career and, in 1979 he, together with his old adversary, Martin Brereton, claimed bronze medals at the European Junior Championships which were held in Rimini, Italy.

The next step in McGuigan's progression was the Olympic Games, which were scheduled to be held in Moscow in 1980. Unfortunately, in the run up to the Games he broke his hand in a contest and it was a race against time to be ready. With the hand on the mend Barry was duly picked to wear the green vest in the featherweight division. In the first round, McGuigan was afforded a bye and in his first outing he defeated Issack Mabushi of Tanzania after the referee had stopped the contest in third round. However, his moment of victory proved pyrrhic, since his hand injury had come back to haunt him.

"I remember after the decision was announced I was going over to the corner to see the coaches and I heard the BBC commentator Harry Carpenter say that I seemed to be having no problems with my injured hand. I knew that there was still a problem, as in my sparring I was having difficulty with my timing and accuracy due to the injury since, I knew, it had not healed completely. Just as I heard Harry mention that my hand seemed okay, I was advising Gerry Storey that I was in pain and having problems with it. In those days the solution was to freeze the hand with an injection of anaesthetic that would see you through your bout without pain."

The medicine was duly administered for Barry's next bout against the Zambian Winfred Kabunda, but the damage had been done to McGuigan's frame of mind and he lost the bout on points.

"The fight with Kabunda was one of only three fights I lost as a senior amateur fighter and I was very disappointed to be out. In his next bout, the Zambian was in turn defeated by the eventual gold medal winner Rudi Fink from East Germany, so it was a bitter experience. I was only left to think what could have been, but we all fell in to support Hugh Russell and he ended up with a bronze, so that provided me and the team with some consolation."

With the Olympic dream now gone, McGuigan took the plunge into the paid ranks and he signed terms in 1981 with the Co. Tyrone-born and Belfast-based bookmaker, Barney Eastwood. Belfast and Northern Ireland was still going through its nightmare with politics on the street being dictated by events concerning the hunger strikes in the Maze prison. It was a huge gamble at the time for anyone to contemplate the return of professional boxing to the city, but McGuigan's class was worth a gamble. Based in the Eastwood Gym in Castle Street, McGuigan came under the watchful eye of former professional fighter Eddie Shaw.

Barry's first outing came on a cold May night in 1981 at Dublin's Dalymount Park. That bill marked the beginning of the end of Charlie Nash's career, while Selvin Bell was no match for the body punching of McGuigan, and was duly stopped in two rounds. A win over Gary Lucas in four rounds in London was followed by McGuigan's first setback, when he lost a hotly disputed decision in Brighton to Peter Eubank, the elder brother of Chris. Undeterred, the McGuigan machine rolled into Belfast one month later and the Ulster Hall was the arena that was to experience a boxing renaissance.

Victories over Jean-Marc Renard in September, and Terry Pizarro in October, set up the rematch with Eubank that the Belfast public yearned for. Revenge was sweet for McGuigan on the night of 8th December 1981. The Ulster Hall was jam-packed as Eubank was stopped in the eighth and final round.

A series of victories followed, but the tragic death of the Nigerian boxer, Young Ali, after a bout in London with McGuigan, in June 1982, saw the Clones man plunged into grief and despair.

A long depression then engulfed Barry McGuigan and after much soul searching and turmoil, he decided to carry on with his career. A victory against Jimmy Duncan in October 1982 set up a final eliminator for the British title against the tough hitting, and previously undefeated, Hastings-based Paul Huggins. Huggins was duly stopped in the fifth round at the Ulster Hall and in the following April Vernon Penprase offered little opposition as he was stopped in the second round at the Ulster Hall. McGuigan at twenty-two was now British champion and the road to world domination was becoming clearer.

The inevitable progression towards a crack at a world title continued for the 'Clones Cyclone' as he was now nicknamed. The King's Hall in Belfast was resurrected as a boxing venue for McGuigan's European title fight with Valerio Nati in November 1983. A crowd of seven thousand witnessed him stop the Italian in the sixth round, and the class of his opponents was upped considerably as he closed in on the title held by the legendary Eusebio Pedroza.

During 1984, a series of encounters convinced the Belfast public that McGuigan was ready for the highest stage. Four victories at a packed King's Hall, one at the Royal Albert Hall, and a successful defence of his British and European titles against Clyde Ruan, meant that McGuigan was ready for his toughest battle so far.

Jaun Laporte was a classy Puerto Rican fighter who fought out of New York City. He had gone punch for punch with Eusebio Pedroza in a world title bout, only to lose on points. For his endeavours, the World Boxing Council matched Laporte against the Colombian Mario Miranda for the vacant title at Madison Square Garden. Laporte won the bout when Miranda failed to come out for the eleventh round and became world champion. He went on to defend his title twice, winning both on points, before losing out to the legendary Wilfredo Gómez. To say Laporte was to be McGuigan's toughest opponent was a safe bet.

McGuigan fought Laporte in Belfast on Saturday, 23rd February 1985. It turned out to be his hardest battle and he took a vicious punch from Laporte half way into the fight that almost stopped him in his tracks. Barry composed himself to win on points after ten bruising rounds to prove conclusively that he was able to mix it with the best and, most importantly, take a punch.

Belfast and Ireland was engulfed in frenzy as arrangements were finalised for the fight with the reigning WBA champion, Eusebio Pedroza, at Loftus Road in London on Saturday, 8th June 1985. The fight attracted a crowd of over 25,000 to the ground and was beamed live across Britain and Ireland to record audiences. From the rendition of 'Danny Boy' by Pat McGuigan, to the sight of a Leprechaun waltzing through the ring before the fight, the event was surreal for all who witnessed it. In the seventh round, McGuigan caught Pedroza with a sweet right hand and over the champion went. Twice more McGuigan had Pedroza sprawling in the ring, but all the skill and guile acquired over seven years as champion kept him in the fight. Fifteen fraught rounds were fought out in their intensity and as McGuigan was declared the champion, the party began in London. That party carried on across the Irish Sea and engulfed Ireland for a number of days. The scenes in Belfast and Dublin as McGuigan was welcomed home were unsurpassed. Seventeen years after Pat McGuigan had brought Clones to a standstill through his singing ability, a far bigger reception awaited his feted son.

The fact is that in Barry McGuigan's professional career, those nights in June 1985 were to be the pinnacle of his achievements. The old adage goes that, once you reach the top, there is only one way things can go. Defeat, acrimony, comebacks and court cases all followed in the wake of the glory. However, in those nights in the 1980s, all was well; and maybe that is the way that it should be remembered.

Today, Barry McGuigan is a credit to the world of boxing and his punditry is sought after and is considered second to none.

In retrospect, he is proud of his career and achievements – and why not? When speaking to him you cannot mistake his obvious warmth and knowledge of the game he loved. On a philosophical note, Barry McGuigan has plenty of considered advice for any young lad wanting to go into boxing today.

"I would say to anybody that boxing is a great sport and by all means give it a go. If it's not for you, then it's not for you, but at least you gave it a try. Boxing can open up a world of travel and excitement for boys who could not even dream of such things. I have seen many lads who may have gone off the rails somewhat become great lads due the discipline that adhering to the rules of boxing can give you. It teaches respect for life and respect for people and some of the greatest friendships are made in boxing. No other sport can give you that or has the ability to transform a person the way boxing can. There are guys out there who have dedicated their life to the sport and helped out so many others for little or no reward; they could not be rewarded enough. If you have the discipline and the determination, I would have no hesitation in recommending boxing to anyone."

Barry McGuigan was in the correct place at the correct time in an era when Northern Ireland was hungry for hope and happiness. He provided that in abundance. That is only half the story though. The Clones Cyclone learned his trade through dedication and a will to succeed. Nobody can take away his achievements nor question the ability that has established him as one of the foremost pundits in modern boxing. On the wall of his gym, as he was learning his trade, a crudely painted slogan told McGuigan what was required to succeed in both boxing and life. It simply read:

Work hard, think fast and you will last!

Wise words that have proved to be true for Barry McGuigan.

Dave 'Boy' McAuley

Pound for Pound, None Better!

Many observers of Irish professional boxing in the 1980s felt that the boom times ended on the night of 23rd June 1986. On that blistering evening in Las Vegas, Barry McGuigan, the principal boxer from the Barney Eastwood stable, lost his title to Steve Cruz. What happened afterwards is well documented and needs no elaboration. Hugh Russell had retired with a Lonsdale Belt the previous year: the future of paid fighting, in Belfast particularly, looked to be uncertain.

However, within ten months, a packed King's Hall witnessed a truly classic clash for the WBA world flyweight title. Larne's Dave 'Boy' McAuley was the man who stepped up to the mark on that occasion when he and the reigning champion, Fidel Bassa, went toe-to-toe in a fantastic battle. Despite being knocked to the canvas within the opening few seconds, McAuley regained his composure to slug it out with the Colombian. By the ninth round, underdog McAuley had the champion floored on three occasions and while the roof of the arena threatened to come off the champion Bassa somehow held on.

By the thirteenth round of the last-ever scheduled fifteen-round world title fight, McAuley was out on his feet through sheer exhaustion, the champion left standing and undefeated, but pride had been restored in Irish professional boxing circles. McAuley was the darling of the King's Hall. Twenty years on and the question still remains – if the fight had been over twelve rounds, would the Larne man have been champion?

Almost a year later, the rematch between McAuley and Bassa was scheduled for the same venue. However, it was not to be for Dave Boy as after another bruising encounter he was beaten unanimously on points. As the crowds left the King's Hall, McAuley considered his career options carefully, but decided to give it a final shot.

In 1989 McAuley secured a crack at the darling of British boxing, Duke McKenzie, for his International Boxing Federation title. Twenty-six-year-old McKenzie had won his IBF title the previous year when he stopped Rolando Bohol of the Philippines in the eleventh round of their bout. After defending this title against Tony De Luca, McKenzie agreed to fight McAuley at Wembley Arena in June. With a third attempt at a world title now

on the horizon, it was a case of drinking at the 'Last Chance Saloon' for David McAuley.

The heights of the Wembley arena and the King's Hall are a world away from St Anthony's boxing club in Larne where Dave 'Boy' McAuley first learnt his boxing trade. Born in the east Antrim town in 1961, Dave followed his older brothers into boxing and a glittering career began in 1970. Ulster and Irish schoolboy and junior titles soon followed, but the breakthrough for the Larne boy came at the start of the Eighties.

In 1980, the year of the Moscow Olympic Games, Dave Boy came of age as an amateur. It was a case of making his mark as the right time as first Ulster and then Irish flyweight titles were won in emphatic style. That February, McAuley caught the headlines at the Ulster Hall as he stopped the reigning national champion Jimmy Carson in the third round of their bout. Up until then the contest had been evenly matched, with no indication given of what McAuley had in store. However, in the last round, Carson was caught by a series of left hooks that had him sprawling in the ring. Eventually referee Jackie Poucher was left with no option but to step in to end the bout. Three weeks later in Dublin, the two protagonists were matched again in the final of the Irish flyweight division and, again, McAuley made no mistake. Dave Boy was quite superb in the National Stadium that night and his place at the Olympic Games seemed to be assured.

Further evidence of McAuley's potential came in the United States in April as both he and Ritchie Foster were the only two of Ireland's representatives to win against the illustrious American Golden Gloves champions. As McAuley recalled, his victory was well received by none other than the President of the Irish Amateur Boxing Association, Felix Jones.

"After that fight in the States I felt great and Felix said to me that I had just secured my place on the Irish team for the Olympic Games," recalled Dave. "I felt personally that I was going to Moscow and with securing a place also at the European junior championships I was very confident."

In May 1980 McAuley was an automatic choice for the Irish team that travelled to Rimini for the European junior championships. While he was defeated in his opening contest, he was still the favourite to get the nomination for Moscow. Nevertheless, it was not to be and the plane left without the Larne man.

> **Left**
>
> Challenger Dodie 'Boy' Penalosa (right) misses with a right hook as champion Dave McAuley (left) leans back during the IBF World Flyweight Championships.

"I remember I was told that when the team was picked I would get a phone call and I was in nerves all day waiting on the call," he said. "The first I knew that I was off the team was when I tuned into the local news and there were pictures of the team leaving for the games. That just destroyed me so much and to be treated like that made me disgusted. Hugh Russell was picked to go in my place and, while I have no problem in hindsight, it was the way that I as champion was overlooked that gutted me. Somebody in the hierarchy put the boot into me that year and even today I would love to know who it was. The net result of this was that I had no option left but to turn professional. At the end of the day, I was married and I needed money and boxing was something that could do that for me."

Dave Boy signed up with the Barney Eastwood stable and came under the guidance of legendary trainer Eddie Shaw. His debut came in October 1983 on the undercard of the Barry McGuigan versus Ruben Harasme bout. McAuley did not impress as his fight with John Mwaimu was declared a draw. His next two outings at the King's Hall saw the Larne man record victories over Dave Smith and Ian Coolbeck. The real breakthrough for McAuley came on the never-to-be-forgotten night of 8th June 1985. On the night that Barry McGuigan claimed the world title from Eusebio Pedroza, Dave Boy won a final eliminator for the British bantamweight crown by stopping Bobby McDermott in the tenth round.

Two more victories followed before McAuley dropped a weight and was matched in October 1986 against Glasgow's Joe Kelly for the British flyweight crown. That fight, for the title vacated by Duke McKenzie, took place in Kelly's hometown, but McAuley was comfortable throughout and took the title with a ninth round knockout. That result set up an early opportunity for a crack at the newly crowned WBA world flyweight champion, Fidel Bassa.

While the two fights with Bassa were exhilarating in the extreme, the two defeats did nothing to diminish McAuley's desire to reach the top. Fully a year after the second Bassa fight, McAuley was called upon as a stand-in opponent against the IBF champion Duke McKenzie at Wembley. To say that the Larne man was the underdog would be an understatement, as odds of five to one were offered on the challenger. Beforehand, McAuley made his views on McKenzie known and the fact was that he did not rate him very highly.

"Duke McKenzie does not impress me one bit," he said. "I have the heart of a lion and this man avoided me like the plague when I was the British champion and now I have my chance. He is not a good champion and I aim to prove it."

That was the opening salvo in a war of words that grew before the fight and tainted the atmosphere as the day approached. McKenzie was the darling of the English media with no defeats in twenty-three outings; McAuley was considered to be a routine opponent. While it was known that Dave could pack a punch, it was felt that McKenzie's jab would overwhelm the Larne man. How wrong the pundits were was about to be proved. Dave emphasised the fact that a fighter with nothing to lose is a very dangerous opponent.

Early in the fight, the champion opened a cut over McAuley's left eye and the signs were ominous. However, Dave Boy was determined and he dug deep to mix it and eventually got on top. McKenzie, who had worn shorts adorned with the name 'Bassa' to taunt McAuley, gradually found out that his opponent was there for one reason only, and that was to win. As the chants of 'Here we go!' got louder, McAuley continued his onslaught and by the final bell he was well ahead. As the verdict was announced unanimously in favour of Dave Boy, many years of frustration were lifted as a world championship belt was placed around his waist.

"I remember that before the fight all that the media were interested in was Duke, and my dressing room was like a ghost-town while you could not get near his for journalists. Afterwards, it was the reverse, as you could not move in mine and his was empty. I slipped out to see Duke to commiserate and I just could not believe the difference that there was all because he lost the fight – but that's boxing for you and losing is a hard medicine."

The following day the town of Larne was out in force to greet its most famous son. There to welcome the returning champion were the most important women in his life; his wife Wendy and baby daughter Sacha. Sporting two stitches on his left eye, McAuley was paraded around the town and feted by the great and the good. The task of defending the hard-won crown now became the objective.

The first defence came in November 1989 against Dodie Boy Penalosa, a former IBF world champion from the Philippines. The fight itself was a tough battle with McAuley coming through on a split decision. The following January, Dave Boy returned to the King's Hall where he topped the bill in a defence against the thirty-two-year-old Louis Curtis of the United States. That fight was won by the Larne fighter in convincing fashion and six months later he was considered lucky in a third defence against

Rodolfo Blanco at the same venue. McAuley rode his luck in the clash with the classy Colombian and was floored twice in the second and once in the third and eleventh rounds. McAuley swung a disputed split decision, but it was not the last time that he was to meet Blanco.

In 1991 McAuley defended his title twice in Belfast where he retained it firstly against Pedro Feliciano and then against Jacob Matlala from South Africa. However, the rematch with Blanco was arranged for Bilbao for June 1992 and a further battle ensued, but this time the challenger was afforded a split decision. The pain of defeat for Dave Boy was heartbreaking, and he took a long time to recover from the set back.

After the defeat to Blanco, Dave Boy made the decision to hang up the gloves and he was never to grace the boxing ring again. He began to concentrate on his business interests and today oversees a hotel in Larne. As a sideline, McAuley has made a name for himself as a boxing pundit and his commentaries with Jimmy Magee on RTÉ are well received and respected. In hindsight, Dave 'Boy' McAuley was a great fighter who never truly was given the opportunity to prove his undoubted talent as an amateur. He was just up and coming as the heights of the McGuigan era were experienced in Belfast, but he continued to bring boxing glory to the city until the 1990s. Dave Boy has been recognised for his achievements with an MBE, and is considered to have been one of the most prolific post-war fighters to have been produced by Ireland or Britain.

In the 1980s and early 1990s, Belfast had one of the greatest professional gyms in the world; Dave 'Boy' McAuley was a true star and won the respect of his peers on the world stage. A career that ended in 1992 is still remembered fondly, but the two bouts with Bassa are still up there with the best clashes of all time. Make no mistake, McAuley mixed it with, and dished it out to, the very best.

Left

A triumphant Dave pictured with manager Barney Eastwood

Billy Walsh

A Model of Past and Future Excellence

On the evening of Friday 2nd February 2007, Wexford's Billy Walsh, together with Kieran Joyce and Gerry Storey, was honoured by the Irish Amateur Boxing Association in front of a packed National Stadium in Dublin. Walsh, who is the Head Coach of the Association's High Performance Unit, was one of the Ireland's most outstanding boxers in the 1980s, competing in ten Irish senior finals, winning seven and losing three. Or as Billy recalls with a smile: "I won ten senior titles in all, but was robbed of three of them."

The man from the Model County competed in the 1982 European junior championships, in addition to the European senior finals in 1983, 1989 and 1991, which were held in Bulgaria, Italy and Sweden respectively. Walsh boxed in the World Senior Championships twice and represented his country with distinction at the 1988 Olympic Games in Korea. He was also an accomplished hurler and Gaelic footballer in his native county, and won a provincial hurling medal at juvenile level for his beloved Wexford in 1977. Today, he is the man responsible for overseeing the development of Ireland's future international boxing stars as coach of the High Performance Unit. His office is in the gymnasium adjacent to the National Stadium – it is from there that the plan to put Irish boxing back on the Olympic map has been formed.

Born in Manchester in 1963, Billy could have represented England on the highest stage but the Walsh family decided to return to Wexford and Billy, with his then Mancunian accent, became involved in the GAA.

"My early years were devoted to hurling and football, as is natural for any lad growing up in Wexford," he said. "I captained two Wexford teams in Leinster hurling finals and played football for the county at all levels including senior."

His early career as a boxer in Wexford saw him display much promise and soon he won county, provincial and national level at various classes. Boxing out of the St Joseph's Club in Wexford Town, Walsh was a determined and proud fighter but one incident in a Leinster juvenile final made Walsh's career take a different turn as he learnt a hard lesson in the ring.

"I fought a boxer by the name of John McDonough, whose brother Seamus – the 'Gorgeous Gael' – went on to fight Evander Holyfield. John caught me with a hard body shot and I went down to the canvas. I got up after the punch and was given a count but the fight was out of my reach by then. After that I swore to improve my boxing and vowed I would never, ever, let myself down like that again. From that day I sorted myself out and over the next fifteen years I appeared in the final of every Irish championship I entered."

Meanwhile, his hurling and football careers continued to flourish. At the same time as he took part in his first competitive Games representing Ireland in the European Junior Boxing Championships held in Schwerin, Germany, during 1982, his hurling career was also in the ascendant. A defeat against Kilkenny in the 1982 Leinster final was such a blow to Walsh that he promised himself on the pitch of Croke Park that he would make it to the Olympic Games.

"That final was such a sickening experience, as we were five points up and Kilkenny in their usual style came back to beat us. I had won a couple of Irish boxing titles at that stage, and the hurt I felt after the hurling game made me so determined to make it one day to the Olympics."

In May 1983 Walsh attended the first of his three European Senior Boxing Championships, which that year took place in Varna, Bulgaria. In his preliminary round bout in the light-welterweight division, he met the eventual bronze medal winner, Bulgarian, Yordan Lesov. The fight went to the judges who found in Lesov's favour. However, Kieran Joyce of Cork made his mark at those Championships by taking bronze in the welterweight division.

A year later Walsh, as Irish light welterweight champion, was overlooked for the Irish team picked for the Los Angeles Olympic Games. That Irish team included Gerry Hawkins, Phil Sutcliffe, Paul Fitzgerald, Kieran Joyce and Coalisland's Tommy Corr. Walsh recalled his omission as something that drove him back into Gaelic games for a while.

"Of course I was very disappointed at not getting selected for Los Angeles," he recalled. "I was in a gym back at home when the team was announced on the radio, and when my name wasn't mentioned, I just couldn't believe it. That was me finished with boxing for a while, and I went back to my GAA club, Sarsfield's, that summer to keep myself active. We won the county football championship that year but I returned to the ring soon after."

In the Irish senior final of 1985 Walsh lost out to Damien Denny. That loss saw Denny replace Joyce on the Irish team at that year's European Championships in Budapest, where Sean Casey at flyweight claimed a bronze.

Having regained his Irish welterweight title in 1986 and 1987, Walsh attended his third European Championships in 1987 in Turin. Along with the Wexford man on that team were Gordon Joyce, Paul Buttimer, John Lowey, Paul Fitzgerald and the up-

and-coming Michael Carruth. There were to be no medals for the Irish team in Turin on that occasion and Walsh was eliminated again by a Bulgarian by the name of Angel Stoyanov.

However, the scene was now set for Walsh to erase the memory of missing the Los Angeles Olympics, as the Games in Seoul stood just twelve months away. He won the Irish light welterweight title in 1988 and the Irish team, this time with Walsh was finalised. The team consisted of Walsh, Wayne McCullough, Joe Lawlor, John Lowey, Patrick Fitzgerald, Michael Carruth and Kieran Joyce. It was a formidable squad and a memorable experience for the Wexford man.

"I was very determined to make the Games and my technique was improving all the time," he recalled. We had been over in Seoul for the pre-Olympics earlier in 1988 but when the real Games began it was a dream come true. The people of Wexford had done an awful lot for me by raising money and I felt that I owed it to them to put in a big performance. In my opening contest I came across the Korean, Song Kyung Sup, and things were close in the opening round. In the second round I suffered a cut eye, and the referee led me to the corner and I was just completely devastated when the doctor said that I was not to fight on. I was pleading with the doctor, begging him not to stop the fight, but he was adamant. I cried for a full week after that and had never been so down, as all the preparations had been for nothing. I felt that I had let everyone down and I was reluctant to phone home. Eventually my mother got in contact with me and that helped, for she told me that everyone was so proud of me back home. In a way my job as the coach of the team today has been helped by the experience of losing in Seoul, as I tell the lads of my devastation and that experience in invaluable."

No Irish boxer claimed medals at the Seoul Games but for Walsh the experience is still the highlight of his career.

"I remember being in the Olympic Stadium and seeing the famous Ben Johnson one-hundred metres final, after which he was disqualified. I recall meeting Carl Lewis, who was my all-time hero, and feeling really privileged. You must remember that we were just a bunch of working-class lads and to be on the greatest stage in the world was unforgettable."

As Walsh's career continued in Ireland, he and wife Christine celebrated the birth, in 1989, of their first daughter, Sarah-Jane. The responsibility that went with fatherhood precluded Billy from attending that year's European championships in Athens.

Two years later in 1991 Walsh, as Irish champion, attended the European championships in Sweden. However, the IABA opted for Michael Carruth as the country's representative at the world championships which were to take place in Bombay but a hand injury sustained by Carruth prior to those Games. W

Walsh called up at the last minute. By this stage the rivalry with Carruth had been established.

The Irish championships of 1991 saw three current champions, namely Walsh, Eddie Fisher and Michael Carruth, all vying for honours in the welterweight division. In the opening round, the first two names out of the hat were Billy Walsh and Michael Carruth.

"Michael and I were and are great mates and we roomed together everywhere we travelled to," said Walsh. "I was like Michael's mother's eleventh son and we sparred and trained together. To have to fight a good friend is a nightmare for a friendship, as it became hard to communicate the way we did since we were then rivals. It was awful and there were only a handful in the Stadium for a fight that would have packed the place on finals' night. However, I beat Michael and then beat Jim Webb and Eddie Fisher to win the title."

That was not to be the last of the Walsh versus Carruth rivalry. In 1992, the year of the Barcelona Olympic Games, the two contenders met in the Irish final in front of a packed National Stadium in what was in essence a box-off for Barcelona.

"It was a close call in the ring that night and Michael got the decision, but there was a bit of debate over it," he said. "For me that was the end of the road and Michael got the nod for Barcelona and the rest is history."

Needless to say, the achievements of Michael Carruth in Barcelona are part of the rich fabric of Irish sporting history. The nation arose early on the Saturday morning of the Barcelona finals to witness Wayne McCullough and Michael Carruth box for gold medals. RTÉ that morning had a live link-up with the Carruth family home and there, in the living room, as a guest of the family sat Billy Walsh. In scenes that the Dublin author Roddy Doyle could only have dreamt about, the family watched as McCullough was beaten. Then the moment of truth came.

"It was completely mad in that house and, to be truthful, I was fearful that Michael was going to lose to Hernandez. I thought of the devastation that there would be if Michael was beaten. So we settled down and I sat in awe and watched as he fought the best fight that he could have had. Michael was a tactical genius in that fight and, even though he got a warning in the second, it suddenly dawned on me that he was going to do it. At the end of the second, Hernandez was getting a rollicking in his corner, and I said that in the last round, if he came out to fight and not box Michael, then the Cuban would play into his hands. He did and Michael frustrated him; I will never forget seeing Michael's hand raised in victory. I cried with joy that morning and to think that one of the lads whom I had boxed with had made it to the top was just immense."

Michael Carruth's moment of glory still drives Billy Walsh in his dedication to Irish boxing. The break-up of the Communist Eastern Bloc has removed the country greatly from those heady days of 1992. Those glory days will be hard to emulate, as the number of countries vying to enter the Olympic Games has grown significantly.

The introduction of qualifying championships has meant that the days when Ireland sent seven or eight boxers to Games are a thing of the past. Irish boxing noted these changes and appointed Billy Walsh in 2003 as its High Performance Coach. He is based in the National Stadium along with his assistant Zauri Antia, who is from Georgia.

His role is to ensure that the best talent in the country is nurtured to the best standards in order to prepare them to represent Ireland on the highest stage in the future. Walsh agrees that the game in which he competed has changed greatly and that the sport must be treated as a science to ensure success.

"The things I look for in a young boxer are attitude, determination and hunger, but in the modern sport these are not enough. You need to have the right philosophy and technique blended with belief and the right self-control to make someone a champion. To be truthful, I was a bit sceptical years ago of the role that science played, but now I know that it is absolutely crucial in a boxer's development. When I look back on my own career I know that on many occasions I was overdoing the training, but the key is to be right physically and mentally when you climb into the ring. We are teaching our boxers excellence, and my view is that you can only achieve the best by believing that you can get there."

On Ireland's future in amateur terms, Walsh is certain that the philosophy of high-performance coaching will pay dividends in the near future.

"Ireland has the talent and if we get those boxers at the right stage and give them schooling in excellence then the future, I'm sure, will be bright."

On the wall of the gymnasium at the National Stadium, there is a notice board that records how many days are left until the qualifying contests for the Olympic Games. Crucially, there is also a note which advises the boxers of how many days there are until the opening of the actual Olympics. There is no doubt that Billy Walsh is aiming to put Irish boxing back on the pedestal it occupied in 1992.

For a man who cried with joy as he watched his good friend Michael Carruth take gold in 1992, there can be no doubt that Billy Walsh has the passion, experience and determination to see that glory repeated.

Michael Carruth

"Dad, Ronnie Delaney's Time's Up!"

On the morning of Saturday, 8th August 1992, most of the population of Ireland rose early to watch sporting history being made in the boxing ring at the Barcelona Olympics. Thirty-six years had passed since Fred Tiedt contested for Ireland's last boxing gold medal at the Melbourne Games and now the country had, not one, but two fighters going for glory. Both Wayne McCullough and Michael Carruth were veterans of the previous Olympic Games held in Seoul. That experience, coupled with skill and determination, had seen them come through their respective divisions. The nation held its breath as the action began just after nine that morning.

The Belfast 'pocket rocket' McCullough was first up against a Cuban opponent, Joel Casamayor. Despite a valiant fight-back in the last round, he had to be content with a silver medal. One hour later and into the ring stepped Michael Carruth to face the classy Cuban Juan Hernandez Sierra in the welterweight final. Fourteen minutes later, his hand was held aloft in triumph and the nation erupted.

Left

Michael Carruth pictured at the Olympic Final in 1992 with Cuban Juan Hernandez Sierra

Carruth had broken the mould in Irish boxing. He had finally claimed an Olympic boxing gold medal for his country. His life would never be the same again as the magical moment was greeted with euphoria back home. The Dubliner was the first to climb the pinnacle and his name will never be erased from the pages of Irish boxing history.

Michael Carruth was born in the Greenhills area of Dublin on 9th July 1967. He, along with Martin and William, was one of a set of triplets born to Austin and Joan Carruth. In total, the Carruth family consisted of ten children. It was through his father that Michael first acquired an interest in boxing.

"Dad looked after the Greenhills Boxing Club along with John Whitehead, who was the treasurer," said Carruth. "I was about five or six when I first went up to the club and I had my first competitive bout at the age of eight."

The young Dubliner soon moved to the famous Drimnagh Boxing Club and it was there that he began to show the class that would eventually see him to Olympic glory.

"At that time, the Drimnagh club was the best club in Ireland and I always looked up to fighters such as Phil Sutcliffe as a hero. I won a few Dublin and Leinster titles back then, and I always had my Dad in my corner and he was a great help."

In 1985 Carruth had enlisted in the Irish Army and was based in Rathmines in Dublin. By 1986 he had qualified for his first Irish senior final, where he lost out to Tommy Tobin. However, a year later he lifted the first national crown, by seeing off Sylvester Furlong at the National Stadium. A call-up for international honours soon followed and he made his debut in a green vest at the 1987 European Championships, where he was eliminated at the quarterfinal stage by the talented Russian, Orzubek Nazarov.

In 1988, with a place at the Seoul Olympic Games at stake, Carruth reclaimed his Irish title and was chosen as Ireland's representative in the lightweight division. A unanimous victory over his Japanese opponent, Satoru Higashi, in the first round was followed by bitter disappointment when he was stopped by the Swede, George Cramme.

"The Swede caught me in the first and I dropped to the canvas but I knew that I had been vulnerable going to those Games. I didn't know how to react as I had never been down before, and my composure just left me and I was stopped. Seoul taught me a sore lesson; that I would never go to a major games again unless I was totally prepared, and that meant fighting at my natural weight."

A trip to the 1990 World Boxing Championships in Cuba saw Carruth eliminated by Havana-born Candelario Duvergel after a tough encounter. However, a trip to Bombay for a further leg of the world championships was halted after Carruth broke his hand in training. With the hand on the mend, Carruth now set his sights on the Barcelona Olympic Games, and after a box-off win over his good friend Billy Walsh, he entered the qualifying stage for the Olympics. Eventually Ireland sent a team of six fighters to those games where glory awaited.

"I had the bitter experience of Seoul to drive me on as I trained for the Barcelona Games. Both Wayne and I had been to an Olympics before and that stood for us in the competition. The Irish team in 1992 had some pedigree as there was Wayne and I, Paul Douglas, John Lowey, Paul Griffin and Paul Buttimer," said Carruth. "I was going out there with the sole intention of taking gold, for if you were not prepared psychologically, then you should just stay at home. I was determined mentally and physically and I felt confident."

The Irish team had a poor start as Carruth joined RTÉ's Jimmy Magee as co-commentator as Drimnagh's Paul Griffin entered the ring to face Steven Chungu of Zambia.

Left

Michael Carruth fights his way through to the medals at the Barcelona Olympics in 1992

"It was live on the air back home and Paul was dropped by a cracking punch and Jimmy asked [me] to comment on the knock-down. It was hard to keep my composure as Paul, a good friend and club mate, was on the canvas and I just wanted to scream at him to get up. Paul lost and that shook me, as did the defeats of Paul Buttimer and Kevin McBride, so it was a poor start."

Michael Carruth was afforded a bye in the opening round of his division. He had to wait a full week to enter the ring when he was drawn to meet Maselino Tuifao from Samoa.

"The banter was great among the Irish team, and they were telling me that I would have no problem against the Samoan, who they said was probably a rugby player in disguise. I had previously sparred with this guy, so I knew it was well within my capability to beat him."

The Barcelona Games, in an attempt to avoid controversial decisions, were the first to introduce computerised scoring. Carruth's fight against the Samoan was won easily on a scoreline of eleven points to two.

"In hindsight, the fight against Tuifao was a handy draw and it eased me into the competition: but my next opponent, the German Andreas Otto, was a class act as he was a European and world silver medallist. This was the same man who had beaten me three years previously on a scoreline of eighteen to one, so I knew he would be tough. When I looked back on that previous fight with Otto, I knew that the score was not a reflection of the bout, and I swore that if he met me again that he'd remember the tear-up he had had with the red-haired Irishman. I recall that he was quite tall and I got at him at close quarters in the Olympic bout, and forty seconds in I caught him in the body with the right and he was given a count. I thought to myself that this was going to be easier than I thought, and I got stuck into the fight and was well ahead at the end of the first. I got hammered into him and then it got scrappy and it ended up at six each as the fight ended. It went to the independent judges but I could just tell that he knew he was beaten and I got the decision."

Half an hour before Carruth's victory, Wayne McCullough had defeated Mohammed Sabo of Nigeria. By Thursday evening, Ireland had two fighters into the semi-finals and had assured itself of at least two bronze medals but rather than basking in the glory, Carruth recalled that the Belfast man had other things on his mind.

"Wayne is the greatest athlete I have ever met, and he said to me when I returned to the village that we should go out for a run. I was absolutely knackered but Wayne was addicted, so I warned him that I would go only if he went at my pace. So there we were in the heat running around the village just an hour after we had both assured ourselves of bronze medals."

With both boxers through, Wayne McCullough was on the end of some minor intimidation by his semi-final opponent, Lee Gwang-Sik.

"Wayne was in the canteen in the village when the Korean guy walked up behind him and hit him a kick. I was the captain of the team and when I heard about it I said to Wayne that I would look after it. For the next day or so Wayne, Kevin McBride, Paul Douglas and I walked around the village and any Korean athlete we saw we stopped them, and asked Wayne was this the guy who had booted him? Luckily we never ran into him."

Retribution or not, the quest for glory had gained momentum and in the semi-final, Carruth was drawn to meet Arkhom Chenglai from Thailand. The favourite from Cuba, Hernandez, had stopped his Swedish opponent in the second round of their quarterfinal and was a sure bet to make the final. For Carruth, the date that Saturday morning with the Cuban was the only match that mattered.

"The semi-final was a bit of a let-down, in boxing terms, as I was always on top and expected a harder fight," he recalled. "Looking back now I feel that Chenglai had been content to get his bronze medal, and the prospect of a clash with the Cuban did not appeal to him. I could sense that he wasn't up for the fight, but I was really physically and mentally on fire by that stage and swung the decision by eleven points to four."

Wayne McCullough had won his bout earlier against the Korean, Lee Gwang-Sik – who had a tendency to use his feet in the canteen – and that meant that two Irish boxers were into the finals on the following Saturday morning.

"The atmosphere had snowballed in the Irish camp but I felt no more pressure than usual," said Carruth. "The Cuban guy, Hernandez, the silver medallist at Seoul, was waiting for me and he was an overwhelming favourite. That Saturday, I was up early with Wayne and we both had our 'Last Supper' together. I have always had this superstition, which made me go to an arena before a fight and get a feel for the canvas, just to assure me. So, I got the bus in with Wayne and we were first to be weighed in and checked through for the fights. The first thing we noticed, however, was that there was a considerable Irish contingent building up in the arena with tricolours everywhere. The Irish all decided to take over a section of the arena near the ring, so the officials had no chance of keeping the original seating arrangements. I decided to go in and see Wayne as he was being gloved up, but as soon as I went into the changing area I was not allowed out to the arena again. There were Cubans everywhere and all the Irish officials left with Wayne, so I was all alone in the changing rooms as the action began."

By 9.00am, the nation held its breath. Wayne McCullough's bout saw the Belfast man lose the opening two rounds to the Cuban Joel Casamayor. A brave fight back in the last saw the score at the end of the contest end up sixteen-eight in favour of the Cuban. It was silver for McCullough; Ireland awaited the Dubliner.

"Wayne's defeat did not increase the pressure on me for, if anything, it meant that I had nothing to lose," said Carruth. "I just caught Wayne's last round from the tunnel and after that it was up to me. I bandaged up and my Dad came into me and he looked at me in the eyes and said 'Your legs, son...your legs will win you that gold medal!' Having my dad in the corner was the ultimate experience for anyone to have, especially on such a stage."

In December 1956, Dubliner Ronnie Delaney had claimed Ireland's last Olympic gold medal in the 1500 metres event. For Carruth, that achievement was in his thoughts as he waited to enter the arena.

"We went out into the tunnel and as I waited I breathed deeply and turned to my Dad and said: 'Dad, Ronnie Delaney's time's up' as I was sure that I was going to win. Later my Dad told me that when I had said that to him every hair on his neck had stood on end. I was about to play the greatest 'chess match' in Irish boxing history."

Part of RTÉ's broadcast that morning included live link-ups from the packed living room of the Carruth family home. Irish Olympic silver medallist Fred Tiedt was joined by Michael's friend and rival, Billy Walsh, in the packed room. Paula, Michael's wife of three months, peeped through her fingers nervously on the sofa. The preliminaries over, the bell sounded for the first round.

"I remember I entered what athletes call 'The Zone'," said Carruth. "For twelve minutes, I was in a trance, lost in my concentration with just one thing on my mind. I was not going to get involved in a brawl with him, so I stood off Hernandez and scored a couple of times in a round that went in a flash. I got back to the corner and looked up at the scoreboard and saw that I was leading four-three after the first; it was then that I began to believe!"

Twenty seconds into the second round, Carruth suffered a serious setback to his ambitions, when the referee gave the Dubliner a warning for holding; a caution that cost him three points.

"I looked at the referee and you couldn't print what I said to him. I knew that I had to get right back at him [Hernandez] and towards the end of the round I caught him with two sweet hooks that I knew had scored."

However, at the end of the round, with Carruth despondent on his stool, he looked up to see that the scores were tied at eight points each. The gods were on his side. Back home in Dublin the tension was rising in the Carruths' living room as Michael now stood just three minutes away from history. In the Cuban corner, Hernandez was being given a rollicking by his seconds, who knew that their man was in deep, deep trouble.

As Carruth recalled, while he was fighting the most important bout of his career, the strangest of thoughts came into his head.

"My Dad was in a frenzy telling me how to fight, but all I could think about was how the family back home was feeling."

The five hundred Irish fans were now in orbit as the two fighters stood for the last round. Carruth's confidence was sky-high.

"The bell went and I got a surge of energy and immediately went straight at Hernandez. They were screaming at me in the corner to stay off him and box to the plan, so I stepped off him," said Carruth. "I was ahead and the Cuban had obviously not been prepared for this situation and was unaware how to fight me. I thought to myself that I must hold on as I was clearly ahead. It was not pretty, but I frustrated him and held on for dear life. He was coming at me but I was able to land counter punches on the break and they were counting. I remember I saw the clock and it read sixteen seconds to go. Eventually, the bell went and I just fell into my father's arms in the corner as the Irish crowd went wild."

The moment of truth was imminent but Carruth, his seconds, and the Irish crowd were confident that the medal had been won.

"I knew by their corner that they knew he had been beaten," he said. "Jack Poucher, who was a judge from Ireland – not at my fight of course – was signalling that I had got the decision by three points. We were too long-in-the-tooth to believe that and eventually the referee called us both to the ring."

Ask any boxer and he will say that you can tell how the decision in a fight has gone by the pressure a referee puts on your wrist. If he grabs it firmly, it's a good sign that he is preparing to raise it in victory when the decision is announced. A limp grip is usually a bad sign. For Carruth, the referee gripped his hand in the ring with a very weak grip.

"I thought to myself 'Oh God no, not again!' The announcer started off in Spanish and I was following as best I could what he was saying. I had rehearsed this moment since I had first entered the Greenhills Club at six years of age, and that moment was now upon me."

Within seconds, Ronnie Delaney's time was indeed up. Carruth's arm was raised in triumph; the Irish crowd went wild and a million homes back home echoed to cheers. History had been made.

"Though I'm not really religious, I had intended to go down on my knees and bless myself, but that was lost in the whole euphoria," said Michael. "I just lost it and jumped for joy and the referee didn't get a chance to raise my arm as I was away. I have been through that moment a million times since it happened, and nothing will ever touch it. It was pandemonium in the arena and when I got back to the changing rooms it was as if the world's media was there to see me."

Half an hour later and Carruth was awarded his medal in a proud arena.

"I dedicated the medal to my young nephew Gary [the Carruths' first grandchild], who had drowned tragically at Blessington Lakes. At the end of the fight as I am going over to the Cuban, I looked at the sky and that was me acknowledging my nephew for helping me through and inspiring me. The first thing I couldn't believe about the medal was the sheer weight of it around my shoulders. Pandemonium again erupted in the changing rooms but I was exhausted and my Dad asked me what I was doing for the rest of the day? I said that I fancied a beer or two and sure enough after two beers I was really tired. Dad said not to drink anymore that day as it was important that I savoured the whole experience, for it was the greatest day of my life. Eventually, after many hours I got a phone call through to the family home. The phone had not stopped since I had won the medal, and when I got through my sister Orla answered and asked who was calling? I said: 'Michael', to which she replied 'Michael who?' When she realised it was me she started crying, and then Siobhan my other sister took the phone and she started crying also."

The next morning, Carruth and McCullough faced the media again in a packed press centre. The gold medallist recalled one question from a journalist – the answer to which confused the assembled press pack.

"The guy asked me had Hernandez been the hardest-ever fighter I had faced," said Michael. "I thought about this and after a while gave my response, which was 'Nah, Hernandez wasn't the hardest, for have you ever heard of a guy from Wexford called Billy Walsh?' The media all began to scratch their heads but Billy was, let me tell you, a lot harder than Hernandez."

The medallists' return to Dublin was a triumph. McCullough and Carruth spent the next number of months travelling to civic receptions across Ireland. Summer turned to autumn, autumn to winter, and the moment was still fresh in the minds of Ireland's populace. Michael Carruth stayed in the army, tried his hand at the professional game and retired from boxing in 2000. The highlight of 1992 was never to be repeated.

I met Michael on a bright February day in a bar in Coolock on the north Side of Dublin. He is still a very fit man, whose entry into the bar was greeted by appreciative nods and winks from the imbibers present. A true son of Dublin he will always be. His moment of glory may have happened fifteen years before our meeting but he relates the story as if it were just yesterday.

That 'Carruth Moment' ranks up there with 'That O'Leary Penalty', 'That Ray Houghton Goal' or, for those who can remember, 'That Ronnie Delaney Gold'. He was the first and, hopefully, not the last, of our Olympic boxing champions. However, in real terms, sad as it may seem, it may be some years before an Irish boxer will enter an Olympic boxing final and have the chance to say: 'Michael Carruth, your time's up!'

Wayne McCullough

"What more can I say son? Absolute Genius!"

There lives in Belfast, in a part of the Upper Crumlin Road known locally as the 'Turn of the Road', a man in his eighties by the name of Al Gibson. He is a proud man steeped in Ulster boxing history and wisdom, having enjoyed a fine record as a professional in bygone days. Al Gibson is a walking encyclopaedia of Ulster and Irish boxing. He speaks with passion of the sport he loves. As he rhymes off the names of the fighters whom he has known over the decades, he speaks in hushed tones as he describes their evident greatness.

When he talks of the recent past, he gets to the name of one Wayne McCullough and pauses. Then, with a sharp intake of breath, Al Gibson's eyes widen, as he takes of his glasses and says with a knowing smile:

"Now, Wayne McCullough, there's a proud boy and a half!" says Al. "He has it all and proved it on the very highest stages, and when I think of that fight in Japan. What more can I say son? Absolute Genius!"

Wise words from a gentleman of Ulster boxing, who lives not two miles from the street where Wayne McCullough was born on 7th July 1970. Percy Street, between Belfast's Shankill and Falls Roads, was in the eye of the political storm that had erupted in the city that previous August. Indeed, the week of Wayne's birth coincided with a pivotal event of the Troubles known as the Lower Falls Curfew. Community relations in the city were at a low and worsened considerably over the succeeding years. The McCullough family, which consisted of three brothers and four sisters, soon relocated to the Highfield Estate at the top of the Shankill Road. Highfield was situated perfectly for young boxers as the Albert Foundry Club stood off the nearby West Circular Road. At the age of seven, Wayne found himself at the club under the watchful eye of trainer Harry Robinson.

"My two brothers Noel and Alan were boxing, and I couldn't wait to join them," he recalled. "I was about seven when I started and Harry Robinson guided me in the early days when I must have had over a hundred fights by the age of twelve. Davy Larmour, who went on to be a British bantamweight champion, was at the club as a professional and he was always someone to look up to."

At the age of eleven, McCullough passed his eleven plus examination and left Springhill Primary to join the local secondary school, Cairnmartin. His career in the ring continued unabated, with his sole aim to turn professional at the earliest opportunity. In 1986, the Highfield boxer won his first Ulster senior boxing crown, with a convincing win over the vastly experienced PJ O'Halloran. An international debut against Scotland followed in which he stopped his opponent Donald Glass.

By 1988 Wayne McCullough had acquired Ulster and Irish titles in the light-flyweight division. At eighteen years of age, he was on his way to Seoul as the youngest representative of Ireland's Olympic squad. It had been traditional for the youngest member of the squad to be asked to carry the Irish Tricolour at the opening ceremony, but, for a lad from the greater Shankill area, this honour was not as straightforward as it seemed.

Boxing is an all-Ireland sport and always has been. The border is an irrelevancy in the sport, as it is in rugby, cricket and hockey. However, the sight of a lad from the loyalist Highfield Estate parading the flag of the Irish Republic became a political football in the North.

"The whole flag issue was blown out of proportion, as I was doing it for sporting reasons and nothing else," said Wayne. "Pat McCrory, our coach, came to me and asked if I would carry the flag, which to be truthful put me in bit of a position. I said that I would do it for sporting reasons alone, and entering that stadium is one of the most unforgettable moments of my life."

In his opening bout, McCullough was paired with the lanky Ugandan fighter, Fred Mutuweta. The Belfast fighter was awarded a unanimous decision after he floored the African in the second round. In his next fight, Wayne was drawn against the Canadian Scotty Olsen, the reigning Commonwealth champion. After receiving two standing counts during the bout, McCullough's Olympic dream was at an end. On his return, the Shankill Road threw a party for its favourite son: nobody mentioned the carrying of the flag.

After Seoul, McCullough was persuaded to bide his time before entering the paid ranks. A trip to the 1990 Commonwealth Games in Auckland, New Zealand, saw him victorious in the flyweight division, where he defeated Nokuthula Tshabangu of Zimbabwe for the gold medal. More memorable than McCullough's win was the medal ceremony, which did not go as smoothly as the organisers had anticipated.

As Wayne was standing on the podium, with his gold medal around his neck, the recording of 'Danny Boy' jammed in the tape player to a deafening silence in the arena. However, cometh the hour, cometh the man, and into the ring jumped Northern Ireland expatriate and Games official Bob Gibson. With microphone in hand, he sang the

traditional air unaccompanied to steal the show and create a long lasting friendship with Wayne. Indeed, soon after, Bob Gibson was the special guest of honour at Belfast's Europa Hotel as Wayne fought at a Golden Gloves evening, where he repeated his feat to an appreciative crowd.

Soon after he returned from the Games, Wayne was to meet his soul mate and future wife Cheryl Rennie. In November 1990, McCullough travelled to the World Cup in Bombay where he battled his way to claim a bronze medal, again at the expense of his Seoul opponent Fred Mutuweta. McCullough duly followed this achievement with a trip to the 1991 World Championships in Sydney. There, he blazed a trail through his division and was unlucky to lose in the quarterfinals against the eventual silver medallist, Enrique Carrion from Cuba.

At the Barcelona Olympics in 1992, McCullough's experience and pedigree made him favourite to lift a medal. He travelled with high expectations as Ireland's bantamweight representative in August that year. The swimmer Michelle Smith carried the flag on that occasion, and it was to prove to be a memorable Games for Irish boxing.

As the Irish boxing team were eliminated one by one, both McCullough and team captain, Michael Carruth, found themselves fighting for gold medals on finals' morning. McCullough in his opening bout had seen off – yes, you've guessed it – the Ugandan Fred Mutuweta on a comfortable twenty-eight to seven scoreline. He followed that victory with a win over the Iranian Ahmad Ghanim and was then drawn to meet Mohammed Sabo of Nigeria.

McCullough negotiated that fight with relative ease, and had assured himself of at least a bronze medal. In his semi-final bout, he was drawn to meet the Korean Lee Gwang-Sik and nine minutes of pugilistic warfare ensued. McCullough's all-action style and volume of punches won the day on a scoreline of twenty-one to sixteen points. Both he and Carruth were now into the finals. Ireland, north and south, waited with bated breath.

Wayne's fight with the classy Cuban Joel Casamayor proved to be a painful experience, in more ways than one. A typically slow start by McCullough saw him trail six-one after the first round. In the second, a scoring jab to Wayne's face by the Cuban caused him serious discomfort.

"He hit me with the jab and I felt the pain in my cheekbone," recalled Wayne. "My face was numb and in reality I should not have fought on."

Trailing by ten points to two at the end of the second, McCullough bravely went out for the last and out-boxed the Cuban convincingly. Despite a storming comeback he was defeated on a scoreline of fourteen to eight.

175

"I was determined to finish the fight and by the end there was blood coming out of the corner of my eye. I had lost after giving it my best shot but the damage to my face was a huge price to pay as I didn't fight again for a year."

An hour after his defeat, Wayne watched Michael Carruth make history.

"I remember that I saw Michael's fight on the television in the medical room in the arena as I was taking a drugs test; it was a truly special moment."

With an Olympic silver medal to add to his other amateur accolades, Wayne McCullough had gone as far as he could in unpaid boxing. Unfortunately, for him, the glory days of Barry McGuigan had passed and the professional ranks in Belfast were going through a lull in the early 1990s. His only option was to leave his native city to pursue a professional career in the United States under the management an American television executive called Matt Tinley. A move to Las Vegas followed for Wayne and Cheryl, and his rise through the world bantamweight rankings was swift.

By the turn of 1995, under the legendary trainer Eddie Futch, McCullough had gone fifteen fights undefeated. A victory over Geronimo Cardoz in March that year secured him a crack in Japan at the reigning World Boxing Championship holder Yasuei Yakushiji. Only the keenest and closest accompanied the Belfast boy, and to the serenade of Bob Gibson singing 'Danny Boy', he left his Tokyo hotel for his ultimate moment. Dedication and training in the freezing Albert Foundry gym during the 1970s had finally brought McCullough to his ultimate hour. By the time he returned to the hotel, he would be the champion of the world.

At the end of twelve fabulous rounds, the two boxers, bruised and battered, came to the centre of the ring to await their fate. To Wayne, the Japanese announcer went through the formalities which made sense to all but one hundred of the 10,000 crowd. After an age, the announcer paused and roared out his rough translation of the name McCullough. The boy from the Shankill had just become the champion of the world. Tears, joy and pandemonium erupted in the ring as the dream became reality.

In many ways, it can be argued that the fact that McCullough went to Yakushiji's hometown to fight for and win the world title

elevated what he achieved. On the other side of the world, in an intimidating arena, he was to fight the greatest twelve rounds that any Irish fighter had ever fought. One thinks of John Caldwell fighting Eder Jofre in Sao Paulo in 1962 as the only comparable experience for an Irish fighter. Caldwell lost that night; in 1995, McCullough won.

In December 1995 Wayne McCullough defended his title at the King's Hall, the shrine of Belfast boxing. That night in front of a packed hall he stopped the Dane, Johnny Bredahl, in the seventh round. The homecoming as champion was complete.

McCullough defended his title again in March 1996 with a points victory over Jose Luis Bueno, before vacating the belt and moving up a weight to challenge Daniel Zaragoza for the world super-bantamweight crown. That fight in January 1997 was a tremendous battle. The bout went to a split decision and McCullough lost narrowly. It was his first defeat and he was devastated by the experience. That fight left McCullough with a broken jaw, minus two wisdom teeth. However, even darker days lay ahead.

In 1998, McCullough fought Naseem Hamed in Atlantic City for the IBO world featherweight title. A points defeat for the Belfast man was a considerable setback in his attempt to climb the world rankings. In October 1999 he fought Erik Morales for the super-bantamweight crown, losing again on points.

In October 2000, a fight was arranged in Belfast for McCullough. Prior to the fight he attended the Royal Victoria Hospital for his yearly brain-scan, which was obligatory under the British Boxing Board's rules. Two days before the fight, he was told that a cyst had been discovered on his brain. In essence, a punch to the head could end his life.

"That was the lowest point in my life," recalled Wayne. "Cheryl and I could only sit about the house and I became very depressed. But I am a fighter and it was a case of trying to establish the extent of the problem and making sure that it was addressed."

In Las Vegas, the Nevada Boxing Commission suggested that McCullough consulted with a specialist based at the Department of Neurosurgery at University of California in Los Angeles. After an examination, he was advised that the cyst was not actually on his brain, but in the narrow space between the brain and the skull, and this should not impact on McCullough's career. Accordingly, the Nevada Commission relicensed McCullough and, in 2002, he once again entered the ring, to face Alvin Brown, whom he stopped in two rounds. Eventually the British Board relented and McCullough was authorised to fight in Britain. Wayne McCullough's last fight took place in July 2005, when he fought Oscar Larios for the second time and lost on points again.

Left

Wayne McCullough squares up to a show-boating Naseem Hamed at the Featherweight Championship, Atlantic City

Living and training fighters in Las Vegas has given Wayne McCullough a nice life in the sport he loves. After all his trials and tribulations it is not surprising that he had found great faith in God.

"Sure I miss Belfast but it was boxing that took me here and we are settled in Las Vegas. Cheryl took me to her church in Belfast soon after we started dating, and my faith is something that has grown with me ever since. When you enter a ring you really need someone to look after you and for me that someone is God. I am good friends with George Foreman, who is a preacher, and he has been a great influence on me."

Wayne's career in boxing continues unabated. He has scaled the heights in both amateur and professional ranks. His memories of his early days are vivid; even though Las Vegas is a long way from the Belfast he grew up in.

"Belfast was a hard city to grow up in, especially if you were from the generation that I came from," he said. "I was lucky as the fact is that boxing bridged all the religious stuff, and we trained and fought anywhere in the city. Now I have a number of Mexican fighters in my gym and they are so like the Belfast fighters. For what they lack in skill, they more than make up for in guts and determination. These boys have a survival instinct: that same instinct has helped Belfast and Ireland produce so many good fighters. However, I think the Michael Carruth was a true great – if not the greatest – amateur to come out of Ireland. Having won a gold medal at the Olympics, he did what no other boxer from Ireland did. I read a recent article where he stated that he thought me going to Japan to win the belt was the best achievement of any Irish boxer. The feeling's mutual as his achievement in Barcelona was immense."

Wayne McCullough, his wife Cheryl and daughter Wynona live a contented life in Las Vegas. We have not heard the last of him in boxing terms. He has been an exemplary and brave fighter who represented the best attributes of the sport.

Steve Collins

The Celtic Warrior

Where were you on the night of Saturday, 18th May 1995? If you had a passing interest in the world of boxing, you were most likely glued to the television for the first instalment of Steve Collins' clash with the strutting arrogance that was Chris Eubank. The town of Mill Street in Co. Cork, with its magnificent Green Glens Arena packed to the rafters, was to witness the highest of drama as the showman met the hardman in a never to be forgotten battle. Drama, 'codology' and sheer brutality was to ensue as Collins dethroned the-then reigning World Boxing Organisation super middleweight champion with a sublime display of aggression. Eubank may have been self-styled as "Simply the Best" but it was Collins who took that mantle and engraved his name forever on the list of Irish boxing greats.

Steve Collins was born in Cabra in Dublin on 21st July 1964. The sport of boxing was in his blood from an early age as his uncle, Jack O'Rourke, won three Irish senior titles during the sixties, while his father, Pascal, was a very accomplished fighter in his day also. Another uncle, Terry Collins, had a notable victory over the East End gangster Reggie Kray to his name so it was natural that Steve Collins would enter the ring at some stage. In 1986, as an amateur, Steve emulated his uncle Jack by winning the Irish senior middleweight crown but due to the weak Irish economy he left Ireland to make a living in Boston. Collins took the well-worn route of most Irish immigrants to the States back then and made a living through a number of low-paid jobs to keep his family solvent.

While living in Massachusetts, Collins turned professional and joined the world-famous gym of the Petronelli brothers who had in their ranks none other than Marvin Hagler. Under various trainers, Steve's first paid fight saw him stop the comparative novice Julio Mercado in the third round of their contest in October 1986. Six further victories followed within eighteen months and a fight with Sam Storey for the Irish middleweight title was set for Boston in March 1988. The previously undefeated Storey was dispatched on a unanimous decision after ten gruelling rounds and five straight victories thereafter saw Collins matched with Kevin "Killer" Watts, who at that stage was rated number 5 in the world, for the USBA middleweight crown. That fight in Atlantic City in 1989 saw Collins in classic slugging style and he took he title despite being dropped to the canvas in the eleventh round. Despite ploughing a lonely furrow in the United States, Collins was gaining valuable exposure on network television and quite a following in the Boston area.

A successful defence of his middleweight title led to a crack – when Michael Watson was unable to fulfil the original match – against the legendary Jamaican Mike McCallum in 1990 for his

WBA middleweight title. While he had the 'home' advantage of a Boston venue, Collins went the distance only to lose his unbeaten record on a unanimous decision. However, Collins had given the Jamaican such a battle that he expressed his reluctance to put his title on the line again against the Celtic Warrior. Professional boxing is a cruel sport and in the aftermath of the defeat to McCallum, Collins found himself back making a living behind a bar in Boston. Undeterred, the Dubliner continued to make his mark and in August 1989 he knocked out Fermin Chirino in the sixth round of their bout at the Boston Sheraton hotel. After a further win in Boston against the tough Eddie Hall, Collins decided to move home and signed up with the Belfast gym of Barney Eastwood.

In April 1992, Collins secured a second crack at the then vacant WBA middleweight title when he was matched against Reggie 'Sweet' Johnson in a fight scheduled for East Rutherford, New Jersey. The title had been vacated when Mike McCallum had opted to fight James Toney for the IBF crown and with Collins ranked as number one contender and Johnson number two, a battle royal was anticipated. At the age of twenty-eight, Collins was at his peak and the fight with Johnson was a classic with Collins considered unlucky to lose on a majority decision.

"The death of my father at the time of the fight was a low point in my life and affected me very deeply. The Johnson defeat was so devastating for me. I had a lot going on a personal level and it was hard to come to terms with it. I really had to dig deep to find the inspiration to continue my career after that."

It was the second defeat of his career and his next outing was against the undoubted class of Sumbu Kalambay for the EBU championship in his adopted home of Italy. A third defeat was recorded – again on a split decision – by the Celtic Warrior in Italy and soon after Collins split with the Eastwood stable with amicable agreement and signed up with the London-based Barry Hearne. Within a year, Collins had captured the WBA Penta-Continental middleweight title with a knockout over the South African Gerhard Botes at Earl's Court in London. Collins' star was rising in Britain and he was to capture the WBO middleweight crown a year later when he knocked out the champion Chris Pyatt. Going into that bout, Collins was considered to be the underdog as the classy Pyatt was defending his title for the fourth time. However, Collins made no mistake with a display of controlled aggression to stop the champion in the fifth round.

At this time in Britain, Sky Sports was making its mark with its football and boxing coverage. The super-middleweight scene was flourishing with Chris Eubank, Michael Watson and Nigel Benn all setting the pace on the satellite channel during the decade. In 1990, the Brighton-based Eubank defeated Nigel Benn by a knock-out in Birmingham to claim the world super middleweight crown and he went on to defend it twice against Michael Watson. The second fight with Watson ended in near tragedy after Eubank caught his challenger with an uppercut that caused a brain injury which ended Watson's career. Many observers felt that Eubank, who considered quitting the ring after the Watson fight, was a different fighter after that ill-fated clash. His reluctance in future bouts to go for a knockout became evident and his style became one of going the distance to grind out points' victories.

Irish interest in the super middleweight scene was to occur initially in the shape of Belfast's Ray Close. As Irish and European Boxing Union champion, the Barney Eastwood managed Close had fought Eubank to a standstill in Glasgow in 1993 and came away with a draw. The scene was set for a rematch in the King's Hall in Belfast May 1994 and a packed arena witnessed a bloodthirsty encounter that the champion shaded in a split verdict. The fight in Belfast did not resolve the matter and a third episode in the Close and Eubank affair was arranged for March 1995. Unfortunately, a routine brain scan on Close showed up some irregularities that forced the hand of the British Boxing Board of Control to ban the Belfast fighter. However, waiting in the wings for his chance was Steve Collins and the fight with Eubank was arranged for Mill Street in Cork on St Patrick's weekend 1995.

Irish sport in the 1990s threw up a number of notable occasions in which, if not present, the general public can recall with absolute clarity where they where when the event took place. The famous David O'Leary penalty against Romania in the 1990 World Cup, together with Michael Carruth's triumph in the 1992 Olympic Games, were just two occasions that had the nation glued to the television; the Eubank versus Collins match was to be the third of the decade. Tickets for the clash at the 9,000 seater arena in rural Cork had sold out within hours of going on sale and with Sky Sports hyping the fight to the heavens the scene for the drama was set.

Showmanship is one of the great traits of professional boxing and the then unbeaten Chris Eubank was the ultimate showman. His style outside the ring was ridiculed as he adopted the persona of the monocled country gentleman. Indeed, he had bought for himself the aristocratic title of Lord Brighton, such was his devotion to the class system. Collins was having none of it and went out to match the showman in the mind games. A few

days prior to the clash, word seeped out that Collins had visited a number of hypnotherapists to help him with his preparations for Eubank. Collins let it be known that he had been 'programmed' to fire two punches for every one thrown by Eubank and the war of minds was on.

As the fighters entered the ring, the psychological war had been won by Collins. Sitting in his corner, listening obliviously to his Walkman, Collins displayed the greatest of indifference as Eubank made his usual over the top journey to the ring. To say that Eubank was affected deeply by the whole episode would be a correct assumption.

The fight began in whirlwind style with the undefeated Eubank posing and choosing his shots against the game Dubliner. Collins kept chasing the champion and had the arena in uproar as he gave Eubank a torrid time. By the tenth round, Eubank seemed to be slightly ahead on points when he threw caution to the wind and floored Collins with a right. With Collins hurt, Eubank was unable to finish his opponent and Collins stormed back.

With the capacity crowd now on their feet, Collins continued his onslaught and the sight of Eubank's trainer Ronnie Davies slapping his face in the corner told the tale. Collins chased and harried Eubank and exposed his showboating time and time again. The bell went and the decision went to the judges and Collins was declared the winner. Eubank had lost his unbeaten record and Collins was now the star of Irish sport. In the rematch, the following September, Collins was a comfortable winner. The unanimous verdict in Collins' favour led to Eubank quitting the sport and Collins now set his sights on defending the title.

"That was undoubtedly the highlight of my career," said Steve. "You cannot believe how intense things were between us and there was no love lost I can tell you. I got so much pleasure in that victory and it was sweet."

Two further defences for Collins followed within nine months. A win at the Point Depot over Cornelius Carr was followed by a knockout victory at Mill Street over Neville Brown. However, Nigel Benn was still a contender for a crack at Collins' title and the two were matched in July 1996 in Manchester. Collins won the fight when Benn retired on his stool at the start of the sixth round. A rematch was set for November but Benn was not the fighter he had once been and retired in his corner after six rounds.

In February 1997, Collins retained his title when his fight with Fred Seillier was stopped due to cuts sustained by the challenger. At the Kelvin Hall in Glasgow in July, Collins, despite being down in the first round, stormed back to stop Craig Cummings in the third round of their bout. That was Collins' seventh successful defence of his title and he seemed to be untouchable in the division.

In Collins' next defence, he was matched with Joe Calzaghe, but the Celtic Warrior was forced to withdraw at a late stage before the bout due to injury. The WBO then took severe action and stripped Collins of his title and he duly retired. In a parting shot, Collins claimed to have lost his motivation to step into the ring. He felt that his only viable option had been a unification bout against Roy Jones Jr, but this had been denied and a fight with Calzaghe would do nothing for him.

Two years later Collins decided to come out of retirement to face Joe Calzaghe. The clash with Calzaghe was arranged for Cardiff on 5th June, but Collins blacked out during sparring with the British middleweight champion Howard Eastman and underwent a CAT scan. The result was that doctors told Collins that a further blow to the head could result in his death. Collins had no option left and he retired from the ring for the second time.

"It was over and I just had to accept it. I had enjoyed my career and been lucky enough to work with Marvin Hagler my all-time hero. He and Jake La Motta were the two men I always tried to emulate and my style was based on them."

Although the glory years of the mid-1990s are remembered fondly, the probability was that Collins, Eubank and Benn were not at their peak when they formed their rivalries. The WBO title was a class away from the WBA and WBC titles, yet it served its purpose and kept the British and Irish public enthralled. Steve Collins was an honest strong contender, and proved to be an honest strong champion. Today he remains a personality of note in Dublin and Ireland.

Tough as nails, he once boasted that Readymix Concrete wanted to sponsor his chin. A showman, a fighter and without a doubt a hard man, Steve Collins caught the imagination and admiration of the British and Irish public and is still fondly remembered.

Left

Steve Collins throws a right at Chris Eubank for the WBO Supermiddleweight title, Cork

Gerry Storey

Bravery, Boxing and the Belfast Blitz

The name of Gerry Storey has been woven through this book like the stitching which binds its chapters together. He has overseen the careers of a significant number of boxers, many of whose stories are told within. His record as a coach has guaranteed him the highest respect from all across Ireland, and in 2005 he was honoured on the world stage.

Storey has taken several Irish teams to Olympic Games, countless squads to Commonwealth Games and even taught the paramilitaries in Long Kesh how to box. He has been the beacon of light that saw the Holy Family Boxing Club in Belfast's New Lodge Road survive and thrive throughout the Troubles. The club has produced over one hundred Irish champions, numerous Olympians and three outright winners of the Lonsdale Belt. Storey brought his magic touch to inspire lads to the heights, while retaining his unassuming nature throughout.

Born in Artillery Street in 1936, to Bobby and Nellie, Gerry Storey's family soon moved the short distance to Vere Street, which was adjacent to the York Street Mill. In April 1941 the area was blitzed by the German Luftwaffe, and the wall of the mill collapsed onto both Sussex and Vere Streets, killing all who had stayed in their homes. The Storey family had a very lucky escape due to Nellie Storey's sixth sense.

"We went into small bomb shelters in the houses and I remember that my mother Nellie had some sort of premonition and was never happy in the shelter," he said. "Eventually we moved out and on the night of the blitz, our former shelter was the only one that took a direct hit. It was near to the York Street Mill and its wall collapsed on to Sussex and Vere Streets and everyone was killed. I was very young but I remember the whole experience as really terrifying."

After the war, Storey joined the Holy Family gym where trainer Jimmy McStravick was his tutor. The club boasted names such as Mickey Harte, Gerry McStravick, Dickie Ferguson and Tommy Maguire. Storey was quick to learn his trade.

Storey won the Ulster and Irish titles but in his early twenties, his career was ended when an eye condition came to the attention of the medics.

"I always was having sight problems with my bad eye and the doctors told me that they were refusing to let me go on. Luckily, I was given the opportunity to help out at the club and do a bit of coaching and that's where it all began."

Left

Over-seeing talent in the ring – a lifetime's work

By 1962, Storey had progressed as a coach and took charge of his first Ulster team. In 1966 Gerry brought the Irish team to the Royal Albert Hall for a match with England. A year later, he trained the Irish team that went to the European Championships in Italy and in 1972 he oversaw the squad at the Munich Olympics.

Storey was in the corner with Ireland at every Olympics from Munich to Moscow. He saw numerous Ulster and Irish champions follow his instructions and success was second nature. His memories though are tinged with tales of poor decisions and boxing politics that saw some of Ireland's greatest deprived of a medal.

"Looking back on the Munich Olympics, I always thought that Mick Dowling was very unlucky not to get a medal. He was a real victim of politics that night in his quarterfinal battle with the Cuban, Orlando Martinez. Ireland has always had some unlucky decisions at the Games and the same went for Davy Larmour in Montreal against the American Leo Randolph. But that was all part and parcel of the game and we just accepted it and got on with things."

Belfast during the 1970s was a virtual no-go area for foreign sporting teams. However, in the Holy Family club, Storey was fighting to keep boxing alive, and sought to attract quality opposition to the city. One day, a call came to Storey from a group of loyalist paramilitaries on the Shankill Road, who wanted to promote a boxing tournament at a club. They sought Storey's advice and gave assurances regarding safety. Storey then persuaded a Canadian Select to fight an Ulster team coached by him. The night was a resounding success and further international teams followed in the Canadians' wake.

"I remember the East Germans came to the Shankill and there had been a lot of money placed on local boy Gerry Hamill to win his bout. Gerry hit his guy in the second round and he went over and the referee, who was a German also, was telling him to stay down and he would disqualify Gerry. Our interpreter overheard this and before there could be a riot, one of the local guys present grabbed the microphone and said that all bets on Hamill would be paid out in full. That kept the lid on things that night, but it was scary."

In 1978 Gerry Storey oversaw the preparations of the Northern Ireland Commonwealth Games team bound for Canada. The Ulster bantamweight champion that year was Barry McGuigan and his father, Pat, delivered the young Clones lad religiously to the Storey household every Friday.

"Barry stayed with us, and my wife Belle looked after him like another son while I prepared the team for the Games. He always was a bit special and I got to know him well, and he always wanted to do that bit extra to be the best. He won the gold at

the Games and I remember one morning coming out of Mass in Chapel Lane when Barney Eastwood approached me and asked who I could recommend to him as a professional fighter. I had no hesitation and said 'Barry McGuigan', but I told him to leave him until after the Olympic Games in Moscow and then he would be truly ready. I told Barney that if he bided his time with McGuigan then I would guarantee him that he would win the world title. Barney was surprised that I was so certain, but McGuigan was the best prospect that Ireland had and, in my view, he was even better at that stage than John Caldwell had been."

In 1985 at Loftus Road in London, Storey's prediction came true when McGuigan beat the legendary Eusebio Pedroza to lift the WBA crown.

Hugh Russell was another fighter to come from the Storey stable. As Gerry remembered, 'Little Red' was so keen to join the club that he must have lied about his age.

"Hugh was the only boy I knew who was eleven years of age four years in a row. We always had a strict rule in the club that you were not allowed to join until you were ten years old. Every time we asked Hugh for a birth certificate he would disappear for a few weeks and then he would come back when he thought that the coast was clear. I remember when he was eleven and I took him to Dublin for the all-Ireland boys' championships and he was so small on the stool that I had to use my knee to stop him falling off. He was judged to be the best boxer in the championships and that was some achievement. Hugh was an excellent boxer, very fast and skilful, and his record proved how good he was. His achievements in boxing have given me immense pleasure, when I think that I have known him since he was just another kid knocking about outside the club."

During the 1981 Hunger Strikes, Storey was asked by representatives of the Northern Ireland Office to teach the prisoners in the Maze Prison how to box.

"I was told that the prisoners on both sides had requested me specifically," said Storey. "Boxing has no politics or religion and I was more than happy to go and help out. I went in with republicans and loyalists who shared an interest in boxing, and they were a product of the times in which we lived."

Storey has never waned in his dedication to the sport of boxing and recalls the moment that he first wanted to involve himself.

"I remember seeing footage of Jersey Joe Walcott fighting Joe Louis in 1947 and I was hooked from that day. There was a shop in the New Lodge area and in the window there was a book entitled: *How to Box* by Joe Louis, and I saved up my coppers to buy it. Back then, to think that when I would become a coach – that I would meet all those champions – was something that never could have contemplated."

The Holy Family in Artillery Street stands as a testament to the dedication of Gerry Storey. Throughout the Troubles, the club welcomed fighters from all over Ireland and never was a person asked their religion. The gym, featured in the Daniel Day-Lewis film *The Boxer*, and has been an oasis of calm in a district that has suffered much since 1969.

International recognition for his selfless dedication came in 2005, when he was awarded the prestigious Sport for Good award at the Laureus World Sports Awards in Portugal. Storey joined the ranks of such notables as Roger Federer, Kelly Holmes, Ellen MacArthur and Maria Sharapova in accepting this accolade. Fittingly, the award was presented to Storey by Barry McGuigan and Marvin Hagler.

"That was a great honour for me and for Ireland, and it meant so much that people recognised the work we have done," said Storey. "I never started training kids to become the National Coach of Ireland. We wanted to offer the lads in the area an alternative to what was going on and the parents were happy that we were giving them a real alternative. When things were really bad, the parents were happy to know that their sons were safe in this club. It was an award for everyone in Irish boxing who has sacrificed themselves for the sport."

Suitably, he is reluctant to choose one fighter who he considered to have been the best he had ever handled. Even his own son Sam – one of three Lonsdale Belt winners to come out of the club – receives no preferential treatment. To Storey, all the boys were treated equally and given the same tuition regardless of class, creed or ability.

"If I wanted to pick someone who has stood out I would be very reluctant to name anyone in particular. Olympians and Lonsdale Belt winners have all been produced in this club but every achievement has been special in its own way."

On Ireland's future in international boxing, Storey agreed that the country has an uphill task ahead if it is to achieve Olympic success.

"It's going to be very hard, but it is by no means impossible. I always felt that the best way to learn is from the world leaders in the game, such as the Cubans. Training and technique along with determination will tell in the end."

As it is, the Holy Family is still striving under the watchful eye of Gerry Storey. Times have changed in Belfast and the shackles of the past have loosened. He remains as dedicated as the day he first entered his local boxing club. His selfless and proud record is one from which all coaches could learn. For the boy who survived the worst excesses of Hitler's Luftwaffe, training champions is just a way of life.

Left

Gerry Storey at the start of a promising career which was to be curtailed by eye problems.

Acknowledgements

This book has been a labour of love which has brought me great pleasure in its compiling. It would never have come to fruition had not have been for the kind and generous assistance of so many, a number of whom I would wish to thank. Initially, I would pay tribute to each and every personality whose story is contained within these pages. Their kindness and help was never in question and I am grateful to them.

To my father, Tony Flynn, whose knowledge and chauffeuring skills were a joy to behold, I would record my gratitude. Mr Liam McBrinn, my father-in-law, was a mine of information who kept the facts straight, as he perused each story diligently.

The staff at *The Irish News*, especially Thomas Hawkins, Ann McManus and Hugh Russell, were very kind and helpful in my research. In addition, I would pay tribute to the staff at the *Andersonstown News* and Mairtin O'Muilleoir and Conor McLoughlin in particular. Other journalists and media stalwarts whom I would like to mention are the legend that is Mr Jack Magowan, Paul Kelly, and the BBC's Adam Coates, Brian Johnston and Padraig Coyle. Also, Paul Carson at the photographic library in the *Belfast Telegraph* was always a pleasure to deal with.

To Pat McCrory and Jack Monaghan, I would record my appreciation for your advice and comment. To my former work colleague, Mr John Goodall, I am eternally grateful. John is a master of the English language whose undoubted skill in this field is bettered only by his kind nature and wonderful personality. John Dunne was forever a source of knowledge and memorabilia. I wish to acknowledge John Murphy, Jean Brown, Stuart Wilkinson and the staff of Appletree Press for their help and guidance through every word. Finally, to my wife Katrina and to our two daughters, Meabh and Deirbhile, there is nothing that can be written to express my love and gratitude.

Barry Flynn

Right

Hugh Russell (*right*) in action against Yo Ryon Sik of North Korea